SIDE by SIDE

Plus

Book & eText 4

- Life Skills & Test Prep
- Career & Academic Readiness
- Expanded Reading & Writing
- Digital FunZone & Audio

Steven J. Molinsky • **Bill Bliss**

Illustrated by Richard E. Hill

Side by Side Plus Book & eText 4

Pearson Education, 10 Bank Street, White Plains, NY 10606

Staff credits: The people who make up the *Side by Side Plus* team, representing content creation, design, manufacturing, marketing, multimedia, project management, publishing, rights management, and testing are Pietro Alongi, Allen Ascher, Rhea Banker, Elizabeth Barker, Lisa Bayrasli, Elizabeth Carlson, Jennifer Castro, Tracey Munz Cataldo, Diane Cipollone, Aerin Csigay, Victoria Denkus, Dave Dickey, Daniel Dwyer, Wanda España, Oliva Fernandez, Warren Fischbach, Pam Fishman, Nancy Flaggman, Patrice Fraccio, Irene Frankel, Aliza Greenblatt, Lester Holmes, Janet Johnston, Caroline Kasterine, Barry Katzen, Ray Keating, Renee Langan, Jaime Lieber, José Antonio Méndez, Julie Molnar, Alison Pei, Pamela Pia, Stuart Radcliffe, Jennifer Raspiller, Kriston Reinmuth, Mary Perrotta Rich, Tania Saiz-Sousa, Katherine Sullivan, Paula Van Ells, Kenneth Volcjak, and Wendy Wolf.

Contributing authors: Laura English, Meredith Westfall

Text composition: TSI Graphics, Inc.

Illustrations: Richard E. Hill

Photo credits: Original photography by Paul I. Tañedo and Pearson Education. Page 14c Exactostock/Superstock; p. 46a (top left) Paul Popper/Popperfoto/Getty Images, (top right) Bettmann/Corbis, (middle) Bettmann/Corbis, (bottom left) Bettmann/Corbis, (bottom right) Hulton-Deutsch Collection/Corbis; p. 46c (top) Bettmann/Corbis, (middle right) Bettmann/Corbis, (middle left) Bettmann/Corbis, (bottom) AP Images; p. 46c (left) DAVID FURST/AFP/Getty Images/Newscom, (right) Reuters/Corbis; p. 47 (top right) Everett Collection Historical/Alamy, (top left) Corbis, (middle right) Morphart/Fotolia, (middle left) Pictorial Press Ltd/Alamy, (bottom right) Pictorial Press Ltd/Alamy, (bottom left) akg-images/Newscom; p. 48 (top left) donyanedomam/Fotolia, (top middle) Konstantin Kulikov/Fotolia, (top right) Gail Johnson/Fotolia, (middle left) rnl/Fotolia, (middle) Rudolf Tepfenhart/Fotolia, (middle right) MasterLu/Fotolia, (bottom left) tonyv3112/Fotolia, (bottom middle) Heritage Image Partnership Ltd/Alamy, (bottom right) Russell Kord/Alamy; p. 49 Rafael Ben-Ari/Fotolia; p. 50b (top) Jan-moritz Baudach/Glow Images, (middle) John Gaffen/Alamy, (bottom) Ilona Ignatova/Shutterstock; p. 50c (left) Hemis/Alamy, (right) Dario Lopez Mills/AP Images; p. 50d John Birdsall/AGE Fotostock; p. 64a (1) svetavo/Fotolia, (2) JIANG HONGYAN/Shutterstock, (3) vetkit/Fotolia, (4) popoimagen/Fotolia, (5) magraphics.eu/Fotolia, (6) vilax/Shutterstock; p. 64c (top) Juanmonino/E+/Getty Images, (middle) Ijansempoi/Shutterstock, (bottom) John Henley/Corbis; p. 79 (top left) WENN.com/Newscom, (top right) ZUMA Press, Inc./Alamy, (middle left) AP Images, (middle right) Everett Collection, (bottom left) ZUMA Press, Inc./Alamy, (bottom right) Bettmann/Corbis, (far bottom left) Pictorial Press Ltd/Alamy; p. 80 (clover) Jon Beard/Shutterstock, (moon) Lynne Carpenter/Shutterstock, (well) SW Productions/Stockbyte/Getty Images, (candles) Dmitry Vereshchagin/Fotolia, (nut) Mamuka/Fotolia, (grape) DLeonis/Fotolia, (leaf) Springfield Gallery/Fotolia, (lightning) valdezrl/Fotolia, (wishbone) Blend Images/Shutterstock, (full moon) jovica antoski/Fotolia, (fountain) art_zzz/Fotolia, (star) Jill Fromer/Photodisc/Getty Images; p. 81 (top left) Andres Rodriguez/Fotolia, (top middle) George Wada/Fotolia, (top right) Aaron Amat/Fotolia, (left) Kadmy/Fotolia, (bottom left) Vibe Images/Fotolia, (bottom middle) Monkey Business/Fotolia, (bottom right) Christopher Meder/Fotolia; p. 82b (top left) Gavran333/Shutterstock, (top right) Rob hyrons/Fotolia, (helmut) Bruce Au/Shutterstock, (glasses) Coprid/Fotolia, (fountain) John Krstenansky/Alamy, (bottom) Jim West/Alamy; p. 82d (top) Redchopsticks/Corbis, (bottom) Rene Mansi/E+/Getty Images; p. 94c Comstock/Exactostock/SuperStock; p. 108c (top left) Kelpfish/Fotolia, (middle left) uckyo/Fotolia (middle right) Anna Sedneva/Shutterstock, (bottom right) 6493866629/Shutterstock; p. 108d Sherry Yates Young/Shutterstock; p. 125 Monkey Business/Fotolia; p. 126 (top left) Gino Santa Maria/Fotolia, (top right) nyul/Fotolia, (bottom left) Top Photo Corporation/Top Photo/Corbis, (bottom middle) apops/Fotolia, (bottom right) Tetra images RF/Getty Images; p. 127 Media Bakery13/Shutterstock; p. 128b (top left) Monkey Business Images/Shutterstock, (top middle) Alistair Berg/Digital Vision/Getty Images, (top right) micromonkey/Fotolia, (bottom left) Firma V/Shutterstock, (bottom middle) UpperCut Images/Alamy, (bottom right) michaeljung/Shutterstock; p. 128c (left to right) Triff/Shutterstock, sandroscuba/Fotolia, sumnersgraphicsinc/Fotolia, Kzenon/Fotolia, Aleksandr Bryliaev/Shutterstock, Rudchenko Liliia/Shutterstock; p. 128d iofoto/Shutterstock; p. 144c (left to right) Philippe TURPIN/Glow Images, Fuse/Getty Images, Goodluz/Shutterstock, Rido/Fotolia, Michaeljung/Fotolia; p. 158a (top) A. Ramey/PhotoEdit, Inc, (bottom) Kayte Deioma/PhotoEdit, Inc; p. 158b (top) Roberto Schmidt/Getty Image, (bottom) Ron Chapple/Getty Images; p. 158c (top) The Star-Ledger/Jennifer Brown/The Image Works, (bottom) Bonnie Kamin/PhotoEdit, Inc; p. 159 (top left) Ewing Galloway/Alamy, (top right) Stephen Coburn/Fotolia, (bottom left) ClassicStock/Alamy, (bottom right) AVAVA/Shutterstock; p. 160 (top left) Susan Liebold/Alamy, (top right) YOSHIKAZU TSUNO/AFP/Newscom, (top middle left) HUY NGUYEN/KRT/Newscom, (top middle right) Schalk van Zuydam/AP Images, (bottom middle left) apops/Fotolia, (bottom middle right) Alvey & Towers Picture Library/Alamy, (bottom left) David Eulitt/KRT/Newscom, (bottom right) sima/Fotolia; p. 161 (top left) Hero Images/Getty Images, (top middle) Ulrich Baumgarten/Getty Images, (top right) michaeljung/Fotolia, (left) Jacek Chabraszewski/Fotolia, (bottom left) Darren Baker/Fotolia, (bottom middle) B. Boissonnet/BSIP/Corbis, (bottom right) spotmatik/Shutterstock; p. 162c (top) MISHELLA/Shutterstock, (bottom) Ariel Skelley/Blend Images/Getty Images; p. 162d Lisa F. Young/Alamy.

The authors gratefully acknowledge the contribution of Tina Carver in the development of the original *Side by Side* program.

Side by Side Plus Book & eText with Audio CD 4: ISBN 13 – 978-0-13-382905-1; ISBN 10 – 0-13-382905-7

CONTENTS

Red type indicates standards-based lessons.

Red type indicates standards-based lessons.

Dear Friends,

Welcome to *Side by Side Plus*—a special edition for adult learners that offers an integrated standards-based and grammar-based approach to language learning!

Flexible Language Proficiency *Plus* Life Skills

The core mission of *Side by Side Plus* is to build students' general language proficiency so they can use English flexibly to meet their varied needs, life circumstances, and goals. We strongly believe that language teachers need to preserve their role as true teachers of language even as we fill our lesson plans with required life-skill content and prepare students for standardized tests. Our program helps you accomplish this through a research-based grammatical sequence and communicative approach in which basic language lessons in each unit lead to standards-based lessons focused on students' life-skill roles in the community, family, school, and at work.

Keys to Promoting Student Persistence and Success

STUDENT-CENTERED LEARNING The core methodology of *Side by Side Plus* is the guided conversation—a brief, structured dialog that students practice in pairs and then use as a framework to create new conversations. Through this practice, students work together to develop their language skills "side by side." They are not dependent on the teacher for all instruction, and they know how to learn from each other. This student-centered methodology and the text's easy-to-use format enable students to study outside of class with any speaking partner—a family member, a friend or neighbor, a tutor, or a co-worker, even if that person is also an English language learner. If students need to attend class intermittently or "stop out" for a while, they have the skills and text material to continue learning on their own.

MEANINGFUL INSTRUCTION RELEVANT TO STUDENTS' LIVES Throughout the instructional program, civics topics and tasks connect students to their community, personalization questions apply lesson content to students' life situations, and critical-thinking activities build a community of learners who problem-solve together and share solutions.

EXTENDING LEARNING OUTSIDE THE CLASSROOM The magazine-style Gazette sections in *Side by Side Plus* provide motivating material for students to use at home. Feature articles, vocabulary enrichment, and other activities reinforce classroom instruction through high-interest material that

students are motivated to use outside of class. A bonus Audio CD offers entertaining radio program-style recordings of key Gazette activities. (See the inside back cover for a description of other media materials and software designed to extend learning through self-study.)

SUFFICIENT PRACTICE + FREQUENT ASSESSMENT = SUCCESS Students need to experience success as language learners. While other programs "cover" many learning objectives, *Side by Side Plus* offers students carefully-sequenced intensive practice that promotes mastery and the successful application of language skills to daily life. Students can observe their achievement milestones through the program's frequent assessments, including check-up tests and skills checklists in the text and achievement tests in the accompanying workbook.

THE "FUN FACTOR" We believe that language instruction is most powerful when it is joyful. There is magic in the power of humor, fun, games, and music to encourage students to take risks with their emerging language, to "play" with it, and to allow their personalities to shine through as their language skills increase. We incorporate these elements into our program to motivate students to persist in their language learning not only because they need it, but also because they enjoy it.

MULTILEVEL INSTRUCTION *Side by Side Plus* provides exceptional resources to support multilevel instruction. The Teacher's Guide includes step-by-step instructions for preparing below-level and at-level students for each lesson and hundreds of multilevel activities for all students, including those above-level. The accompanying Multilevel Activity & Achievement Test Book and CD-ROM offer an array of reproducible multilevel worksheets and activities.

We hope your students enjoy using *Side by Side Plus*. We are confident that these resources will help them persist and succeed through a language learning experience that is effective . . . relevant to their lives . . . and fun!

Steven J. Molinsky
Bill Bliss

Guide to Life Skills, Standards, & Test Prep Features

Side by Side has helped over 25 million students worldwide persist and succeed as language learners. Now, in this special edition for adult learners in standards-based programs, *Side by Side Plus* builds students' general language proficiency *and* helps them apply these skills for success meeting the needs of daily life, work, and continuing education.

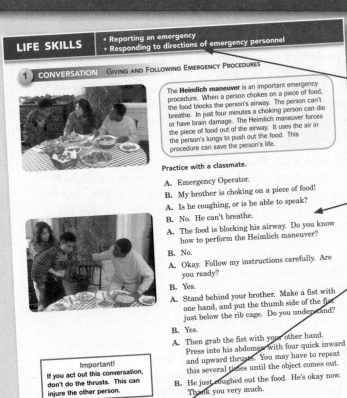

LIFE SKILLS • Reporting an emergency • Responding to directions of emergency personnel

1 CONVERSATION GIVING AND FOLLOWING EMERGENCY PROCEDURES

The **Heimlich maneuver** is an important emergency procedure. When a person chokes on a piece of food, the food blocks the person's airway. The person can't breathe. In just four minutes a choking person can die or have brain damage. The Heimlich maneuver forces the piece of food out of the airway. It uses the air in the person's lungs to push out the food. This procedure can save the person's life.

Practice with a classmate.

A. Emergency Operator.
B. My brother is choking on a piece of food!
A. Is he coughing, or is he able to speak?
B. No. He can't breathe.
A. The food is blocking his airway. Do you know how to perform the Heimlich maneuver?
B. No.
A. Okay. Follow my instructions carefully. Are you ready?
B. Yes.
A. Stand behind your brother. Make a fist with one hand, and put the thumb side of the fist just below the rib cage. Do you understand?
B. Yes.
A. Then grab the fist with your other hand. Press into his abdomen with four quick inward and upward thrusts. You may have to repeat this several times until the object comes out.
B. He just coughed out the food. He's okay now. Thank you very much.

Important!
If you act out this conversation, don't do the thrusts. This can injure the other person.

2 TEAMWORK CPR (CARDIOPULMONARY RESUSCITATION)

With a classmate, find out the basic procedures to follow for CPR (cardiopulmonary resuscitation). Then practice giving and following the directions.

COMMUNITY CONNECTIONS Where can you take a course in CPR and other first-aid procedures in your community? (The Red Cross, hospitals, and other institutions often offer these courses.) Share the information as a class.

Standards-based lessons at the end of every unit apply students' language learning to their life-skill roles in the community, family, school, and at work. Students develop the key competencies included in CASAS, BEST Plus, EFF, SCANS, Model Standards, and other major state and local curriculum frameworks and assessment systems.

Real-life conversation practice in authentic life-skill situations gets students talking through interactive pair work. **Extensive photographs and illustrations** provide clear contexts and support vocabulary learning.

Teamwork activities promote cooperative learning as students work together in pairs, groups, or as a class to share information and complete tasks.

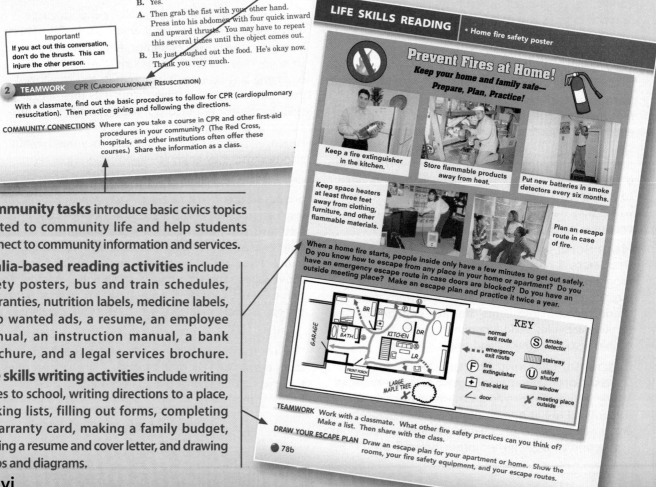

LIFE SKILLS READING • Home fire safety poster

Prevent Fires at Home!
Keep your home and family safe— Prepare, Plan, Practice!

Keep a fire extinguisher in the kitchen.

Store flammable products away from heat.

Put new batteries in smoke detectors every six months.

Keep space heaters at least three feet away from clothing, furniture, and other flammable materials.

Plan an escape route in case of fire.

When a home fire starts, people inside only have a few minutes to get out safely. Do you know how to escape from any place in your home or apartment? Do you have an emergency escape route in case doors are blocked? Do you have an outside meeting place? Make an escape plan and practice it twice a year.

GARAGE · BR · BATH · KITCHEN · DR · LR · FRONT PORCH · LARGE MAPLE TREE

KEY
→ normal exit route
(S) smoke detector
→ emergency exit route
stairway
(F) fire extinguisher
(U) utility shutoff
+ first-aid kit
window
↙ door
X meeting place outside

TEAMWORK Work with a classmate. What other fire safety practices can you think of? Make a list. Then share with the class.

DRAW YOUR ESCAPE PLAN Draw an escape plan for your apartment or home. Show the rooms, your fire safety equipment, and your escape routes.

78b

Community tasks introduce basic civics topics related to community life and help students connect to community information and services.

Realia-based reading activities include safety posters, bus and train schedules, warranties, nutrition labels, medicine labels, help wanted ads, a resume, an employee manual, an instruction manual, a bank brochure, and a legal services brochure.

Life skills writing activities include writing notes to school, writing directions to a place, making lists, filling out forms, completing a warranty card, making a family budget, writing a resume and cover letter, and drawing maps and diagrams.

Making a Monthly Budget Changed Their Lives

Last year Eduardo and Isabel Soriano decided to do something about their financial situation. They often ran out of money at the end of the month, and they kept asking themselves, "Where did the money go?" The problem was that they didn't really keep track of what they were spending. As a result, they often didn't have enough money for their expenses, and their monthly bill payments were sometimes overdue. They finally decided to take control of their finances by setting up a budget to help them manage their money, pay their bills on time, and save for the future.

The Sorianos knew the amount of their monthly take-home pay, but they needed to make a list of their expenses. So for two months, they wrote down everything they spent. It wasn't difficult keeping a record of their *fixed* expenses, such as rent and car payments, because these expenses were the same every month. But they needed to collect receipts to help them keep track of their *variable* expenses—expenses that change from month to month—such as groceries and clothing. They made sure to include insurance, taxes, repairs, and other expenses that occur less frequently. They figured out how much they spent on each of these items in a year, and then they divided this amount by twelve for a monthly average.

According to Isabel, setting up a budget wasn't very difficult. "We compared our monthly expenses with our monthly take-home pay to make sure we weren't spending more than we earned. We looked at all our expenses carefully to see how we could reduce our spending and cut out waste. For example, one month our grocery bills were high, so we decided to save money by using coupons and shopping at wholesale stores. We also realized that we were spending money on certain things we didn't really need, such as premium cable TV channels and fast-food lunches near our workplaces. Now we just have basic cable service, and we take lunches to work from home."

Eduardo adds, "Once we figured out how to trim costs, we wrote a new budget based on these amounts. We made room in our budget for an emergency fund. We try to put 5% to 10% of our income into this fund each month so we're prepared in case one of us loses our job or there's an illness in the family."

The Sorianos also decided that it was important for them to make room in their budget for a family vacation. For years their children had been saying, "We wish we could go to Disney World!" The Sorianos have kept to their budget because they know how much this trip means to their children. This July, the family will finally travel to Disney World. "We all have dreams," says Isabel, "and budgeting wisely can help to make them come true."

1. _____ is a fixed expense.
   A. Clothing
   B. Food
   C. A vacation
   D. Rent

2. *Overdue* in paragraph 1 means _____.
   A. late
   B. too many
   C. expensive
   D. paid

3. In the past, the Sorianos ran out of money because _____.
   A. they had a budget
   B. they had overdue bills
   C. they didn't keep track of their expenses
   D. they didn't have any take-home pay

4. *Waste* in paragraph 3 refers to _____.
   A. recycling
   B. unnecessary purchases
   C. necessary expenses
   D. paper

5. You can save money if you _____.
   A. trim costs
   B. spend more than you earn
   C. divide your expenses by twelve
   D. don't have an emergency fund

6. According to the Sorianos, you can d_____
   things you like if you _____.
   A. spend money on things you don'_____
   B. collect receipts
   C. compare your monthly expense_____
   D. budget carefully

Narrative reading passages offer practice with simple magazine and newspaper articles on topics such as parenting, interactions with the police, consumer rights, budget-planning strategies, health safety tips, and career advancement. **Academic lessons** in school textbook formats prepare students for success in continuing education through subject-matter content including civics, history, and health.

Reading comprehension exercises in multiple-choice formats help students prepare for the reading section of standardized tests.

Critical thinking and **problem-solving activities** throughout the text help students focus on issues and problems and share ideas, experiences, and solutions.

Check-up tests allow a quick assessment of student achievement and help prepare students for the kinds of test items found on standardized tests.

More complete **Achievement Tests** for each unit, including listening test items, are available as reproducible masters and printable disk files in the Teacher's Guide with Multilevel Activity & Achievement Test Book and CD-ROM. They are also available in the companion Activity & Test Prep Workbook.

Vocabulary checklists and **language skill checklists** help students review words they have learned, keep track of the skills they are developing, and identify vocabulary and skills they need to continue to work on. These lists promote student persistence as students assess their own skills and check off all the ways they are succeeding as language learners.

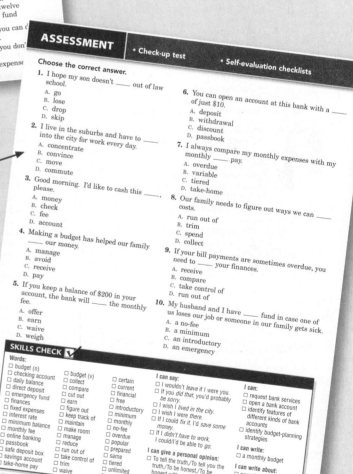

Choose the correct answer.

1. I hope my son doesn't _____ out of law school.
   A. go
   B. lose
   C. drop
   D. skip

2. I live in the suburbs and have to _____ into the city for work every day.
   A. concentrate
   B. convince
   C. move
   D. commute

3. Good morning. I'd like to cash this _____, please.
   A. money
   B. check
   C. fee
   D. account

4. Making a budget has helped our family _____ our money.
   A. manage
   B. avoid
   C. receive
   D. pay

5. If you keep a balance of $200 in your account, the bank will _____ the monthly fee.
   A. offer
   B. earn
   C. waive
   D. weigh

6. You can open an account at this bank with a _____ of just $10.
   A. deposit
   B. withdrawal
   C. discount
   D. passbook

7. I always compare my monthly expenses with my monthly _____ pay.
   A. overdue
   B. variable
   C. tiered
   D. take-home

8. Our family needs to figure out ways we can _____ costs.
   A. run out of
   B. trim
   C. spend
   D. collect

9. If your bill payments are sometimes overdue, you need to _____ your finances.
   A. receive
   B. compare
   C. take control of
   D. run out of

10. My husband and I have _____ fund in case one of us loses our job or someone in our family gets sick.
   A. a no-fee
   B. a minimum
   C. an introductory
   D. an emergency

SKILLS CHECK ✓

Words:

☐ budget (n)
☐ checking account
☐ daily balance
☐ direct deposit
☐ emergency fund
☐ finances
☐ fixed expenses
☐ interest rate
☐ minimum balance
☐ monthly fee
☐ online banking
☐ passbook
☐ safe deposit box
☐ savings account
☐ take-home pay

☐ budget (v)
☐ collect
☐ compare
☐ cut out
☐ earn
☐ figure out
☐ keep track of
☐ maintain
☐ make room
☐ manage
☐ reduce
☐ run out of
☐ take control of
☐ trim
☐ waive

☐ certain
☐ current
☐ financial
☐ free
☐ introductory
☐ minimum
☐ monthly
☐ no-fee
☐ overdue
☐ popular
☐ prepared
☐ same
☐ tiered
☐ unlimited
☐ variable

I can say:
☐ I wouldn't *leave* if I were you.
☐ If you did that, you'd probably be sorry.
☐ I wish I *lived* in the city.
☐ I wish I *were* there.
☐ If I could fix it, I'd save some money.
☐ If I didn't have to work, I could/I'd be able to go.

I can give a personal opinion:
☐ To tell the truth,/To tell you the truth,/To be honest,/To be honest with you,/If you ask me,

I can:
☐ request bank services
☐ open a bank account
☐ identify features of different kinds of bank accounts
☐ identify budget-planning strategies

I can write:
☐ a monthly budget

I can write about:
☐ something I wish for

94d

Scope and Sequence

Unit	Topics & Vocabulary	Grammar	Functional Communication	Listening & Pronunciation	Writing
1	• Describing actions that have occurred • Describing actions that haven't occurred yet • Discussing duration of activity • Discussing things people had done • Parent-school communication • Notes to school • Writing a personal letter • Parenting	REVIEW: • Present perfect tense • Present perfect continuous tense • Past perfect tense • Past perfect continuous tense	• Expressing ability • Asking for & reporting information • Expressing surprise • Sharing news	• Listening to a narrative about tasks accomplished & indicating these tasks on a checklist • Pronouncing reduced *have*, *has*, & *had*	• Writing about something you had worked hard to prepare for • Making a list of reasons parents go to the office at a child's school • Making a list of problems children sometimes have in school • Identifying parts of a letter: date, salutation, body, closing, signature • Writing notes to school to explain a child's absence, to excuse a child for a medical appointment, & to communicate concerns to a teacher • Filling out a parent school volunteer form

2	• Evaluating people's activities
	• Job interviews
	• Expressing possibility
	• Making deductions
	• Expressing concern about others
	• Apologizing
	• Recounting difficult situations
	• Driving rules
	• Directions
	• Drawing a map
	• Bus & train schedules
	• Interactions with the police
		• Perfect modals:
		  Should have
		  Might have
		  May have
		  Could have
		  Must have
			• Asking for & reporting information
			• Expressing possibility
			• Agreeing
			• Apologizing
			• Making a deduction
			• Expressing obligation
				• Listening to conversations & reaching conclusions about what people should have done
				• Pronouncing reduced *have*
					• Writing about how to do well at a job interview
					• Writing a story about your English teacher
					• Writing about something you should have done differently
					• Writing out directions to your home & drawing a map
					• Filling out a traffic accident report
					• Filling out a driver's license application form

3	• Discussing creative works • Describing work tasks accomplished • Discussing things that have happened to people • Describing accomplishments • Securing services • Automobile repairs • Historical narratives • Discussing opinions • Civics: U.S. history • Making a timeline	• Passive voice • Relative pronouns	• Expressing opinions • Agreeing • Asking for & reporting information • Offering to do something • Sharing news • Small talk • Reacting to good & bad news • Expressing empathy • Expressing opinions	• Listening & choosing the best line to continue a conversation • Pronouncing reduced auxiliary verbs	• Writing about the history of the place where you were born or a place where you have lived • Writing about students' rights & responsibilities in your school • Creating a history timeline • Creating an autobiographical timeline of life events
Gazette Reading & Writing Workshop	• Inventions that changed the world • Timeline of major inventions • Culture concept: Ancient & modern wonders of the world • Interview with a photojournalist • Social Studies: Architectural wonders of the world	• Passive voice	• Reporting about events • Telling about places you would like to visit • Describing background, education, & life events • Using idiomatic expressions	• Listening to radio news reports & interpreting the facts	• Writing an e-mail or instant message to tell things that have happened to you recently • Punctuation • The Writing Process

CORRELATION and PLACEMENT KEY

Side by Side Plus 4 correlates with these standards-based curriculum levels and assessment system score ranges.

For correlation keys to other major state and local curriculum frameworks, please visit:
http://pearsoneltusa.com/molinskyandbliss

NRS (National Reporting System) Educational Functioning Level	High Intermediate
BEST Plus 2.0 (Basic English Skills Test)	485–524 (SPL 5)
BEST Literacy	68–75 (SPL 5)
CASAS Reading	211–220
CASAS Listening	210–218
CASAS Writing	226–242
TABE CLAS-E Reading & Writing	515–556
TABE CLAS-E Listening & Speaking	526–558

LIFE SKILLS, CIVICS, TEST PREPARATION, CURRICULUM STANDARDS AND FRAMEWORKS

Life Skills, Civics, & Test Preparation	EFF	SCANS/Employment Competencies	CASAS	LAUSD	Florida*
• Parent/school communication • Making requests at a school office • Meeting with a child's teacher • Problems children have in school • Critical thinking: Bullying in school • Parenting skills: Helping children succeed in school • Critical thinking/Culture concept: How parents in different countries participate in their children's education	• Interact in a way that is friendly • Create & pursue vision & goals • Define what one is trying to achieve • Identify family relationships • Meet family needs & responsibilities • Reflect & evaluate • Cooperate with others	• Identify goal-relevant activities • Identify human resources (occupations, work skills) • Understand an organizational system (workplace operations) • Problem solving • Participate as a member of a team	0.1.2, 0.2.2, 0.2.3, 2.5.5, 2.7.2, 3.5.7, 4.8.1, 4.8.7	3, 4a, 6, 10a, 10b	4.01.01, 4.02.07, 4.02.08, 5.01.01, 5.02.08
• Driving rules • Getting pulled over by the police • Asking for & giving directions • Drawing a map • Interpreting bus & train schedules • Calling for information about a bus or train schedule • Finding transportation schedule information on the Internet • Interactions with the police • Critical thinking: Ways the police & people in the community can help each other • Planning a trip using a map • Interpreting movie listings in a newspaper	• Seek input from others • Plan: Set a goal • Reflect & evaluate • Interact in a way that is tactful • Identify community needs & resources • Reflect & evaluate	• Acquire & evaluate information	0.1.2, 2.2.1, 2.2.3, 2.2.4, 2.2.5, 2.6.1, 2.6.2, 2.6.3, 4.1.5, 4.1.7, 5.3.5, 5.3.7, 5.5.6, 7.2.2	5b, 9, 13, 16a, 16b, 18, 35b, 35c	4.01.01, 4.06.01, 4.06.02, 4.06.03, 5.01.01, 5.06.01, 5.06.02, 5.06.05
• Civics: U.S. history—World War I, the Great Depression, the New Deal, World War II, the United Nations, the Cold War, the Civil Rights Movement, September 11, 2001, the War in Iraq • Study skill: Creating a history timeline	• Interact in a way that is friendly • Analyze & use information	• Sociability • Identify goal-relevant activities • Serve clients/customers • Interpret & communicate information • See things in the mind's eye (Interpret a timeline; Draw a timeline)	0.1.2, 0.2.4, 4.8.1, 4.8.3, 5.2.1, 5.2.3	1a, 5a, 5b, 8a, 38b	4.01.01, 4.06.05, 5.01.01, 5.01.03
• Interpreting a narrative reading about famous inventions & their inventors • Interpreting a timeline of major inventions • Interpreting facts in radio news reports	• Analyze & use information • Respect others & value diversity	• Acquire & evaluate information • Work with cultural diversity	2.7.2, 4.8.7, 5.2.5	6, 43	4.01.01, 4.01.03, 5.01.01

EFF: Equipped for the Future (Content standards, Common activities, & Role maps)
SCANS: Secretary's Commission on Achieving Necessary Skills (U.S. Department of Labor)
CCRS: College and Career Readiness Standards for Adult Education (U.S. Department of Education)
CASAS: Comprehensive Adult Student Assessment System
LAUSD: Los Angeles Unified School District (ESL Intermediate High content standards)
Florida: Adult ESOL High Intermediate Standardized Syllabi

(* Florida standards beginning with prefix "4" indicate Low Intermediate benchmarks included for re-teaching or review. Florida standards beginning with prefix "5" indicate High Intermediate benchmarks.)

Scope and Sequence

Unit	Topics & Vocabulary	Grammar	Functional Communication	Listening & Pronunciation	Writing
4	• Asking for information • Indicating uncertainty • Referring people to someone else • Reporting a crime • Reporting a missing person • Returning & exchanging defective products • Requesting product repair services • Warranties • Consumer complaints	• Embedded questions	• Asking for information • Indicating that you don't know • Inquiring about permissibility • Describing a person	• Listening & deciding where a conversation is taking place • Pronouncing reduced *you*	• Writing about things you wonder about the future • Making a list of items bought in a store & reasons one might return them • Filling out a product warranty card
5	• Describing plans & intentions • Consequences of actions • Discussing future events • Expressing hopes • Asking for & giving reasons • Making deductions • Emergencies • Reporting an emergency • Responding to directions of emergency personnel • Home fire safety • Smoke detector instructions	• Conditional: Present real (If ___ will) Present unreal (If ___ would) • Hope-clauses	• Expressing agreement • Asking for & offering advice • Expressing hopes • Making a deduction	• Listening & making deductions based on information heard • Pronouncing contractions with *would*	• Writing about what you would do if you won a million dollars • Making a list of fire safety practices • Drawing an escape plan for an apartment or home
Gazette **Reading &** **Writing** **Workshop**	• The expression of wishes & hopes in music • Interpreting a table with number facts • Culture concept: Traditions & customs for making wishes around the world • Interviews with people about hypothetical plans for the future • Employment: Workplace safety	• Present real conditional • Present unreal conditional • Hope-clauses • Passive voice • Embedded questions	• Making hypothetical statements about the future • Describing traditions • Using idiomatic expressions	• Listening to an automated telephone system & determining the correct number to press for specific needs	• Writing an e-mail or instant message to tell about your weekend plans • The Writing Process
6	• Advice • Expressing wishes • Job satisfaction • Expressing ability • Asking for & giving reasons • Life in cities & suburbs • Requesting bank services • Opening a bank account • Bank brochures • Budget-planning strategies	• Present unreal conditional • Wish-clauses	• Asking for & offering advice • Giving a personal opinion • Expressing wishes	• Listening & making deductions based on information heard • Pronouncing reduced *would*	• Writing about something in your life you wish for • Filling out a bank account application form • Making a monthly household budget
7	• Making deductions • Discussing unexpected events • Expressing wishes & hopes • Consequences of actions • Rumors • Describing symptoms • Following medical advice • Community health care services • Nutrition & food labels • Over-the-counter medicine • Medicine labels • Safety procedures at work	• Past unreal conditional (If ___ would have) • Wish-clauses	• Asking for & giving reasons • Making a deduction • Expressing wishes • Empathizing • Expressing hopes	• Listening to conversations & making deductions based on information heard • Pronouncing reduced *have*	• Writing about a rumor at school or at work • Writing about something in your life you wish you had done, but didn't • Making a list of community health care providers • Filling out a medical history form • Filling out a workplace accident report

Life Skills, Civics, & Test Preparation	EFF	SCANS/Employment Competencies	CASAS	LAUSD	Florida*
• Explaining problems to store personnel • Returning & exchanging defective products • Requesting product repair services • Critical thinking: Comparing repair policies at different stores in the community • Interpreting product warranties • Problem-solving: Determining whether problems with products are covered by limited warranties • Consumer rights • Identifying ways to make consumer complaints • Math: Word problems about estimating cost; Interpreting charts & prices	• Identify community needs & resources • Cooperate with others • Gather information • Understand, interpret, & work with numbers • Use math to solve problems	• Serve clients/customers • Participate as a member of a team • Acquire & evaluate information • Problem solving	0.1.2, 1.6.2, 1.6.3, 4.8.1, 4.8.3, 5.2.1	21a, 21b	4.01.01, 4.04.01, 4.04.03, 4.04.05, 4.07.02, 5.01.01, 5.04.01, 5.04.02, 5.04.06
• Reporting an emergency • Heimlich maneuver • Responding to directions of emergency personnel • CPR (Cardiopulmonary resuscitation) • Identifying places in the community to learn CPR & other first-aid procedures • Interpreting a home fire safety poster • Interpreting & drawing a diagram of a home escape plan • Identifying home fire safety practices • Interpreting a smoke detector instructional manual • Drawing a floor plan & identifying locations of smoke detectors • Interpreting a rental agreement	• Seek input from others • Create & pursue vision & goals • Interact in a way that is friendly • Provide for family members' safety & physical needs • Cooperate with others • Use technology	• Identify goal-relevant activities • Self-management: Set personal goals • Sociability • Participate as a member of a team • See things in the mind's eye (Interpret & draw a diagram) • Use technology	0.1.2, 0.1.3, 1.4.3, 1.4.5, 1.4.8, 2.5.1, 3.1.1, 3.4.2, 4.3.3, 4.8.1, 7.2.2	5b, 7c, 9, 12, 24, 30b, 32	4.01.01, 4.07.01, 5.01.01, 5.01.06, 5.02.05, 5.04.05
• Interpreting a narrative reading about music that expresses wishes & hopes • Interpreting statistical information in a chart • Interpreting information & instructions on an airline automated telephone system	• Analyze & use information • Understand, interpret, & work with numbers • Respect others & value diversity • Create & pursue vision & goals • Use technology	• Acquire & evaluate information • Work with cultural diversity • Work with technology	2.2.3, 2.6.3, 2.7.2, 4.8.7	6, 13, 43	4.01.01, 5.01.01, 5.01.02
• Requesting bank services • Opening a bank account • Identifying banks in the community • Types of bank accounts: Savings, checking • Interpreting a bank brochure & chart comparing different accounts offered • Budget-planning strategies • Math: Word problems with money; Interpreting utility bills	• Seek input from others • Create & pursue vision & goals • Cooperate with others • Analyze & use information • Identify community resources • Manage resources • Meet family needs & responsibilities • Understand, interpret, & work with numbers • Use math to solve problems	• Self-management: Set personal goals, Assess self accurately • Serve clients/customers • Participate as a member of a team • Acquire & evaluate information • Allocate money	0.1.2, 0.1.3, 1.4.4, 1.5.1, 1.5.3, 1.8.1, 1.8.2, 1.8.3, 4.8.1, 4.8.3	5a, 7c, 19, 20a, 20b, 22b, 22c	4.01.01, 4.04.01, 5.01.01, 5.01.02, 5.01.03, 5.04.01, 5.04.08
• Describing symptoms • Following medical advice • Identifying community health care providers & services • Nutrition • Interpreting nutrition facts on food labels • Critical thinking: Determining healthy & unhealthy ingredients in food • Over-the-counter medicine • Interpreting warnings on medicine labels • Interpreting a workplace safety poster • Identifying safety procedures at work • Interpreting a map of hurricane evacuation procedures • Interpreting safety signs & symbols	• Meet family needs & responsibilities • Identify community resources • Gather information • Analyze & use information • Understand, interpret, & work with numbers • Understand & interpret symbolic information	• Identify goal-relevant activities • Acquire & evaluate information • See things in the mind's eye (Interpret a chart)	0.1.2, 2.5.3, 3.1.1, 3.1.3, 3.2.1, 3.3.1, 3.3.2, 3.3.3, 3.4.2, 3.5.1, 3.5.9, 4.3.1, 4.3.3, 4.3.4, 4.4.3, 7.2.2	9, 28, 29, 30a, 30c, 31, 32, 33, 39b	4.01.01, 4.03.08, 4.05.01, 4.05.04, 4.05.06, 4.07.01, 5.01.01, 5.01.02, 5.02.05, 5.03.08, 5.05.01, 5.05.02, 5.05.03, 5.05.04

Scope and Sequence

Unit	Topics & Vocabulary	Grammar	Functional Communication	Listening & Pronunciation	Writing
8	• Reporting what people have said • Reporting information • Leaving, taking, & conveying messages • Job interviews • Discussing feelings • Advice • Job interviews: Talking about personal qualities Asking appropriate questions Answering difficult questions • Help wanted ads • Resumes	• Reported speech • Sequence of tenses	• Reporting information • Expressing surprise • Indicating lack of prior knowledge • Asking for & giving reasons	• Listening to conversations & making deductions based on information heard • Pronouncing reduced *to*	• Writing about a time when you needed advice • Making a list of abbreviations in help wanted ads and their full-word equivalents • Filling out a job application • Making a personal timeline of work experience • Writing a resume • Writing a cover letter
Gazette Reading & Writing Workshop	• Job interview skills • Interpreting a pie chart with information about job search strategies • Determining appropriate job interview behavior • Culture: Job interviews around the world • Interview with a human resources manager • Career Education: Exploring & planning a career	• Imperatives • Passive voice • Reported speech • Sequence of tenses	• Describing job interviews • Using idiomatic expressions	• Listening to voice-mail messages at work	• Writing an e-mail or instant message to tell about an interesting conversation you have had • Quotation marks • Writing a business letter
9	• Verifying • Reporting information • Expressing opinions • Writing a personal letter • Writing a business memo • Feedback on job performance • Following procedures • Employee benefits • Career advancement • Work-related values	• Tag questions • Emphatic sentences	• Asking for & reporting information • Expressing surprise • Expressing opinions • Sharing news • Congratulating • Initiating topics • Expressing agreement	• Listening to conversations & making deductions based on information heard • Pronouncing tag intonation	• Writing a personal letter • Writing a work memo • Writing about positive feedback you have received • Writing procedures for doing things at work or at school
10	• Invitations • Expressing disappointment • Decision-making • Consequences of actions • Expressing concern about people • Asking for assistance • Civic rights & responsibilities • Community legal services	REVIEW: • Verb tenses • Conditionals • Gerunds	• Invitations • Expressing disappointment • Calling attention to people's actions • Apologizing • Giving reasons • Making a deduction • Empathizing • Offering to help	• Listening & making deductions about where conversations are taking place • Pronouncing *would you* & *could you*	• Writing about an important decision you had to make & the advice people offered • Making a list of community legal services
Gazette Reading & Writing Workshop	• Technology in our lives • Interpreting a table with number facts • Culture concept: Technology in action around the world • Interviews with people about how technology has changed their lives • Civics: Social media & today's citizens	• Verb tense review • Prepositional phrases	• Describing innovations in technology • Describing the influence of technology in people's lives • Using idiomatic expressions	• Listening to a store service department's automated telephone system & determining the correct number to press for specific needs	• Writing an instant message using common abbreviations • The Writing Process

Life Skills, Civics, & Test Preparation	EFF	SCANS/Employment Competencies	CASAS	LAUSD	Florida

• Job interviews:
  • Talking about personal qualities
  • Asking appropriate questions
  • Answering difficult interview questions
• Critical thinking:
  • Personal qualities important for job applicants
  • Ways to learn about a company before an interview
  • Appropriate questions to ask during an interview
• Interpreting help wanted ads
• Interpreting a resume & cover letter
	• Identify family relationships
	• Develop & express sense of self
	• Cooperate with others
		• Exercise leadership
		• Identify goal-relevant activities
		• Identify human resources (occupations)
		• Identify human resources (work skills)
		• Self-esteem
		• Participate as a member of a team
			0.1.1, 0.1.2, 0.2.1, 0.2.3, 4.1.2, 4.1.3, 4.1.5, 4.1.6, 4.1.7, 4.1.8, 4.4.1, 4.4.2, 4.6.5, 4.8.1, 7.1.3, 7.5.1, 7.5.2	1a, 3, 4b, 34, 35, 36, 37, 41	4.01.01, 4.03.02, 4.03.03, 4.03.04, 5.01.01, 5.03.02, 5.03.03, 5.03.04

• Interpreting a narrative reading about tips for a successful job interview • Interpreting statistical facts in a pie chart • Comparing two applicants' job prospects based on their interview behavior • Interpreting voice-mail messages at work	• Analyze & use information • Define what one is trying to achieve • Develop & express sense of self • Interact in a way that is friendly & courteous • Understand, interpret, & work with numbers • Respect others & value diversity • Use technology	• Acquire & evaluate information • Self-esteem • See things in the mind's eye (Interpret a pie chart) • Work with cultural diversity • Work with technology	0.1.1, 0.1.2, 2.7.2, 4.1.3, 4.1.5, 4.1.6, 4.1.7, 4.1.8, 4.8.7	6, 34, 35, 36, 43	4.01.01, 4.01.06, 5.01.01, 5.01.06
• Feedback on job performance • Following work procedures • Interpreting employee benefits information in a new employee manual • Career advancement • Identifying work-related values • Interpreting a pay stub	• Develop & express sense of self • Seek input from others • Work together • Create & pursue vision & goals • Understand, interpret, & work with numbers	• Self-esteem • Self-management: Assess self accurately • Identify human resources (work skills) • Participate as a member of a team • Identify goal-relevant activities	0.1.2, 0.2.3, 4.2.1, 4.2.4, 4.4.1, 4.4.2, 4.4.4, 4.5.1, 4.5.4, 4.6.1, 4.8.1, 4.8.2, 7.1.3, 7.5.1, 7.5.2	4a, 5a, 5b, 8c, 8d, 38a, 40a, 40b, 41	4.01.01, 4.03.06, 4.03.07, 4.03.10, 5.01.01, 5.01.03, 5.03.06, 5.03.07, 5.03.09, 5.03.10
• Civics: Civic rights & responsibilities—obeying laws, paying taxes, keeping informed, getting involved, voting in elections, serving on a jury • Critical thinking: Important civic responsibilities • Interpreting a community legal services brochure • Project: Compiling a list of community legal services	• Reflect & evaluate • Exercise rights & responsibilities • Identify community needs & resources • Gather information • Meet family needs & responsibilities	• Acquire & evaluate information	0.1.2, 0.1.3, 2.1.1, 2.5.1, 2.5.2, 4.8.1, 5.3.2, 5.6.1, 5.6.2, 5.6.3, 7.2.2	8a, 9, 26a, 26b, 26c	4.01.01, 4.02.04, 5.01.01, 5.02.04, 5.02.07
• Interpreting a narrative about technology in our lives • Interpreting statistical facts in a line graph • Interpreting a store service department's automated telephone system & determining the correct number to press for specific needs	• Analyze & use information • Understand, interpret, & work with numbers • Understand, interpret, & work with symbolic information • Use technology	• Acquire & evaluate information • See things in the mind's eye (Interpret a line graph) • Work with technology	2.7.2, 4.8.7	6, 43	4.01.01, 5.01.01

1

Review:
Present Perfect Tense
Present Perfect Continuous Tense
Past Perfect Tense
Past Perfect Continuous Tense

- Describing Actions That Have and Haven't Occurred
- Discussing Duration of Activity
- Discussing Things People Had Done

- Parent/School Communication
- Notes to School
- Writing a Personal Letter
- Parenting

VOCABULARY PREVIEW

Things to Do Today

☐ 1. take inventory

☐ 2. write a report

☐ 3. speak to the boss

☐ 4. go to the bank

☐ 5. eat lunch

☐ 6. give out the paychecks

☐ 7. set up the meeting room

☐ 8. see the personnel officer

☐ 9. get gas

☐ 10. drive to the gym

☐ 11. swim

☐ 12. do sit-ups

Things I've Done Today: I've . . .

- ☑ 1. taken inventory
- ☑ 2. written a report
- ☑ 3. spoken to the boss
- ☑ 4. gone to the bank
- ☑ 5. eaten lunch
- ☑ 6. given out the paychecks
- ☑ 7. set up the meeting room
- ☑ 8. seen the personnel officer
- ☑ 9. gotten gas
- ☑ 10. driven to the gym
- ☑ 11. swum
- ☑ 12. done sit-ups

I've Sung for Many Years

(I have)	I've
(We have)	We've
(You have)	You've
(They have)	They've
(He has)	He's
(She has)	She's
(It has)	It's

> eaten.

A. Can you sing?

B. Yes. I've sung for many years.

1. *swim*
swum

2. *draw pictures*
drawn

3. *drive trucks*
driven

4. *speak French*
spoken

5. *fly airplanes*
flown

6. *take inventory*
taken

7. *grow corn*
grown

8. *ride horses*
ridden

9. *write speeches*
written

Have You Eaten Lunch Yet?

Have { I / we / you / they } eaten?
Has { he / she / it }

Yes, { I / we / you / they } have.
{ he / she / it } has.

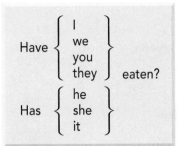

eat ate eaten

eat lunch

A. Have you **eaten** lunch yet?

B. Yes, I have. I **ate** lunch a little while ago.

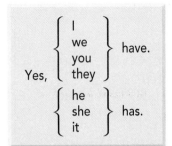

write wrote written

write her composition

A. Has Tina **written** her composition yet?

B. Yes, she has. She **wrote** her composition a little while ago.

go went gone

1. *you*
   go to the post office

give gave given

2. *Dan*
   give out the paychecks

take took taken

3. *you and Susan*
   take a break

do did done

4. *you*
   do Room 24

see saw seen

5. *the employees*
   see the new copy machine

feed fed fed

6. *Michael*
   feed the monkeys

No, They Haven't

Have { I / we / you / they } eaten?

Has { he / she / it }

No, { I / we / you / they } haven't.

{ he / she / it } hasn't.

I / We / You / They haven't (have not) eaten.

He / She / It hasn't (has not)

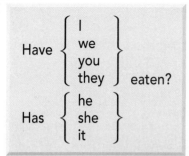

give
gave
given

give blood

A. Have you **given** blood recently?

B. No, I haven't. I haven't **given** blood in a long time.

go
went
gone

go fishing

A. Has your father **gone** fishing recently?

B. No, he hasn't. He hasn't **gone** fishing in a long time.

write
wrote
written

1. *you*
   write in your journal

be
was/were
been

2. *Dorothy*
   be sick

get
got
gotten

3. *your son*
   get a haircut

run
ran
run

4. *you and your wife*
   run in a marathon

have
had
had

5. *you*
   have a medical checkup

wear
wore
worn

6. *Anthony*
   wear his tuxedo

 4

How Long?

for	since
five years	five o'clock
a week	last week
a long time	2001
many years	he started college

A. How long have you known how to water-ski?

B. I've known how to water-ski for many years.

A. How long has Alexander been a vegetarian?

B. He's been a vegetarian since he started college.

1. *be married*
   ten years

2. *have a toothache*
   ten o'clock this morning

3. *be in the hospital*
   last week

4. *own this car*
   thirty-two years

5. *have a British accent*
   she moved to London

6. *know each other*
   2001

7. *play the violin*
   he was in first grade

8. *like hip hop music*
   a long time

9. *want to be an actress*
   she was four years old

A VERY BUSY DAY AT THE OFFICE

Things to Do Today

- ☑ go to the bank
- ☐ take the mail to the post office
- ☐ write my monthly report
- ☑ meet with the personnel officer about my maternity leave
- ☐ speak to the boss about my salary
- ☑ send a fax to the company's office in Tokyo
- ☐ read the office manager's memo about recycling
- ☐ see the training video about the new computer system

Allison is having a very busy day at the office. She has done some of the things she has to do today, but there are many other things she hasn't done yet. She has gone to the bank, but she hasn't taken the mail to the post office yet. She also hasn't written her monthly report. She has already met with the personnel officer about her maternity leave, but she hasn't spoken to the boss yet about her salary. She has sent a fax to the company's office in Tokyo. She hasn't read the office manager's memo about recycling. And she hasn't seen the training video about the new computer system. Allison is probably going to stay late at the office today so she can do all the things she hasn't done yet.

 READING *CHECK-UP*

Q & A

Allison's co-workers are asking her about the things she has done today. Using this model, create dialogs based on the story.

A. Allison, have you _____ yet?

B. { Yes, I have. }
{ No, I haven't. }

LISTENING

Carl is going to have a party at his apartment this Saturday night. This is the list of things that Carl needs to do to get ready for the party. Check the things on the list that Carl has already done.

- ___ go to the supermarket
- ___ clean the apartment
- ___ get balloons at the party store
- ___ buy some new dance music
- ___ hang up the decorations
- ___ make the food
- ___ tell the neighbors about the party
- ___ give the dog a bath

They've Been Dancing for Ten Hours

(I have)	I've
(We have)	We've
(You have)	You've
(They have)	They've
(He has)	He's
(She has)	She's
(It has)	It's

been working.

A. How long have your friends been dancing?

B. They've been dancing for ten hours.

1. *wait for the bus*
since 8 o'clock

2. *study*
for five hours

3. *work here*
for thirty-five years

4. *argue*
since we got here

5. *go out*
for three months

6. *leak*
since last week

7. *live in Florida*
since they retired

8. *snore*
all night

9.

What Have They Been Doing?

(I have)	I've	
(We have)	We've	
(You have)	You've	
(They have)	They've	written.
(He has)	He's	
(She has)	She's	
(It has)	It's	

(I have)	I've	
(We have)	We've	
(You have)	You've	
(They have)	They've	been writing.
(He has)	He's	
(She has)	She's	
(It has)	It's	

A. Cynthia looks tired. What has she been doing?

B. She's been taking orders.

A. How many orders has she taken?

B. She's taken more than one hundred.

A. Wow! That's a lot of orders!

B. That's right. She's never taken that many orders before.

Ted

you

Amy and Rick

1. *give tennis lessons*
   more than 20

2. *write memos*
   more than 25

3. *assemble cell phones*
   at least 75

4. *draw portraits*
around 30

5. *read resumes*
more than 200

6. *deliver packages*
over 50

7. *sing songs*
at least 40

8. *sell tee shirts*
well over 300

9. *do sit-ups*
at least 90

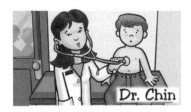

10. *see patients*
around 45

11. *build sandcastles*
10 or 11

12. *make smoothies*
more than 150

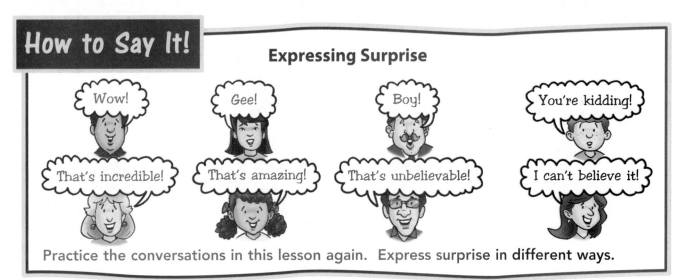

How to Say It!

Expressing Surprise

Wow! / That's incredible!

Gee! / That's amazing!

Boy! / That's unbelievable!

You're kidding! / I can't believe it!

Practice the conversations in this lesson again. Express surprise in **different ways.**

INTERVIEW *How Long Have You ...? / How Long Did You ...?*

Interview another student. Then tell the class about the student you interviewed.

Where do you live now?
How long have you lived there?
Where did you live before?
How long did you live there?

Where do you (work/go to school) now?
How long have you (worked/gone to school) there?
Where did you (work/go to school) before?
How long did you (work/go to school) there?

They Had Done That Before

the day before

I	
He	
She	
It	} had eaten.
We	
You	
They	

A. Did Andrew eat lunch at Burger Town yesterday?

B. No. He didn't want to. He had eaten lunch at Burger Town the day before.

the weekend before

1. Did Sheila drive to the beach last weekend?

the night before

2. Did you go dancing last night?

the morning before

3. Did Paul make pancakes for breakfast yesterday morning?

the day before

4. Did your children have peanut butter and jelly sandwiches for lunch yesterday?

the evening before

5. Did you and your friends see a movie yesterday evening?

the Saturday before

6. Did the Browns take their children to the aquarium last Saturday afternoon?

It Had Already Begun

A. Did Alan get to the movie on time?

B. No, he didn't. By the time he got to the movie, it had already begun.

1. *plane*
take off

2. *bank*
close

3. *play*
start

4. *game*
begin

5. *meeting*
end

6. *train*
leave the station

7. *ferry*
sail away

8. *space launch*
happen

9. *graduation ceremony*
finish

They Had Been Going Out for a Long Time

I
He
She
It
We
You
They

} had been working.

A. Is it true that Dave and his girlfriend broke up?

B. Yes, it is.

A. I'm sorry to hear that. How long had they been going out?

B. They had been going out for a long time.

Is it true that . . .

1. you had to cancel your trip to Hawaii?
plan it

2. your husband got laid off at the factory?
work there

3. your grandparents had to sell their house?
live there

4. your daughter injured herself and couldn't participate in the gymnastics competition?
train for it

5. your son got sick and couldn't perform in the school play?
rehearse for it

6. you came down with the flu and you couldn't take the SAT test?
prepare for it

IT WASN'T THE WEDDING THEY HAD PLANNED

Albert and Helen Porter had worked very hard to prepare for their daughter Ashley's wedding last July. Ashley had always wanted to get married at home in an outdoor ceremony. Albert and Helen had spent months planning the wedding and getting their house ready for the celebration.

On the night before the wedding, as Albert and Helen went to sleep, they felt totally prepared for this special day. They had repainted the house. They had planted new flowers and bushes in the yard. They had even taken down the rusty old swing set that Ashley had played on as a child. They had rented a tent and a dance floor. They had set up tables and chairs. And they had hung decorations all around the yard.

However, when Albert and Helen woke up early on the morning of the wedding, they couldn't believe what had happened. There had been a big thunderstorm during the night. The tent had fallen down. The tables and chairs had tipped over. And all the decorations had blown away. And it was still raining!

Albert and Helen, not to mention Ashley, were extremely upset. But they quickly decided to move the celebration indoors. It wasn't the wedding they had planned, but it was still a wonderful day, and all their family and friends had a great time.

✔ READING *CHECK-UP*

TRUE, FALSE, OR MAYBE?

Answer True, False, or Maybe (if the answer isn't in the story.)

1. Ashley got married last spring.
2. She didn't want to get married indoors.
3. Ashley doesn't have any brothers or sisters.
4. The night before the wedding, Albert and Helen felt they had done everything to prepare for the wedding.
5. It had stopped raining by the time Albert and Helen woke up.

Sometimes we work hard to prepare for something—a test, a performance, a party, a special event, or something else. Sometimes things go well, and sometimes they don't. Write in your journal about something you had worked hard to prepare for. What was it? How long had you prepared for it? How had you prepared? What happened?

PRONUNCIATION Reduced *have, has, & had*

Listen. Then say it.

How long have you been married?

How long has he owned this car?

How long had he been rehearsing for it?

Say it. Then listen.

How long have we been waiting?

How long has she been sick?

How long had they been living there?

GRAMMAR FOCUS

PRESENT PERFECT TENSE

(I have)	I've	
(We have)	We've	
(You have)	You've	
(They have)	They've	eaten.
(He has)	He's	
(She has)	She's	
(It has)	It's	

I		
We	haven't	
You		
They		eaten.
He		
She	hasn't	
It		

Have	I we you they	eaten?
Has	he she it	

Yes,	I we you they	have.
	he she it	has.

No,	I we you they	haven't.
	he she it	hasn't.

PRESENT PERFECT CONTINUOUS TENSE

(I have)	I've	
(We have)	We've	
(You have)	You've	
(They have)	They've	been working.
(He has)	He's	
(She has)	She's	
(It has)	It's	

PAST PERFECT TENSE

I He She It We You They	had eaten.

PAST PERFECT CONTINUOUS TENSE

I He She It We You They	had been eating.

Choose the correct answer.

1. I (went   have gone) to the bank an hour ago.

2. (He had   He's had) a cold since yesterday.

3. My roof is leaking. It (has   had) been leaking since last week.

4. We didn't want to see a movie last night. We (have   had) seen a movie the night before.

5. He (has   had) been writing memos since 9:00. He's already (been writing   written) more than fifty.

1 CONVERSATION MAKING REQUESTS AT THE SCHOOL OFFICE

Practice conversations between a school secretary and a parent.

A. How may I help you?

B. I'm here to _____.

1. meet with my child's teacher

2. pick up my son in the nurse's office

3. volunteer in my daughter's classroom

THINK & SHARE Think about all the reasons that parents go to the office at their children's school. As a class, make a list of the reasons. Then practice conversations between a parent and a school secretary.

2 CONVERSATION MEETING WITH A CHILD'S TEACHER

Practice conversations between a parent and a teacher.

A. Has my son/daughter been having any problems in school?

B. Yes, actually. _____

A. Really? I had no idea. I'll talk to him/her about it.

B. That would be very helpful.

1. He's been forgetting to hand in his homework.

2. She's been falling asleep during class.

3. He's been getting into fights on the playground.

TEAMWORK What other problems do children sometimes have in school? Work with a classmate and make a list of problems. Then practice conversations between a parent and a teacher.

14a

Parents often write notes to school to explain their children's absences or to communicate with teachers. We usually write a note in the form of a short personal letter.

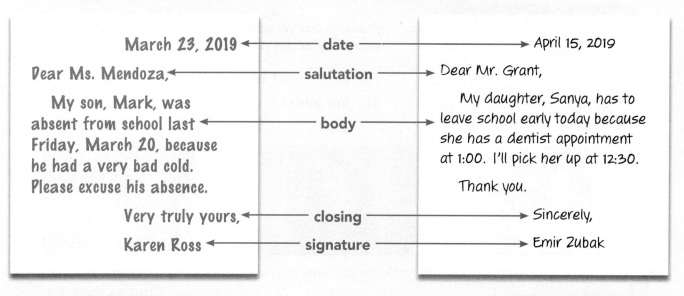

March 23, 2019 ← date → April 15, 2019

Dear Ms. Mendoza, ← salutation → Dear Mr. Grant,

My son, Mark, was absent from school last Friday, March 20, because he had a very bad cold. Please excuse his absence. ← body → My daughter, Sanya, has to leave school early today because she has a dentist appointment at 1:00. I'll pick her up at 12:30.

Thank you.

Very truly yours, ← closing → Sincerely,

Karen Ross ← signature → Emir Zubak

What are the different parts of this note?

May 21, 2019

Dear Ms. Wu,

My son, Adam, has been very unhappy lately, and I'm worried about him. He says that other children in the school have been teasing him and calling him names. A few of his classmates have even started fights with him. He's afraid to go to school because of this bullying.

Can we please meet as soon as possible to talk about this problem? You can call me at 786-369-2548 (home phone) or 786-567-0921 (cell phone).

Thank you.

Sincerely,

Lucy Martin

Write a note to the teacher about each of these situations. Make sure each note contains a date, a salutation, a closing, and your signature.

1. Your daughter had the flu. She was absent for a week.
2. Your son has a doctor's appointment tomorrow at 11:00.
3. Your son was late for school today because your car wouldn't start.
4. Your daughter has been having trouble with her math homework. You want to discuss this with her teacher.
5. Your son's class is going to the zoo next Monday. You're giving him permission to go on the trip.
6. You can't attend the parent-teacher conference next Wednesday because you have to work. You'd like to set up a meeting for another time to discuss your daughter's progress.
7. Next Thursday is a religious holiday. Your son won't be going to school.
8. Your daughter's grandmother is visiting. She will pick up your daughter from school today.
9. Your son has permission to go home with his friend, Alfonso Rivera, after school today. Mrs. Rivera will be picking them up after school.

THINK & SHARE Discuss as a class: Is bullying a problem in schools you know?

Read the article and answer the questions.

Help Your Children Succeed in School!

You want the best for your children! You want them to do well in school so they can have all the opportunities that a good education provides. Fortunately, there are many things you can do to help your children succeed.

Make sure your children have a good night's sleep and a nutritious breakfast before they leave for school in the morning. This will give them the energy they need to pay attention in class. Breakfasts that are high in protein and low in sugar will keep children strong and alert until lunchtime.

Show your children that you value learning. Take an interest in what they are learning at school. Show them how they can use this knowledge in their daily life. For example, follow recipes together and talk about the math involved. Show your children that you, too, are a learner. Let them see that you're interested in the world around you. Talk to them about your interests.

Encourage your children to read. Begin reading to them when they're very young, and read to them often. Take your children to the library. Get them their own library cards. Make reading an important part of family life. Show your children that you enjoy reading. Keep books, newspapers, and magazines around the house. Limit TV-watching to no more than ten hours a week. Children who watch too much television do poorly at school.

Make sure that each child has a special place for homework and studying, a quiet place in your home with good lighting. If possible, children should do homework at the same time each day. Children need to give full attention to their homework. They shouldn't watch TV or talk to friends (on the phone or online through instant messaging) while they're doing their homework.

Talk to your children about their school day to show that you care and to find out how you can help and support them. The best way to get a conversation going is to ask specific questions about teachers, classes, and activities instead of just asking, "How was your day?" If you show that you're really interested and really listen, your children will be more willing to talk honestly and openly.

Pay attention to what your children say about school and how they behave. Look for signs of trouble at school. These can include learning problems such as doing poorly in school or being unable to concentrate, social problems such as having no friends or getting into fights, or physical problems such as having trouble reading what's on the chalkboard. If a child is having any of these problems, contact your child's teacher. The two of you can work together to come up with a plan that may include extra help for your child, a meeting with a counselor, or a doctor's examination.

Keep the lines of communication open between you and your children's teachers. Attend parent-teacher conferences and contact teachers whenever you have a question or a concern. Participate in school activities and events. Join the Parent-Teacher Association. If you have time, volunteer to help in the classroom.

Get involved in your children's education! You'll enjoy doing it, and you'll make a big difference in their school success!

1. What is a nutritious breakfast?
2. Why is a nutritious breakfast important?
3. How can you encourage your children to read?
4. How much television should you allow?
5. Where should children do their homework?
6. How can you get your children to talk to you about their school day?
7. What are some signs that your child is having trouble at school?
8. When should you talk to your child's teacher?

THINK & SHARE Discuss as a class: How do parents in different countries participate in their children's education? What are their responsibilities? How is this different from the role of parents in the United States?

Choose the correct answer.

1. I'm looking forward to attending my daughter's graduation _____.
   A. competition
   B. ceremony
   C. composition
   D. launch

2. Brenda recently spoke with the personnel officer of her company about her maternity _____.
   A. celebration
   B. job
   C. leave
   D. department

3. Oliver speaks with a British _____.
   A. speech
   B. system
   C. accident
   D. accent

4. Parents should _____ their children's television viewing.
   A. limit
   B. set up
   C. help
   D. contact

5. You need to take _____ in what your children are learning at school.
   A. an opportunity
   B. knowledge
   C. an interest
   D. place

6. I've been _____ in my daughter's classroom this year.
   A. volunteering
   B. joining
   C. paying attention
   D. planning

7. Children need to do their homework in a quiet place that has good _____.
   A. learning
   B. lighting
   C. nutrition
   D. messaging

8. I always _____ my children to read.
   A. succeed
   B. value
   C. involve
   D. encourage

9. My son is upset because some of his classmates have been _____ him.
   A. behaving
   B. participating
   C. teasing
   D. concentrating

10. Isabel wasn't able to come to school yesterday. Please excuse her _____.
    A. activity
    B. absence
    C. concern
    D. permission

SKILLS CHECK ✓

Words:
- [ ] be – was/were – been
- [ ] begin – began – begun
- [ ] blow – blew – blown
- [ ] do – did – done
- [ ] draw – drew – drawn
- [ ] drive – drove – driven
- [ ] eat – ate – eaten
- [ ] fall – fell – fallen
- [ ] fly – flew – flown
- [ ] get – got – gotten
- [ ] give – gave – given
- [ ] go – went – gone
- [ ] grow – grew – grown
- [ ] know – knew – known
- [ ] ride – rode – ridden
- [ ] run – ran – run
- [ ] see – saw – seen
- [ ] set – set – set
- [ ] sing – sang – sung
- [ ] speak – spoke – spoken
- [ ] swim – swam – swum
- [ ] take – took – taken
- [ ] wear – wore – worn
- [ ] write – wrote – written

I can ask & answer
- [ ] Have you *gone there* recently?
- [ ] Have you *done it* yet?
- [ ] How long have you *been here*?
- [ ] How long have you been *waiting*?
- [ ] How long had you been *planning it*?
- [ ] Where do you live now?
- [ ] How long have you lived there?
- [ ] Where did you live before?
- [ ] How long did you live there?
- [ ] Where do you work now?
- [ ] How long have you worked there?
- [ ] Where did you work before?
- [ ] How long did you work there?

I can:
- [ ] make requests at a school office
- [ ] meet with my child's teacher
- [ ] identify ways to help children succeed in school

I can write:
- [ ] notes to school

I can write about:
- [ ] something I had worked hard to prepare for

2

Perfect Modals:
Should Have
Might Have
May Have

Could Have
Must Have

- **Evaluating People's Activities**
- **Job Interviews**
- **Making Deductions**
- **Expressing Concern About Others**
- **Apologizing**

- **Recounting Difficult Situations**
- **Driving Rules**
- **Directions**
- **Drawing a Map**
- **Bus and Train Schedules**
- **Interactions with the Police**

VOCABULARY PREVIEW

1. answer the phone
2. apologize
3. daydream
4. fail
5. get lost
6. get stuck in *traffic*
7. hand over
8. oversleep
9. refuse
10. shake hands
11. skip *dessert*
12. yell

15

He Should Have Spoken Louder

| I
He
She
It
We
You
They | should have eaten. |

A. Did Richard speak loud enough at the meeting this morning?

B. No, he didn't. He **should have spoken** louder.

1. Did Gail run fast enough during the marathon?

faster

2. Did Fred drive carefully enough during his driving test?

more carefully

3. Did Mr. and Mrs. Lopez get to the airport early enough?

earlier

4. Did you and your classmates study hard enough for the science quiz?

harder

5. Did Jason write legibly enough on his employment application?

more legibly

6. Did you take the cookies out of the oven soon enough?

sooner

7. Did Sally speak confidently enough at her job interview?

more confidently

8. Did Brian dance well enough at the audition?

better

She Shouldn't Have Driven to Work Today

| I He She It We You They | shouldn't have eaten. |

A. Why is Alice upset?

B. She thinks she **shouldn't have driven** to work today. She **should have taken** the train.

1. *buy a typewriter*
get a computer

2. *take Advanced French last semester*
take Beginning French

3. *cook vegetable stew for my guests*
make a salad

4. *see a movie last night*
stay home and watch TV

5. *wear jeans to a job interview today*
wear a suit

6. *go on a safari for their vacation*
go to the beach

7. *write her composition on the bus*
do it at home

8. *eat an entire cake for dessert*
have just one piece

THEY DIDN'T DO AS WELL AS THEY SHOULD HAVE

Barry didn't do as well as he should have at a job interview today. He didn't get the job, and he now realizes that he should have done a few things differently. He should have spoken more confidently, he should have told more about his previous experience, and he probably should have worn more conservative clothes.

In addition, he shouldn't have arrived late for his appointment. He shouldn't have asked questions only about vacations and sick days. And he DEFINITELY shouldn't have eaten his lunch in the interviewer's office. Barry will certainly do a few things differently the next time he has a job interview!

Vicky didn't do as well as she should have in a tennis tournament yesterday. She didn't win, and she now realizes that she should have done a few things differently. She should have practiced more during the week, she should have done more warm-up exercises before the tournament, and she probably should have gotten a good night's sleep the night before.

Furthermore, she shouldn't have used her old tennis racket. She shouldn't have eaten such a large breakfast that morning. And she DEFINITELY shouldn't have gone out dancing with her friends the night before. Vicky will certainly do a few things differently the next time she plays in a tennis tournament!

✔ READING CHECK-UP

True, False, or Maybe?

Answer True, False, or Maybe (if the answer isn't in the story).

1. Barry didn't speak confidently about himself at the interview.
2. He didn't get the job because he didn't have previous experience.
3. Barry likes to go on vacations and gets sick very often.
4. Vicky didn't get a good night's sleep the night before the tournament.
5. She used her old tennis racket during the tournament.
6. Vicky goes out dancing with her friends very often.

How About You?

Tell about a time when you didn't do as well as you should have. What was the situation? What should you have done differently?

LISTENING

Listen and choose the best answer based on the conversation you hear.

1. a. They should have gotten to the party earlier.
   b. They should have left later.

2. a. He should have spoken more softly.
   b. He shouldn't have spoken softly.

3. a. He should have dressed more comfortably.
   b. He should have spoken more confidently.

4. a. He should have studied harder.
   b. He should have written more legibly.

5. a. He shouldn't have left them in the oven.
   b. He shouldn't have taken them out of the oven.

6. a. She should have gotten a good night's sleep last night.
   b. She should have gotten up earlier this morning.

IN YOUR OWN WORDS

For Writing and Discussion

What should you do if you want to do well at a job interview?

What should you talk about?
What should you ask about?
What should you wear?
What should you take with you?
When should you arrive?

(In your answers, use "You should . . .")*

* "You should" = "a person should."

She Might Have Gone to the Bank

I He She It We You They	might have may have	eaten.

A. I wonder why Sheila hasn't come back from lunch yet.

B. I'm not sure. She {**might have** / **may have**} **gone** to the bank.

A. Hmm. Maybe you're right.

I wonder why . . .

1. Bob was late for the meeting
get stuck in traffic

2. Professor Jones didn't come to class yesterday
be sick

3. Mr. and Mrs. Lane didn't come to our party
forget about it

4. Jimmy was late for school this morning
miss the bus

5. Peggy didn't want to go to the play with us
see it already

6. the neighbors haven't returned our ladder
break it

7. Dad left the rock concert early
have a headache

8. Grandma and Grandpa aren't answering their phone
go away for the weekend

GEORGE HASN'T COME TO ENGLISH CLASS

George hasn't come to English class this evening, and all the students in the class are wondering why.

Henry thinks he might have gotten sick. Linda thinks he might have had a doctor's appointment. Mr. and Mrs. Kim think that one of George's children may have caught a bad cold. Carla thinks he may have had to work overtime. Mr. and Mrs. Sato think he might have gone to the airport to meet his relatives who are arriving from overseas. And Maria thinks he may have decided to study in another school.

All the students are curious about why George hasn't come to English class this evening . . . and they're a little concerned.

COMPLETE THE STORY

Complete this story about your English teacher. In your story, use names of students in your class.

Our English teacher hasn't come to class today, and all the students are wondering why.

_____ thinks _____.

_____ thinks _____.

_____.

_____.

_____.

And I think _____.

We're all curious about why our English teacher hasn't come to class today . . . and we're a little concerned.

He Could Have Gotten Lost!

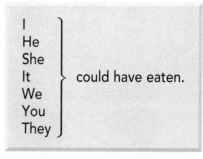

I
He
She
It
We
You
They
} could have eaten.

A. If you ask me, Jack shouldn't have gone hiking by himself in the mountains.

B. You're right. He **could have gotten lost**!

1. *swim to the other side of the lake*
   drown

2. *play baseball in the rain*
   catch a bad cold

3. *ride her bicycle downtown during rush hour*
   get hurt

4. *move his piano by himself*
   break his back

5. *use her computer during a thunderstorm*
   be electrocuted

6. *go skating on the town pond*
   fall through the ice

7. *shovel all the snow in the driveway*
   have a heart attack

8. *argue with a police officer*
   wind* up in jail

9.

* wind – wound – wound

22

He Must Have Overslept

I	
He	
She	
It	must have eaten.
We	
You	
They	

A. Richard came to work late today.

B. I'm really surprised to hear that. He NEVER comes to work late!

A. I know. He **must have overslept**.

B. You're probably right.

1. Maria missed English class all last week.
be very sick

2. Gary skipped dessert at the restaurant today.
go on a diet

3. Mrs. Grimsley smiled at her employees this morning.
be in a very good mood

4. Peter handed in his homework late this morning.
have a problem with his computer

5. Beverly yelled at me this morning.
be very upset

6. Walter was in a terrible mood today.
"get up on the wrong side of the bed"

7. You talked in your sleep last night.
have a bad dream

8. Rover refused to eat his dinner.
eat too many dog biscuits during the day

23

I		
He		
She	must have	
It	might have	eaten.
We	may have	
You		
They		

A. Timmy looks frightened! He **must have seen a scary movie** today.

B. I'm not so sure. He ⎰ **MIGHT have** ⎱ **seen a scary movie**, but that doesn't
⎱ **MAY have** ⎰ usually make him so frightened.

A. I'm a little concerned. Maybe we should talk to him.

B. That's a good idea.

A. Janet looks tired! She **must have worked overtime** today.

B. I'm not so sure. She ⎰ **MIGHT have** ⎱ **worked overtime**, but that doesn't
⎱ **MAY have** ⎰ usually make her so tired.

A. I'm a little concerned. Maybe we should talk to her.

B. That's a good idea.

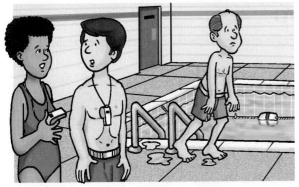

1. Mr. Jenkins looks exhausted!
   swim fifty laps

2. Rachel looks upset!
   fail an exam

3. Steve looks angry!
   have a fight with his landlord

4. Margaret looks tired!
   jog for a long time

5. Wayne looks upset!
   have an argument with the boss

6. Our English teacher looks disappointed!
   find a lot of mistakes in our homework

7. Rick looks exhausted!
   do a lot of sit-ups

8. Senator Wilson looks tired!
   shake* a lot of hands

* shake – shook – shaken

I Want to Apologize to You

A. I want to apologize to you.

B. What for?

A. You must have been very angry with me yesterday.

B. I don't understand. Why should I have been angry with you?

A. Don't you remember? We had planned to **see a movie** yesterday, but I completely forgot!

B. Don't worry about it. Actually, I owe YOU an apology.

A. You do? Why?

B. I couldn't have **seen a movie** with you anyway. I had to **take care of my little sister** yesterday . . . and I completely forgot to tell you.

A. That's okay. Maybe we can **see a movie** some other time.

A. I want to apologize to you.

B. What for?

A. You must have been very angry with me yesterday.

B. I don't understand. Why should I have been angry with you?

A. Don't you remember? We had planned to _____ yesterday, but I completely forgot!

B. Don't worry about it. Actually, I owe YOU an apology.

A. You do? Why?

B. I couldn't have _____ with you anyway. I had to _____ yesterday . . . and I completely forgot to tell you.

A. That's okay. Maybe we can _____ some other time.

1. *go to the beach*
   study for my final exams

2. *have lunch*
   go to an important meeting

3. *take a walk in the park*
   visit a friend in the hospital

4.

How to Say It!

Apologizing

I want to apologize to you.

I need to apologize to you.

I owe you an apology.

I apologize.

I'm sorry.

Practice the conversations in this lesson again. Use different expressions for apologizing.

LUCKY PEOPLE

Gary must have been daydreaming while he was driving to work yesterday. He drove through a red light at the busiest intersection in town. Fortunately, he didn't hit anyone. Gary was lucky. He could have caused a terrible accident.

Howard must have been extremely irritable this morning. He was rude to his supervisor when she pointed out a mistake he had made. Fortunately, his supervisor was in a good mood, and she didn't get angry. Howard was lucky. His supervisor could have fired him.

Mr. and Mrs. Gray must have had a lot of financial problems last year. They were never able to pay their rent on time. Fortunately, their landlord was very understanding. Mr. and Mrs. Gray are pretty lucky. Their landlord could have evicted them.

Mrs. Chen must have been very scared yesterday. There was a big, mean dog outside while she was putting out the garbage. Fortunately, the dog didn't see her. Mrs. Chen was lucky. That big, mean dog might have bitten her.

Ms. Kendall must have been feeling very brave last night. She refused to hand over her purse to a man who was trying to mug her. Fortunately, the man got scared and ran away. Ms. Kendall was very lucky. She might have gotten hurt.

Irwin must have been very lonely yesterday. All evening he made long-distance phone calls to his friends throughout the country. Fortunately, most of his friends weren't home. Irwin was very lucky. He could have run up quite a big phone bill.

✔ READING CHECK-UP

TRUE, FALSE, OR MAYBE?

Answer True, False, or Maybe (if the answer isn't in the story).

1. Gary wasn't paying attention while he was driving to work.
2. Gary caused a terrible accident.
3. Mrs. Chen doesn't like dogs.
4. The dog didn't bite Mrs. Chen.
5. Howard was in a good mood yesterday.
6. Howard's supervisor is rarely in a bad mood.
7. Ms. Kendall didn't give her purse to the man.
8. Ms. Kendall had a lot of money in her purse.
9. Mr. and Mrs. Gray couldn't pay their rent on time last year.
10. The landlord evicted Mr. and Mrs. Gray.
11. Irwin's friends live throughout the country.
12. Irwin never communicates with his friends by e-mail.

WHICH WORD IS CORRECT?

1. Mr. and Mrs. Johnson didn't get to the train station on time. They (should have   must have) left their house earlier.
2. Alan was late for work today. He (should have   must have) overslept.
3. You're very lucky. You (could have   must have) gotten hurt.
4. I (may have   couldn't have) gone skiing with you anyway. I had to work.
5. Susan was an hour late for the meeting this morning. She (might have   should have) gotten stuck in traffic.
6. Arnold's cake tasted terrible! He (may have   should have) taken it out of the oven sooner.
7. I shouldn't have taken chemistry. I definitely (must have   should have) taken biology.
8. Janet wasn't paying attention. She (must have   should have) been daydreaming.
9. My cousin Ronald (shouldn't have   couldn't have) swum to the other side of the lake. He (must have   could have) drowned!
10. Roberta didn't come to the company picnic last Saturday. She (should have   may have) forgotten about it.

{ **How About You?** }

Tell about a time when something bad *could have* happened to you, but didn't. What was the situation? What could have happened?

Tell about a time when you were
. . . lonely.
. . . scared.
. . . irritable.
. . . brave.

PRONUNCIATION Reduced *have*

Listen. Then say it.

He should have spoken louder.

She might have been sick.

They may have gone away.

Say it. Then listen.

You could have gotten hurt.

I must have overslept.

We shouldn't have gone there.

Write in your journal about a time when you did something and then you thought later that you should have done it differently. What did you do? What do you think you should have done?

GRAMMAR FOCUS

PERFECT MODALS:

SHOULD HAVE

I He She It We You They	**should have** eaten.

SHOULDN'T HAVE

I He She It We You They	**shouldn't have** eaten.

MUST HAVE

I He She It We You They	**must have** been upset.

MIGHT HAVE/MAY HAVE

I He She It We You They	**might have** **may have**	eaten.

COULD HAVE

I He She It We You They	**could have** gotten lost.

Choose the correct word.

1. Edward arrived a half-hour late for his job interview. He (must have   should have) gotten up earlier.

2. I'm surprised Carla missed the meeting this morning. She (should have   may have) gotten stuck in traffic.

3. Jack (shouldn't have   couldn't have) worn jeans to his interview. He (must have   should have) worn a suit.

4. Aunt Emma didn't come to the family picnic on Sunday. She (mustn't have   might have) been sick.

5. Marc (may have   shouldn't have) moved his sofa by himself. He (could have   mustn't have) hurt his back.

6. Paul almost got into an accident while he was driving today. He (must have   mustn't have) been daydreaming. He's lucky nothing happened. He (must have   may have) been badly hurt.

1 CONVERSATION   GETTING PULLED OVER BY THE POLICE

Practice conversations between a police officer and a driver.

A. Let me see your license and registration.

B. Here you are, Officer.

A. Do you know what you did wrong?

B. _____

A. That's right. You could have caused an accident. Stay in the vehicle while I check your information.

B. Yes, sir. / Yes, ma'am.

1. I drove through a stop sign.

2. I went through a red light.

3. I made an illegal left turn.

4. I was speeding.

5. I was driving too fast in a school zone.

6. I was driving the wrong way on a one-way street.

2 CONVERSATION   ASKING FOR & GIVING DIRECTIONS

Practice the conversation.

A. Excuse me. Can you tell me how to get to Redwood Avenue?

B. To Redwood Avenue? Sure. Go straight two blocks, turn right, and then make the first left.

A. Go straight two blocks, turn right, and then make the first left?

B. That's correct.

A. Thanks very much.

Now practice with other students. Ask for and give directions to places in your community. Repeat the directions to make sure you understand them.

3 WRITING   GIVING DIRECTIONS & DRAWING A MAP

Give your classmates directions to your home. Write out the directions and draw a map.

Trailside Lines — Bus Number 534

LOCATION	ARRIVES	DEPARTS
Miami, FL		9:20pm
Miami North, FL	9:40pm	9:40pm
Ft Lauderdale, FL	10:05pm	10:20pm
W Palm Beach, FL	11:10pm	11:20pm
Ft. Pierce, FL	12:20am	12:40am
Orlando, FL	2:40am	3:30am
Jacksonville, FL	6:00am	7:30am
Brunswick, GA	8:45am	8:45am
Savannah, GA	10:05am	10:35am
Manning, SC	12:35pm	1:05pm
Fayetteville, NC	3:10pm	4:40pm
Raleigh, NC	5:45pm	6:05pm
Richmond, VA	8:55pm	10:00pm
Baltimore, MD	12:45am	1:15am
New York, NY	4:50am	

Trailside Lines — Bus Number 109

LOCATION	ARRIVES	DEPARTS
New York, NY		6:30pm
Newark, NJ	7:00pm	7:10pm
Baltimore, MD	10:40pm	11:51pm
Richmond, VA	1:55am	3:00am
Raleigh, NC	5:50am	6:05am
Fayetteville, NC	7:10am	8:15am
Manning, SC	10:20am	10:40am
Savannah, GA	12:40pm	1:20pm
Brunswick, GA	2:40pm	2:40pm
Jacksonville, FL	3:55pm	5:00pm
St Augustine, FL	5:45pm	5:45pm
Daytona Beach, FL	6:50pm	7:00pm
Orlando, FL	8:05pm	9:00pm
Ft. Pierce, FL	11:00pm	11:20pm
W Palm Beach, FL	12:25am	12:35am
Ft Lauderdale, FL	1:30am	1:40am
Miami North, FL	2:05am	2:05am
Miami, FL	2:25am	

TEXAS EAGLE

Chicago • St. Louis • Little Rock • Dallas •
Fort Worth • San Antonio • Los Angeles

21/421 Daily — Read Down		◀ Train Number ▶ / ◀ Days of Operation ▶		22/422 Daily — Read Up
1 45P	Dp	Chicago, IL	Ar	2 14P
2 40P		Joliet, IL		1 11P
4 04P		Bloomington, IL		11 43A
4 37P		Lincoln, IL		11 00A
5 14P		Springfield, IL		10 30A
6 22P		Alton, IL		9 18A
7 21P	Ar	St. Louis, MO	Dp	8 30A
8 00P	Dp		Ar	7 39A
12 37A		Walnut Ridge, AR		1 36A
3 10A		Little Rock, AR		11 34P
4 20A		Arcadelphia, AR		9 57P
8 15A		Marshall, TX		7 31P
9 00A		Longview, TX		6 15P
12 00N	Ar	Dallas, TX	Dp	3 40P
12 20P	Dp		Ar	3 20P
1 55P	Ar	Ft. Worth, TX	Dp	2 20P
2 40P	Dp		Ar	1 58P
4 30P		McGregor, TX		11 51A
7 00P		Austin, TX		9 31A
7 42P		San Marcos, TX		8 32A
10 25P	Ar	San Antonio, TX	Dp	7 00A
5 40A	Dp		Ar	10 25P
1 24P		Alpine, TX		2 20P
5 10P	Ar	El Paso, TX	Dp	9 00A
5 55P	Dp		Ar	8 16A
12 20A	Ar	Tuscon, AZ	Dp	2 20A
1 05A	Dp		Ar	1 35A
2 22A	Ar	Phoenix, AZ	Dp	11 17P
2 32A	Dp		Ar	11 07P
6 37A		Palm Springs, CA		5 06P
8 15A		Pomona, CA		3 11P
10 10A	Ar	Los Angeles, CA	Dp	2 30P

1. How many stops does Bus 534 make?
2. What states does it stop in?
3. What *additional* state does Bus 109 stop in?
4. How long does each bus stay in the Fayetteville station?
5. On what day does a Monday bus from Miami get to New York? At what time?
6. On what day does a Friday afternoon bus from Georgia get to Miami? At what time?
7. How long is the trip from Orlando to New York?

8. What time does the train leave Chicago?
9. What time does it leave Los Angeles?
10. What time does the train from Chicago arrive in Los Angeles?
11. Which states does the train travel through?
12. How many stops does it make?
13. When does the train from Chicago arrive in Dallas? How long does it stop there?
14. If you leave Los Angeles on Sunday, what day will you get to Chicago?

COMMUNITY CONNECTIONS Where do you want to travel? Call for information about a bus or train schedule to get to this place, or find schedule information on the Internet. Compare information with a classmate.

Police Department Starts New Community Outreach Program

By LISA EVANS

LINVILLE, March 15 – Linville police department's newest community outreach program, an orientation program for newcomers, had its first session on Thursday. More than thirty new Linville residents from many different parts of the world crowded into a meeting room at City Hall to learn what the police do and how to work with the police to make Linville safer.

Officer Hannon, a Linville traffic officer, led the meeting. He talked about safe driving and explained what to do when a police officer pulls you over for a traffic violation. Officer Sorrento gave crime prevention tips and explained to everyone how to report a crime.

Officer Hannon came up with the idea for the orientation program a month ago after an encounter with a frightened immigrant driver. He was on traffic patrol and noticed a car with a burnt-out taillight bulb. He flashed his lights, and the driver, Juan Mendoza, pulled over to the side of the road.

This should have been a routine matter, but Mr. Mendoza was scared and confused. Instead of waiting in his car, he got out and walked towards the police officer, and Officer Hannon got ready to draw his gun. He told Mr. Mendoza to stand against his car while he checked to see if Mr. Mendoza was carrying a weapon. Then he ordered him back into his car and asked to see his driver's license, registration, and proof of insurance. Officer Hannon called in all the information. When it checked out, he gave Mr. Mendoza a ticket and told him to get the light bulb fixed, submit a receipt for the repair, and then the ticket would be cancelled.

According to Officer Hannon, "I could have walked away after I issued the ticket, but I was concerned. Mr. Mendoza was shaking like a leaf. I asked him what was wrong. He told me that this was his first experience with the police in the United States, and he didn't feel safe. He

Juan Mendoza and Officer Hannon at City Hall.

explained that police officers in his country could arrest you if you disagreed with the government, and that everyone feared them. That's when I realized that we needed to find a way to convince people from other countries that our police department is here to help them. I hope that this program encourages people to cooperate with the police and to come forward and report crimes. We need the community's help to make their neighborhoods safer."

Mr. Mendoza, who worked with the police department to let people in the community know about the meeting, says that this experience has changed his life. "I feel so much safer because I know that I can turn to the police for help. I hope other community members will feel the same way."

The police department is planning to hold another orientation meeting for newcomers on April 15 at 6:00 P.M.

What to Do If a Police Officer Pulls You Over

- Pull over to the right as soon as you can get there safely.
- Stay in your car. Get out of your car only if a police officer asks you to.
- Keep your hands on the steering wheel so the police officer can see them.
- Answer the police officer's questions politely.

---

1. Who attended the orientation meeting?
2. What did they talk about at the meeting?
3. Why did Mr. Mendoza get a ticket?
4. What mistake did Mr. Mendoza make when Officer Hannon pulled him over?
5. Why was Mr. Mendoza afraid?
6. Why did Officer Hannon decide to start an orientation program for newcomers?
7. What did Mr. Mendoza do to help?
8. When is the next meeting?

THINK & SHARE What can the police and the people in your community do to help each other?

Choose the correct answer.

1. You need to get a good night's ____ before tomorrow's important test.
   A. dream
   B. oversleep
   C. sleep
   D. dinner

2. When the president came into the room, he ____ everybody's hand.
   A. skipped
   B. shook
   C. shoveled
   D. stood

3. I'm sorry I forgot to call you. I ____ you an apology.
   A. owe
   B. return
   C. give
   D. tell

4. The officer asked to see my license and ____.
   A. prevention
   B. violation
   C. orientation
   D. registration

5. You drove through a stop sign! You could have ____ an accident!
   A. issued
   B. caused
   C. checked
   D. realized

6. A lot of people attended the first ____ of the orientation program.
   A. outreach
   B. encounter
   C. session
   D. information

7. The train makes several ____ between Orlando and Baltimore.
   A. states
   B. schedules
   C. stays
   D. stops

8. A police officer ____ on the highway because I was speeding.
   A. pulled me over
   B. checked to see
   C. called in
   D. noticed

9. The police encourage people to report ____ in their neighborhoods.
   A. communities
   B. crimes
   C. experiences
   D. newcomers

10. The police officer said the ticket would be cancelled if I repaired my taillight and submitted ____ for the repair.
    A. proof of insurance
    B. a ticket
    C. a receipt
    D. a check

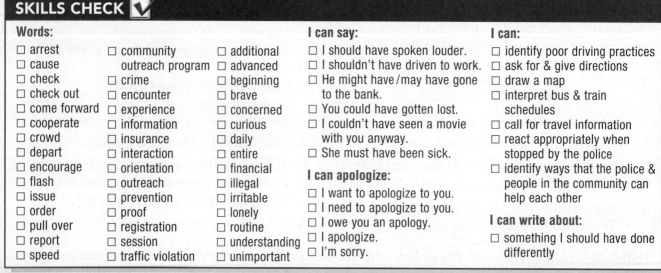

SKILLS CHECK ✓

Words:

☐ arrest
☐ cause
☐ check
☐ check out
☐ come forward
☐ cooperate
☐ crowd
☐ depart
☐ encourage
☐ flash
☐ issue
☐ order
☐ pull over
☐ report
☐ speed

☐ community outreach program
☐ crime
☐ encounter
☐ experience
☐ information
☐ insurance
☐ interaction
☐ orientation
☐ outreach
☐ prevention
☐ proof
☐ registration
☐ session
☐ traffic violation

☐ additional
☐ advanced
☐ beginning
☐ brave
☐ concerned
☐ curious
☐ daily
☐ entire
☐ financial
☐ illegal
☐ irritable
☐ lonely
☐ routine
☐ understanding
☐ unimportant

I can say:

☐ I should have spoken louder.
☐ I shouldn't have driven to work.
☐ He might have / may have gone to the bank.
☐ You could have gotten lost.
☐ I couldn't have seen a movie with you anyway.
☐ She must have been sick.

I can apologize:

☐ I want to apologize to you.
☐ I need to apologize to you.
☐ I owe you an apology.
☐ I apologize.
☐ I'm sorry.

I can:

☐ identify poor driving practices
☐ ask for & give directions
☐ draw a map
☐ interpret bus & train schedules
☐ call for travel information
☐ react appropriately when stopped by the police
☐ identify ways that the police & people in the community can help each other

I can write about:

☐ something I should have done differently

Passive Voice
Relative Pronouns

- Discussing Creative Works
- Describing Work Tasks Accomplished
- Discussing Things That Have Happened to People
- Describing Accomplishments

- Securing Services
- Automobile Repairs
- Civics: U.S. History
- Making a Timeline
- Historical Narratives
- Discussing Opinions

VOCABULARY PREVIEW

1. bicyclist	6. flowerpot	11. poodle
2. casserole	7. identification card	12. puddle
3. courier	8. invention	13. sidewalk
4. decorations	9. mural	14. uniform
5. dinosaur skeleton	10. pickpocket	15. windowsill

This Is a Very Scary Short Story!

Edgar Allan Poe wrote this short story.
This short story **was written** by Edgar Allan Poe.

A. This is a very scary short story!

B. I think so, too.

A. Who wrote it?

B. I'm not sure. I think it **was written** by Edgar Allan Poe.

A. This is a very elegant uniform!

B. I think so, too.

A. Who wore it?

B. I'm not sure. I think it **was worn** by Napoleon.

1. This is a very old airplane!
fly • *the Wright Brothers*

2. This is a beautiful sonata!
compose • *Mozart*

3. This is really a fascinating movie!
direct • *Fellini*

4. This is a very funny political cartoon!
draw • *Richard Hill*

5. This is a very interesting invention!
invent • *Thomas Edison*

6. This is a magnificent portrait!
paint • *Rembrandt*

7. This is an amazing dinosaur skeleton!
find • *archeologists in Asia*

8. This is an impressive building!
design • *Frank Lloyd Wright*

9. This is a very good photograph of you!
take • *Uncle George*

10. This is a very sad poem!
write • *Shakespeare*

11. This is an extremely colorful mural!
do • *the students at Central High School*

12. This is a delicious tuna casserole!
make • *Millie Swensen*

It's Already Been Written

> Somebody has written the report.
> The report **has been written**.
>
> Somebody has hung up the decorations.
> The decorations **have been hung up**.

A. Do you want me to write the accident report?

B. No. Don't worry about it. It's already **been written**.

A. Do you want me to hang up the decorations?

B. No. Don't worry about it. They've already **been hung up**.

1. *sweep the floor*

2. *do the dishes*

3. *set the alarm*

4. *set up the meeting room*

5. *give out the paychecks*

6. *distribute the mail*

7. *make the beds in Room 219*

8. *hide the teacher's birthday present*

9. *take out the trash*

10. *send the packages*

11. *feed the monkeys*

12. *sing the National Anthem*

Have You Heard About . . . ?

A. Have you heard about Helen?

B. No, I haven't. What happened?

A. She **was given** a raise last week.

B. That's great! That's the second time she's **been given** a raise this year!

A. Have you heard about Henry?

B. No, I haven't. What happened?

A. He **was hurt** during a football game last week.

B. That's terrible! That's the second time he's **been hurt** during a football game this year!

1. *Maria promoted*

2. *our mail carrier bitten by a dog*

3. *Aunt Martha invited to the White House*

4. *Stuart*
hit by a car

5. *Mr. and Mrs. Tyler*
robbed

6. *Jennifer*
offered a movie contract

7. *Frank*
fired

8. *Mrs. Mendoza*
taken to the hospital

9. *Arthur*
rejected by the army

10. *Diane*
sent to Honolulu on
business

11. *Albert*
chosen "Employee of the
Month"

12.

How to Say It!

Reacting to Good News

That's great!
That's fantastic!
That's wonderful!
That's great news!
That's fantastic news!
That's wonderful news!
I'm happy to hear that!
I'm glad to hear that!

Reacting to Bad News

That's terrible!
That's awful!
That's a shame!
That's a pity!
That's too bad!
What a shame!
What a pity!
How awful!
I'm sorry to hear that!

**Practice the conversations in this lesson again. React to good and bad news in
different ways.**

ALAN ALMOST DIDN'T GET TO WORK THIS MORNING

Alan almost didn't get to work this morning. As he was leaving his apartment building, he was hit on the head by a flowerpot that had just fallen from a windowsill. As he was walking to the bus stop, he was bitten by a dog, stung* by a bee, and splashed by a car that had just driven through a puddle. And while he was waiting for the bus, he was almost run over by a bicyclist who was riding on the sidewalk.

While he was riding on the bus, his wallet was stolen by a pickpocket who was standing behind him. All his money and identification cards were taken. As he was walking into his office building, he was accidentally knocked down by the courier who delivers the overnight mail. And when Alan finally arrived at work an hour late, he was yelled at by a manager who was in a very bad mood.

Poor Alan! What a way to begin the day!

* sting–stung–stung

 READING *CHECK-UP*

TRUE, FALSE, OR MAYBE?

Answer True, False, or Maybe (if the answer isn't in the story).

1. As Alan was leaving his apartment building, he was hit on the head by a windowsill.
2. As he was walking to the bus stop, a dog bit him, a bee stung him, and a car splashed him.
3. A bicyclist almost hit Alan.
4. Alan had a lot of money in his wallet.
5. Alan accidentally knocked down the courier who delivers the overnight mail.
6. Alan was yelled at because he wasn't on time for work.

How About You?

Have you ever had a bad day when everything went wrong? When? How did you feel? What happened?

A VERY EXCITING YEAR

In January Amelia was hired as a secretary by the Inter-Tel Company, which makes international telephone equipment. In March she was sent to school by the company to study statistics and information technology. In April she was given a raise. Just two months later, she was promoted to the position of supervisor of her department.

In August she was chosen "Employee of the Month," which is a great honor at Inter-Tel. In October she was given another raise. In November she was invited to apply for a position in the company's overseas office in Bangkok. And in December she was given the new job and was flown to Thailand to begin work.

Amelia certainly has had a very exciting year. She can't believe all the wonderful things that have happened to her since she was hired just twelve months ago.

✔ READING CHECK-UP

CHOOSE

1. The interviewer liked Amelia's resume, so she was given the _____.
   a. raise
   b. position

2. After Amelia had worked at the company for five months, she was _____.
   a. promoted
   b. hired

3. In August Amelia was _____ "Employee of the Month."
   a. chosen
   b. given

4. In December she was sent overseas _____ her company.
   a. as
   b. by

5. Over one hundred people had _____ the position in Bangkok.
   a. been invited to
   b. applied for

6. Many wonderful things have happened to Amelia since she was _____ twelve months ago.
   a. hired
   b. fired

How About You?

Tell about things that have happened to you during the past twelve months.

It's Being Repaired Right Now

> Somebody is repairing my computer.
> My computer is **being repaired**.

A. Hello. Is this Carol's Computer Repair Shop?

B. Yes, it is. Can I help you?

A. Yes, please. This is Mr. Lopez. I'm calling about my computer. Has it **been repaired** yet?

B. Not yet. It's **being repaired** right now.

A. I see. Tell me, when can I pick it up?

B. It'll be ready in about an hour.

A. Thank you.

A. Hello. Is this _____?

B. Yes, it is. Can I help you?

A. Yes, please. This is _____. I'm calling about my _____. (Has it/Have they) been _____ yet?

B. Not yet. (It's/They're) being _____ right now.

A. I see. Tell me, when can I pick (it/them) up?

B. (It'll/They'll) be ready in about an hour.

A. Thank you.

1. *Ms. Evans*
VCR • fix

2. *Ted Clark*
pants • take in

3. *Mrs. Withers*
will • rewrite

4. *Glen Burns*
poodle • clip

5. *Jennifer Wu*
wedding cake • make

6.

JOE'S AUTO REPAIR SHOP

Wilma Jones has been having a lot of trouble with her car recently, so she decided to take it to Joe's Auto Repair Shop to be fixed. The car is being repaired there right now, and it is receiving a LOT of attention from Joe and the other mechanics at his shop.

The engine is being tuned up. The oil is being changed. The battery is being charged. The brakes are being adjusted. The front bumper is being repaired. The broken headlight is being replaced. The hood is being repainted. The tires are being checked. And the broken rear window is being fixed.

Wilma is aware that she'll probably be charged a lot of money for these repairs. But she's confident that her car will be returned to her in excellent condition by the fine people who work at Joe's Auto Repair Shop.

✔ READING *CHECK-UP*

Q & A

Wilma Jones is calling Joe's Auto Repair Shop to find out about her car. Using this model, make questions and answers based on the story.

A. Have you *tuned up the engine* yet?
B. *It's* being *tuned up* right now.

LISTENING

Listen and choose the best line to continue the conversation.

1. a. Do you want me to send them?
   b. Who sent them?

2. a. Do you want me to make them?
   b. Who made them?

3. a. Was your cat hurt badly?
   b. Was your dog hurt badly?

4. a. Is she going to go?
   b. Is he going to go?

5. a. When will Mrs. Green begin working?
   b. When will Mr. Fleming begin working?

6. a. When will Mrs. Davis start her new job?
   b. When will Ms. Clark start her new job?

7. a. Oh, good. I'll pick it up in an hour.
   b. Oh, good. Call me when it's been fixed.

8. a. Oh, good. I'll pick it up right now.
   b. Oh, good. I'll pick it up when it's ready.

TALK ABOUT IT! *What's Your Opinion?*

> Answers **should be written** in your notebook.
> Students **should be required** to take an examination.
> Camping **shouldn't be allowed** in public parks.

Talk about these issues with other students.

1. Should your native language be spoken during English class?

2. Should students be allowed to use dictionaries in class?

3. Should high school students be required to do community service?

4. Should young men and women be required to serve in the armed forces?

5. Should animals be used for medical research?

6. Should skateboarding be permitted on city streets and sidewalks?

7. Should camping be permitted in public parks?

8. Should children be allowed to see any movies they want to?

A NATIONAL HISTORIC LANDMARK

This building, which is the original headquarters of the Lord and Lady Department Store Company, was designed by the famous architect Archibald Morgan. It was built by the Vanderpool Construction Company. Construction was begun in 1845 and was completed in 1847. The building was officially opened in ceremonies that were held on April 13, 1847. These ceremonies were attended by the mayors of several cities, the governor, and the vice president of the United States.

The building's interior was destroyed by a fire that broke out in the early hours of the morning of February 3, 1895. After the fire, the building wasn't used for several years.

During World War I the structure was used as a warehouse for clothing and other materials that were sent to our soldiers overseas. After the war, the interior was rebuilt. Electric lights and modern plumbing were installed, and the Lord and Lady Department Store was officially reopened on June 17, 1921.

Since its opening day, the Lord and Lady Department Store has been considered one of the finest examples of nineteenth-century American architecture. The store has been visited by the presidents and prime ministers of many countries.

On December 5, 1973, this building was officially registered as a U.S. National Historic Landmark.

✔ READING *CHECK-UP*

WHAT'S THE ANSWER?

1. Who was the building designed by?
2. Who was the building built by?
3. When was construction begun?
4. When was it completed?
5. When was the building officially opened?
6. Who were the opening ceremonies attended by?
7. What happened on February 3, 1895?
8. What was the building used for during World War I?
9. When was the interior rebuilt?
10. When was the building reopened?
11. Since its opening day, what has the building been considered?
12. What happened on December 5, 1973?

CHOOSE

1. Cable TV service was _____ in my apartment this afternoon.
   a. opened
   b. installed

2. Our high school prom was _____ by all the students in our class.
   a. attended
   b. visited

3. The factory downtown was _____ by the fire.
   a. rebuilt
   b. destroyed

4. The construction has been completed, and now the store can be _____.
   a. rebuilt
   b. reopened

5. Our City Hall is _____ by many tourists because it's a very historic building.
   a. visited
   b. registered

6. Their wedding ceremony wasn't _____ outside because it rained.
   a. considered
   b. held

IN YOUR OWN WORDS

FOR WRITING AND DISCUSSION

Tell a story about the history of the place where you were born or a place where you have lived. You might want to use some of the following words in your story:

attacked	discovered
begun	founded
built	invaded
captured	liberated
closed	opened
conquered	rebuilt
destroyed	settled

PRONUNCIATION   Reduced Auxiliary Verbs

Listen. Then say it.

The engine is being tuned.

The brakes are being adjusted.

The store has been rebuilt.

Say it. Then listen.

The oil is being changed.

The tires are being checked.

The construction has been completed.

SIDE by SIDE JOURNAL Write in your journal about students' rights and responsibilities in your school. What are students required to do? What are they allowed to do? What are they not allowed to do?

GRAMMAR FOCUS

PASSIVE VOICE

This short story **was written** by Edgar Allan Poe.
The decorations **have been hung up**.
My computer **is being repaired**.

Students **should be required** to take an examination.
Camping **shouldn't be allowed** in public parks.

RELATIVE PRONOUNS

He was hit by a flowerpot **that** had just fallen.
He was knocked down by the courier **who** delivers the overnight mail.

She was hired by the Inter-Tel company, **which** makes international telephone equipment.

Choose the correct word.

1. I really like this photograph of you. I think (it's being   it was) taken by Dad.

2. You don't need to make the bed. It's already (was   been) made.

3. My wife just got a big promotion. It's the second time (she's been   she has) promoted this year.

4. The floor has (swept   been swept), the decorations have (hung up   been hung up), and the meeting room (is being   has) set up right now.

5. These are very funny cartoons. I think they (have   were) drawn by Richard Dawson.

6. The package to Honolulu has already (sent   been sent). It (has   was) sent this morning.

7. A truck almost (ran over   has been run over) a bicyclist on Main Street this morning.

8. The tires on your car (are   have) already (been   be) checked, and the mechanics are (being adjusted   adjusting) the brakes right now.

9. What's your opinion? Should students (allow   be allowed) to use dictionaries in English class?

10. The new museum was designed by the architect (who   which) had designed the public library.

11. After my accident, I was taken to a new hospital (who   that) had just opened the week before.

12. I was sent by my company on a business trip to Nairobi, (that   which) is the largest city in Kenya.

13. A. This is Ms. Chen. I'm calling about the computer (that   who) I brought in last week.

    B. Sorry. It hasn't (being   been) fixed yet. It's (being   been) fixed right now.

WORLD WAR I

In the early 1900s, European countries were in an intense competition. They competed for political and economic power. This led to the start of World War I in 1914. England, France, and Russia became allies and protected each other from attacks by Germany and Austria-Hungary. The United States entered World War I in 1917 and helped the Allies win the war. The war ended in 1918.

British troops fighting in France, 1916.

THE GREAT DEPRESSION

After World War I ended, the U.S. economy grew quickly. However, factories and farms produced too much, and European countries didn't have money to buy U.S. products. Americans borrowed money and invested in companies through the stock market. On October 29, 1929, the value of company stocks fell suddenly and the U.S. stock market collapsed. This was the beginning of the Great Depression, which lasted from 1929 to 1939. Hundreds of banks closed, and many people lost all or most of their money. By 1932, twelve million people in the U.S. were jobless.

Waiting in a Depression breadline.

THE NEW DEAL

Franklin D. Roosevelt was president from 1932 to 1945. He introduced laws and programs to help the nation. His plan was called The New Deal. The government gave people jobs to build roads, parks, bridges, and buildings. The Social Security system was established to provide people with unemployment, health, and welfare benefits. By 1939, the economy was stronger. However, there were still about 9 million unemployed Americans.

Work Projects Administration workers, 1935.

WORLD WAR II

In the late 1930s, Germany, Italy, and Japan attempted to increase their powers over neighboring countries. England, Russia, France, and other countries formed the Allied nations. The Allies tried to negotiate with Germany, but promises were broken and World War II started in 1939. The Allies fought against Germany, Italy, and Japan.

Nazi Germany, led by Adolf Hitler, invaded and conquered one nation after another. The Nazis also murdered Jewish people and other minorities. This was called the Holocaust. Under the Nazis, over 6 million Jews were killed.

Dresden, Germany after Allied bombing, 1945.

U.S. troops landing in Normandy, France, 1944.

The United States entered World War II in 1941 when Pearl Harbor in Hawaii was bombed by the Japanese. The U.S. declared war on Japan and joined the Allies. In 1945, the U.S. dropped two atomic bombs on Hiroshima and Nagasaki in Japan. The Allied nations won the war in 1945. The war lasted six years, and 70 million soldiers from 40 countries fought in it. World War II was the most expensive war in history, and many cities were destroyed.

A UN General Assembly meeting in New York.

CREATION OF THE UNITED NATIONS

In 1945, a new international organization called the United Nations, or the UN, was formed. The UN was established to keep peace among countries around the world. In addition to its peace-keeping efforts, the UN also provides countries with economic aid and offers education programs, health programs, and other forms of assistance.

THE COLD WAR

By the end of World War II, Russia had formed an enormous nation called the Soviet Union, which controlled many countries in Eastern Europe. The U.S. and the Soviet Union were the new world superpowers. But the two countries had very different political systems. The U.S. had a democratic government, and the Soviet Union had a communist government. The U.S. and the Soviet Union competed with each other politically and economically. Both countries wanted to protect their interests and gain allies around the world. This was called the Cold War.

The Berlin Wall separating East Berlin and West Berlin from 1961 to 1989.

A protest against the Vietnam War, 1968.

During the Cold War, the U.S. fought Communist forces in two wars. From 1950 to 1953, the U.S. fought in the Korean War. The Communist North fought against the non-Communist South. The fighting ended in 1953, and a border still divides North Korea from South Korea. In the 1950s, Vietnam was also divided into North and South. Communists controlled North Vietnam. From 1964 to 1973, the United States fought in the Vietnam War. In the U.S., there were many protests against the war. When the war ended, Vietnam was controlled by the Communist forces of North Vietnam.

In the 1980s, the Soviet Union began to lose power. The Cold War ended in 1991, after the Soviet Union broke up into independent states.

THE CIVIL RIGHTS MOVEMENT IN THE U.S.

During the 1950s and 1960s, the civil rights movement worked to end discrimination against African-Americans in the U.S. The Reverend Martin Luther King, Jr., was the most famous leader of the civil rights movement. He led protests against discrimination in many states. In 1963, he led hundreds of thousands of people in the March on Washington. During the March, he gave a very powerful and beautiful speech called his "I Have a Dream" speech. In his speech, King said, "I have a dream . . . that my four little children will one day live in a nation where they will not be judged by the color of their skin, but by the content of their character."

In 1968, Martin Luther King, Jr., was shot and killed. The civil rights movement and the nation lost a great leader. The U.S. remembers Martin Luther King, Jr., in a national holiday on the third Monday in January every year.

Martin Luther King, Jr. at the March on Washington, 1963.

SEPTEMBER 11, 2001

On September 11, 2001, terrorists hijacked four airplanes from Boston, New Jersey, and the Washington, D.C. area. They crashed two planes into the twin towers of the World Trade Center in New York City, and both towers collapsed. One plane crashed into the Pentagon, the headquarters of the U.S. armed forces, in Arlington, Virginia. Another plane crashed in Pennsylvania. Thousands of people died in the buildings and on the airplanes.

In 2001, President George W. Bush sent American troops to Afghanistan to fight the terrorist organization responsible for the attacks on September 11. Other countries also sent troops. The conflict still continues.

Rescue workers at the World Trade Center, 2001.

U.S. soldiers in Iraq, 2008.

THE WAR IN IRAQ

Iraq had been an important ally to the U.S. and a supplier of oil. But the U.S. believed that Iraq's leader, Saddam Hussein, was a dictator who had killed many of his country's people and who had weapons of mass destruction. The U.S. launched a military attack on Iraq on March 20, 2003. Thousands of U.S. soldiers died in the war. Hundreds of thousands of Iraqis were also killed, including many civilians. Weapons of mass destruction were never found. The U.S. hoped to bring peace and democracy to the people of Iraq.

CHECK YOUR UNDERSTANDING

1. When did the U.S. enter World War I?
2. What event occurred at the beginning of the Great Depression?
3. Who introduced the New Deal?
4. Which three countries were not Allied nations during World War II?
5. Why did the U.S. enter World War II?
6. When and why was the United Nations established?
7. During the Cold War, what was the main difference between the two superpowers?
8. Which war was the U.S. involved in during the 1960s and 1970s?
9. Why is the third Monday in January a national holiday in the U.S.?
10. What happened on September 11, 2001?
11. Why did the U.S. attack Iraq?

TEAMWORK   U.S. HISTORY TIMELINE

Work with a classmate to make a timeline like the one below. Add 12 important events that occurred between 1900 and 2005. Write each event and its year on the timeline.

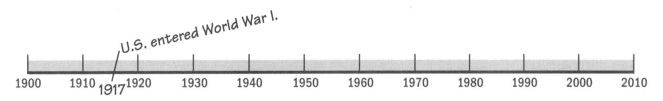

U.S. entered World War I.

1900   1910   1917   1920   1930   1940   1950   1960   1970   1980   1990   2000   2010

Choose the correct answer.

1. I recently _____ for a position at the Blackwell Company.
   A. installed
   B. adjusted
   C. applied
   D. considered

2. I hear they're going to _____ the factory that was destroyed by a fire last year.
   A. rebuild
   B. reject
   C. compose
   D. offer

3. The U.S. and the Soviet Union _____ for political and economic power during the Cold War.
   A. attempted
   B. invested
   C. competed
   D. controlled

4. The U.S. stock market _____ in October of 1929.
   A. conquered
   B. collapsed
   C. divided
   D. broke up

5. During the Great Depression, millions of people were _____.
   A. economic
   B. independent
   C. allied
   D. jobless

6. Unfortunately, many cities were _____ during World War II.
   A. destroyed
   B. produced
   C. launched
   D. increased

7. The United Nations was _____ to keep peace among countries.
   A. negotiated
   B. established
   C. declared
   D. protected

8. There were many _____ against the Vietnam War.
   A. programs
   B. products
   C. protests
   D. weapons

9. The civil rights movement worked to end _____.
   A. discrimination
   B. marches
   C. superpowers
   D. welfare

10. The United States has _____ form of government.
    A. an invaded
    B. an international
    C. a communist
    D. a democratic

SKILLS CHECK ✓

Words:

- ☐ attempt
- ☐ bomb
- ☐ borrow
- ☐ break up
- ☐ compete
- ☐ conquer
- ☐ control
- ☐ crash
- ☐ declare
- ☐ destroy
- ☐ divide
- ☐ drop
- ☐ enter
- ☐ establish
- ☐ fight

- ☐ form
- ☐ gain
- ☐ hijack
- ☐ increase
- ☐ introduce
- ☐ invest
- ☐ judge
- ☐ keep peace
- ☐ kill
- ☐ last
- ☐ launch
- ☐ negotiate
- ☐ produce
- ☐ protect
- ☐ shoot

- ☐ democratic
- ☐ economic
- ☐ enormous
- ☐ independent
- ☐ intense
- ☐ international
- ☐ jobless
- ☐ military
- ☐ national
- ☐ neighboring
- ☐ peace-keeping
- ☐ political
- ☐ responsible
- ☐ unemployed

I can say:

- ☐ I think it was *composed* by *Mozart*.
- ☐ It's already been *written*.
- ☐ I was *promoted* last week.
- ☐ That's the second time I've been *promoted* this year.
- ☐ It's being *repaired* right now.
- ☐ *Dictionaries* should/shouldn't be *allowed*.

I can:

- ☐ identify important events and people in recent U.S. history
- ☐ create a history timeline

I can write about:

- ☐ students' rights and responsibilities

I can react to good news:

- ☐ That's great!/That's fantastic!/ That's wonderful!/That's great news!/ That's fantastic news!/ That's wonderful news!/ I'm happy to hear that!/ I'm glad to hear that!

I can react to bad news:

- ☐ That's terrible!/That's awful!/ That's a shame!/That's a pity!/ That's too bad!/What a shame!/ What a pity!/How awful!/ I'm sorry to hear that!

Feature Article
Fact File
Around the World
Interview
We've Got Mail!

SIDE by SIDE Gazette

Global Exchange
Listening
Fun with Idioms
What Are They
Saying?

Volume 4   Number 1

Inventions That Changed the World

Famous Inventions and Their Inventors

The first known antibiotic, penicillin, was discovered by Alexander Fleming in 1928. It was made from a mold called *penicillin*, which could kill bacteria. Since then, many other antibiotics have been discovered. Millions of lives have been saved by these antibiotics.

X-rays were discovered in 1895 by a German professor, Wilhelm Roentgen. People all over the world were amazed by his invention, the X-ray machine. This invention was so important that Roentgen was awarded the first Nobel Prize for Physics in 1901.

The screw was created over 2000 years ago. It was invented by a Greek named Archimedes. It was first used for watering fields. A person turned the giant wooden screw, which pulled water from lakes or rivers and sent it into fields. The water was used for irrigating crops. Much later, in the 1600s, screws were made by carpenters to hold things together. Today the screw is mass-produced and has an unlimited number of uses.

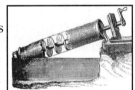

The telephone was invented by Alexander Graham Bell, a doctor and speech teacher for the deaf. The first phone call was made by Bell in 1876. He had spilled acid on his pants and wanted his assistant, Thomas Watson, to help him. The first words spoken on the telephone were "Mr. Watson, come here! I need you!"

Television was invented in 1926 by John Logie Baird, a Scottish inventor. Baird's television certainly didn't look like a television today! It was made out of a box, knitting needles, a cake tin, a bicycle lamp, and a cardboard disc. Electronic televisions like the ones we have today were invented by Vladimir Zworykin in the 1920s in the United States.

The first computer was built in 1946 by two American engineers, J. Presper Eckert, Jr., and John W. Mauchly. It was developed for the army, and it was so large that it took up an entire room! Later, in 1971, the "microchip" was invented, and small home computers were first produced for personal use. Today computers are involved in almost everything we do and are found almost everywhere we go.

FACT FILE

Time Line of Major Inventions

- **3500 B.C.:** the wheel invented
- **3000 B.C.:** toothpaste first used by Ancient Egyptians
- **2000 B.C.:** the sundial first used for telling time
- **1000 B.C.:** kites first flown in China
- **200 B.C.:** the screw invented in Greece for irrigation
- **105:** the first paper created by the Chinese
- **1200:** the abacus, a counting machine, introduced in China
- **1440:** the first printing press set up in Germany
- **1590:** the microscope invented
- **1791:** the first bicycle ridden in France
- **1876:** the telephone invented by Alexander Graham Bell
- **1895:** X-rays discovered by Wilhelm Roentgen
- **1903:** the first airplane flight made by Orville and Wilbur Wright
- **1908:** the first gas-powered cars assembled in the United States
- **1926:** the first television built by John Logie Baird in Scotland
- **1926:** penicillin discovered by Alexander Fleming
- **1946:** the world's first computer turned on
- **1961:** the first manned space flight launched by the Soviet Union
- **1977:** the first cell phones constructed by Bell Laboratory in New Jersey
- **1982:** compact discs introduced by Sony and Philips Corporations
- **1991:** the World Wide Web established

The wheel was invented about 3500 B.C. The first bicycle was ridden in France in 1791. When was the first microscope invented? What happened in 1876? Talk with other students about these major inventions.

Ancient and Modern Wonders of the World

The Pyramids were built as tombs for the kings of ancient Egypt more than 5000 years ago. They were constructed without machines and with very few tools. The kings were buried with many jewels, furniture, and personal treasures.

The Colosseum in Rome, Italy, was completed in 80 A.D. It was built as an amphitheater, a place for people to go to be entertained. Fights between gladiators, fights with beasts such as lions and tigers, and other battles were held there.

Machu Picchu was built high in the Andes Mountains of Peru by Incas during the period 1460 to 1470 A.D. Experts believe it was constructed for religious purposes. It was abandoned in the 1500s, but no one knows why.

Stonehenge is a group of huge stones that were erected in England during the period 2800 to 1800 B.C. No one knows who it was built by or why. Some people think it was used as a sundial to follow the position of the sun. Others think it might have been built as a temple for worshipping the sun.

The Taj Mahal in India was constructed by order of Shah Jahan in the 17th century. It was designed as a tomb for his favorite wife, who had died giving birth to their child. It was built by 20,000 men from many different countries. It is considered one of the most beautiful tombs in the world.

The Temple of Angkor Wat in Cambodia is one of the largest religious structures in the world. It was constructed in the 12th century and took about 30 years to build. The temple was dedicated to the Hindu god Vishnu. Today the site is being repaired and preserved by the United Nations and many countries.

The Great Wall of China was begun in the 3rd century B.C., and it wasn't completed until hundreds of years later. The wall was rebuilt, strengthened, and enlarged in the centuries that followed. It is estimated to be about 6000 kilometers in length. It is said that the Great Wall is even visible from the moon!

Tenochtitlan, an elaborate city in Mexico, was established in 1325 A.D. It was built on an island in the middle of a lake. According to legend, the Aztecs were told by an omen, or sign, to construct the city there. It was inhabited by 200,000 to 300,000 people. Mexico City is located on its ruins.

The Panama Canal was constructed in Panama to connect the Atlantic and Pacific Oceans. In 1901, the United States was given permission to build the canal. It was opened on August 15, 1914. The canal is used by more than 9000 ships a year, and it is maintained by approximately 8000 workers.

Which of these wonders would you like to visit? Why? What are some other wonders of the ancient or modern world that you know about?

Interview

A **Side by Side Gazette** *reporter recently interviewed international photojournalist Sam Turner. Sam has been taking news photographs for twenty years. His photos have been published in newspapers and magazines all over the world.*

Q: Sam, can you tell us a little about yourself?

A: Sure. Both my parents are American, but I was born in Sydney, Australia. My parents both worked for a big American bank, and they were transferred to Australia just before I was born. My parents and I spent a lot of time exploring Australia during our vacations. I was very influenced by those trips. I was really inspired by the natural beauty of the country.

Q: How did you first become interested in photography?

A: I was given a camera for my tenth birthday, and I took it along on a family trip to the Australian Outback. When I showed my photos to people, they were really impressed! I was encouraged to study photography.

Q: So did you go to photography school?

A: Yes, and I was chosen by my teachers as one of the most promising students in the school. One of my photos was selected for a national photo competition, and it won an award.

Q: What has been the most memorable event in your life?

A: I was invited by a group of mountain climbers to travel with them to Mt. Everest and take their photographs at the base camp at the bottom of the mountain. They were wonderful people, and it was a beautiful place.

Q: What photo have you been dreaming about taking someday?

A: I'd like to take a photo from the TOP of Mt. Everest! I'm not physically prepared for that right now, but someday I hope to make that journey. It's my dream!

FUN with IDIOMS

I was given the ax at work today.

Everybody was told about it, but I was left in the dark.

I was held up in traffic.

I was blown away by the mechanic's repair bill.

Do You Know These Expressions?

_____ 1. I was given the ax at work today.

_____ 2. Everybody was told about it, but I was left in the dark.

_____ 3. I was held up in traffic.

_____ 4. I was blown away by the mechanic's repair bill.

a. I was surprised.

b. I was stuck.

c. I was fired.

d. I didn't know.

We've Got Mail!

Dear Side by Side,

We are students in Ms. Baxter's class at the English Language School, and we have a question about the passive voice. It's very confusing for us. It requires different verb forms and different word order in the sentences. Why do we need it?

Sincerely,

"Actively Against the Passive"

Dear "Actively Against the Passive,"

Many students are confused by the passive voice. It is used very commonly in English, especially in written language such as textbooks and newspaper and magazine articles. The passive voice is often used when it isn't known or it isn't important who performs the action. For example:

> The wheel was invented in 3500 B.C.
> The school was built in 1975.
> The paychecks have been given out.
> The computer is being repaired.

When it is known or it is important who performs an action, the passive voice is sometimes used and is followed by a phrase that begins with the word "by." For example:

> The telephone was invented by Alexander Graham Bell.
> This novel was written by Alice Walker.

The passive voice is also used to focus attention on the subject of the passive sentence. For example:

> **The building** was opened in 1847.
> **It** was destroyed by a fire in 1895.
> **It** was reopened in 1921.

So, even if you don't use the passive voice very much when you speak English, you will see it often in print, and you will also hear it being used. As time goes on, we're sure you'll feel more comfortable with the passive voice. Thanks for writing!

Sincerely,

Side by Side

Global Exchange

Kate1: Hi. Sorry I haven't been in touch recently. It's been a very busy time. I have some incredible news! Last month I was chosen "Outstanding Student of the Year" at my school. I was invited to a special ceremony at our city hall. During the ceremony, I was given a beautiful plaque to hang on my wall, and I was offered a college scholarship. The ceremony was attended by the mayor and lots of other important people in our city. My parents and my grandparents were there, and they were very proud. How have you been? What's new?

MarcJ: Hi. It's great to hear from you again. It's been a while. Congratulations on your award. I also have some news, but it isn't good news like yours. Two weeks ago I was hurt badly during a soccer game. I was taken to the hospital in an ambulance. The X-rays showed that my leg was broken in two places, so it was put in a cast. According to my doctor, I won't be allowed to play soccer for the rest of the season. As you can imagine, I'm very disappointed, but I'm confident I'll be back on the team next year. G2G* Talk to you soon.

Send a message to a keypal. Tell about some good or bad things that have happened to you recently.
*G2G = Got to go.

LISTENING   NEWS REPORT

"News Report" True or False?

_____ ①   **a.** A van was hit by a bicyclist.

_____ ②   **b.** Joe Murphy lost the race for mayor.

_____ ③   **c.** Five people were injured in the fire.

_____ ④   **d.** The Terriers defeated the Eagles.

_____ ⑤   **e.** The police discovered the robbery.

What Are They Saying?

. a period	, a comma	' an apostrophe
? a question mark	! an exclamation point	: a colon

Practice these conversations with a classmate.

> This historic building was completed in 1846?

A. Thanks for proofreading my writing. Did you find any mistakes?

B. Yes. I found one error. You shouldn't have used *a question mark* in this sentence.

A. Oh. What punctuation should I have used?

B. You should have used *a period*.

A. I see. Thanks.

> Helens son was bitten by a dog yesterday.

A. Thanks for proofreading my writing. Did you find any mistakes?

B. Yes. I found one error. You're missing punctuation in this sentence.

A. Oh. What punctuation should I have used?

B. You should have used *an apostrophe*.

A. I see. Thanks.

Correct the punctuation error in each sentence. Then practice new conversations about these sentences.

1. When was the first telephone call made by Alexander Graham Bell!

2. The ceremony was attended by the mayor the governor, and the president.

3. I must have been very tired when I took the test:

4. All the tenants apartments were destroyed in the fire.

5. A national holiday in January celebrates Martin Luther King Jr.

6. We're all curious why our English teacher hasn't come to class today?

7. Should animals be used for medical research.

8. I want to visit three wonders of the world Machu Picchu, the Pyramids, and the Great Wall of China.

9. Ms Hernandez was chosen "Teacher of the Year" last week.

10. Alexander Fleming,s discovery of penicillin in 1928 has saved millions of lives.

Architectural Wonders of the World

The Guggenheim Museum Bilbao

Bilbao, one of the largest cities in Spain, had many economic troubles at the end of the 20th century. Politicians and community leaders wanted a world-class museum to bring new life to the city. Three international architects were asked to draw designs for this new museum. The winner, Frank Gehry, a Canadian-American architect, was chosen in 1991. Although the use of computers in architectural design was unusual at that time, Gehry made use of computer technology in bold and innovative ways to create his magnificent museum. The Guggenheim Museum Bilbao opened in 1997, and it was an instant success. The building's graceful design has made it one of the most famous museums in the world.

The museum is built of glass, stone, steel, and titanium, a very strong metal. It is located along Bilbao's Nervion River, in the old industrial area of the city. The museum has 11,000 square meters of exhibit space and 19 different art galleries. Many paintings and sculptures from 20th- and 21st-century artists are displayed there. Since it opened in 1997, the Guggenheim Museum Bilbao has been visited by over ten million people. The museum has brought many tourists to Bilbao, and this has helped to improve the city's economy. The citizens of Bilbao are proud of their city and its beautiful modern museum.

The Petronas Towers

The Petronas Towers are twin skyscrapers in Kuala Lumpur, the capital of Malaysia. The towers were designed by world-famous Argentinian architect Cesar Pelli, and they were completed in 1996. The two modern towers are made of concrete, steel, and glass and rise 1,483 feet into the sky. From 1998 until 2004, the Petronas Towers were the tallest buildings in the world. Each tower has 88 floors.

Many businesses have offices there, including high-tech companies, news agencies, and financial groups.

The two towers are connected by a unique feature—a skybridge that is two floors high and is located at the 41st and 42nd floors. It is 558 feet above the ground. The skybridge is unique because it is not attached to the towers. When there are strong winds, the towers can sometimes move side-to-side several feet. When the towers sway like this, the skybridge is able to move in and out of the towers. Due to its special design, the skybridge cannot be damaged by the movement of the towers. Also, if there is a fire in one tower, occupants can use the skybridge to safely cross over to the other tower. The Petronas Towers are a popular destination for tourists and city residents.

The Burj Khalifa

The Burj Khalifa in Dubai, the United Arab Emirates, is the world's tallest skyscraper. It was designed by American architect Adrian Smith and was completed in 2010. It is over 2,716 feet tall and has more than 160 floors. It also has the world's highest outdoor observation deck, located on the 124th floor. There are 37 floors of office space, over 1,000 residences, a hotel, restaurants, pools, and a fitness club.

The Burj Khalifa represents the new Dubai, a growing city that has become an important part of the international economy. It is a masterpiece of creativity, art, and engineering. The building is shaped like the stem of a desert flower, with wings coming out of the center of the tower. The design of this very modern building, inside and out, has been influenced by traditional culture and art.

The Sydney Opera House

The Sydney Opera House, located in Sydney Harbor, is an enormous arts center in Sydney, Australia. It was designed by Danish architect Jørn Utzon, the winner of a 1957 international design competition. Utzon began working on the plans in 1958. It was a very long and difficult construction process, but the center was finally opened in 1973. Its unique design has white "shells" or "sails" of various sizes and large glass walls. It is one of the most famous performing arts centers in the world.

The Sydney Opera House actually consists of a number of performance spaces. The two largest halls are the Concert Hall and the Joan Sutherland Theatre. There are also several smaller theaters and performance halls, outdoor areas, conference rooms, cafes, restaurants, and stores. Visitors can hear all types of music; watch plays, dance concerts, and opera; and enjoy being at the center. About 3,000 events are held there each year, and the performances are enjoyed by over two million people. Tours of the center are offered to about 200,000 people annually. The Sydney Opera House has made Sydney a world-famous cultural center.

The Baluarte Bicentennial Bridge

The Baluarte Bicentennial Bridge in Mexico is the longest bridge of its kind in the world. It is 3,687 feet long and crosses a deep canyon in the Sierra Madre Occidental Mountains. The bridge is 1,321 feet tall, the tallest bridge in the Western Hemisphere. The bridge is held up by giant steel cables. The cables are attached to the two tall towers of the bridge. The bridge is made of steel and concrete.

The Baluarte Bridge is an incredible accomplishment in modern engineering. It is also a great improvement in highway safety. For decades, the highway going from Mazatlan on the Pacific Coast east to Durango was a long and dangerous trip. The new bridge, which was opened to traffic in 2012, is one of many improvements to the highway. The highway now has a total of 32 bridges and 63 tunnels. The travel time from Mazatlan to Durango has been reduced from 8 hours to 2.5 hours.

DID YOU UNDERSTAND?

1. Who was the Guggenheim Museum Bilbao designed by?
2. What materials is the museum made of?
3. How has the museum helped Bilbao's economy?
4. How tall are the Petronas Towers?
5. What is unique about the towers?
6. Why is the Burj Khalifa called an architectural wonder?
7. What is located on the 124th floor of the Burj Khalifa?
8. When did the Sydney Opera House open?
9. How many events are held at the Sydney Opera House each year?
10. How is the Baluarte Bicentennial Bridge supported?
11. How long does it take to travel from Mazatlan to Durango?

Think & Share

1. Which of the five architectural wonders is the most interesting to you? Why?
2. Describe a famous building or bridge in your area. What is it made of?
3. Every big city has at least one famous building or bridge. Name four big cities and what each one is known for. For example, "San Francisco, California is known for the Golden Gate Bridge."

THE WRITING PROCESS

- Purpose
- Audience
- Pre-writing
- Organizing Ideas
- Writing a First Draft
- Persuasive Essay

Purpose and Audience

Before you write, you need to think about your purpose and your audience.

Purpose: Why are you going to write? Do you want to give information? Do you want to express your feelings or ideas? Do you want to persuade—to convince the reader to agree with you about something?

Audience: Who are you writing for—your teacher? classmates? family members and friends? people in your community?

Pre-writing

Pre-writing is the first step in the writing process. During this step, you **brainstorm**—you write down all your ideas about your topic. Don't write full sentences. Just write words and phrases.

> Farah is preparing to write a persuasive essay about a topic she feels strongly about. She made this list of ideas—facts, reasons, and examples to convince the reader to agree with her opinion.

> Children under age 4 shouldn't watch TV or use tablets.
>
> niece—age 2—too much TV—on all day; doesn't talk
> nephew—age 4—always using tablet; doesn't read books
> need statistic—children's TV watching hours per week
> my job as kindergarten teacher:
>   children don't pay attention
>   children can't sit still
> statistic—percent of children using tablets

Organizing Ideas

The second step in the writing process is to organize your ideas. You look at all the ideas you brainstormed and decide how you want to put them together. **Branching** is a good way to do this. You write your topic on a line at the top, your main ideas on lines below that, and your specific information on the branches. Farah used branching to organize the ideas for her essay.

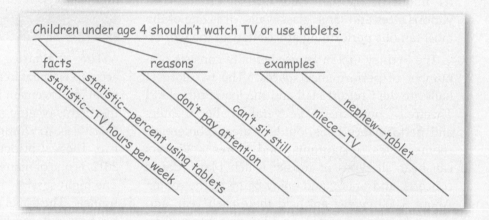

Children under age 4 shouldn't watch TV or use tablets.

facts — statistic—TV hours per week; statistic—percent using tablets

reasons — don't pay attention; can't sit still

examples — niece—TV; nephew—tablet

Write a persuasive essay.

Purpose and Audience: Your purpose is to express an opinion and convince your readers to agree with it. Your audience is your classmates and your teacher.

Pre-write: Brainstorm ideas that support your opinion—facts, reasons, and examples.

Organize your ideas: Use branching to put your ideas in order.

Write a first draft: Share your essay with your teacher and your classmates. Have a class discussion. Do people agree with your opinion?

> *Persuasive essay*: In a persuasive essay, the writer gives an opinion and tries to convince the reader to agree. The writer persuades the reader with facts, reasons, and examples.

Embedded Questions

- Asking for Information
- Indicating Uncertainty
- Referring People to Someone Else
- Reporting a Crime
- Reporting a Missing Person

- Returning and Exchanging Defective Products
- Requesting Product Repair Services
- Warranties
- Consumer Complaints

VOCABULARY PREVIEW

1. conductor
2. flight attendant
3. librarian
4. lifeguard
5. prime minister
6. real estate agent
7. receptionist
8. security guard
9. ticket agent
10. usher
11. birthmark
12. plane ticket
13. restrooms
14. scar
15. tonsils

I Don't Know Where the Cheese Is

Where is the bank?	I don't know where the bank is.
What is he doing?	I don't know what he's doing.
Why were they crying?	I don't know why they were crying.
When can he visit us?	I don't know when he can visit us.

A. Where is the cheese?

B. I don't know where the cheese is.

1. Where are the plane tickets?

2. What was his license number?

3. What are they arguing about?

4. When will the bus from Chicago arrive?

5. Who was the third prime minister of Canada?

6. How long have the Wilsons been married?

7. How long has Alice been working here?

8. Who should I vote for?

9. When is Santa Claus going to come?

Practice the conversations on this page again. Use these expressions instead of "I don't know."

I don't remember . . .	I'm not sure . . .
I can't remember . . .	I have no idea . . .
I've forgotten . . .	

I Don't Know When the Movie Begins

Where does he live?	I don't know where he lives.
How often do they come here?	I don't know how often they come here.
How did she break her leg?	I don't know how she broke her leg.

A. When does the movie begin?

B. I don't know when the movie begins.

1. Where does Mr. Webster work?

2. How much do eggs cost this week?

3. Why did Richard get fired?

4. What time did the plane to Miami leave?

5. How often does the ice cream truck come by?

6. Where did Mom and Dad get married?

7. What does this word mean?

8. What did we do in class yesterday?

9. Why do young people like such loud music?

Practice the conversations on this page again. Use these expressions instead of "I don't know."

I don't remember . . .   I'm not sure . . .
I can't remember . . .   I have no idea . . .
I've forgotten . . .

Do You Know What the Homework Assignment Is?

Where is the park?	Do you know where the park is?
When does the train leave?	Do you know when the train leaves?

A. Do you know what the homework assignment is?

B. I'm sorry. I don't know. You should ask Ronald.
HE can tell you what the homework assignment is.

A. Do you know how much this computer costs?

B. I'm sorry. I don't know. You should talk to that salesperson.
SHE can tell you how much this computer costs.

1. *ask that security guard*

2. *check with the ticket agent*

3. *ask Grandpa*

4. *talk to the boss*

5. *check with the mechanic*

6. *ask your sister*

7. *ask the people next door*

8. *talk with his supervisor*

9. *ask your nurse*

10.

How to Say It!

Asking for Information

Do you know
Can you tell me
Could you tell me
Could you please tell me } *what the homework assignment is?*
Could you possibly tell me
Do you have any idea
Do you by any chance know

Practice the conversations in this lesson again. Ask for information in different ways.

ROSEMARY SMITH WAS ROBBED

Rosemary Smith was robbed about an hour ago while she was walking home from work. She's at the police station now, and she's having some trouble giving information to the police.

She knows that a man robbed her about an hour ago, but she simply can't remember any of the details. She doesn't know how tall the man was. She isn't sure how heavy he was. She can't remember what color hair he had. She has no idea what color eyes he had. She doesn't remember what he was wearing. She has forgotten what kind of car he was driving. She can't remember what color the car was. She has no idea what the license number was. And she doesn't even know how much money was taken!

Poor Rosemary! The police want to help her, but she can't remember any of the details.

✔ READING *CHECK-UP*

Q & A

You're the police officer. You're trying to get information from Rosemary Smith about the robbery. Using this model, make questions and answers based on the story.

A. Can you tell me* *how tall the man was*?
B. I'm sorry. I don't know *how tall he was*.

*Or: Do you know . . . ?	Do you have any idea . . . ?
Could you tell me . . . ?	Do you by any chance know . . . ?

CHOOSE

1. I'm not sure _____.
   a. where do they live
   b. where they live

2. She doesn't know _____.
   a. when the store opens
   b. when does the store open

3. Do you remember _____?
   a. where you put the car keys
   b. where did you put the car keys

4. Could you tell me _____?
   a. why is the boss angry
   b. why the boss is angry

5. I have no idea _____.
   a. how much they spent
   b. how much did they spend

6. He's forgotten _____.
   a. what is her name
   b. what her name is

A "SURPRISE" QUIZ

Mrs. Murphy is giving her students a "surprise" history quiz today, and Jeffrey isn't very happy about it. He has been absent for the past several days, and he's having a lot of trouble answering the questions.

He doesn't know who the nineteenth president of the United States was. He isn't sure when the Civil War ended. He doesn't remember when California became a state. He has forgotten where George Washington was born. He can't remember how many people signed the Declaration of Independence. He doesn't know where Abraham Lincoln was assassinated. He has forgotten why Washington, D.C. was chosen as the capital. And he has no idea what Alexander Graham Bell invented!

Jeffrey is very upset. He's sure he's going to fail Mrs. Murphy's "surprise" history quiz.

✔ **READING** *CHECK-UP*

Q & A

The history quiz is over, and Mrs. Murphy is going over the answers with her students. Using the story as a guide, complete the following conversation.

   A. Who knows who the nineteenth president of the United States was?
   B. I do. It was Rutherford B. Hayes.
   A. And who can tell me _____?
   C. I can. It ended in 1865.
   A. Does anyone know _____?
   D. Yes. It became a state in 1850.
   A. Who remembers _____?
   E. I remember. He was born in Virginia.
   A. Can anybody tell me _____?
   F. Yes. It was signed by 56 people.
   A. Who knows _____?
   G. He was assassinated at Ford's Theater in Washington, D.C.
   A. And who can tell me _____?
   H. It was chosen because the northern and southern states agreed it was a good location for the capital.
   A. And finally, who remembers _____?
   I. I do. He invented the telephone.
   A. Very good, class!

Is Tom in school today?

Do you know { if / whether } Tom is in school today?

I don't know { if / whether } Tom is in school today.

Does Mary work here?

Do you know { if / whether } Mary works here?

I don't know { if / whether } Mary works here.

A. Do you know { if / whether } surfing is allowed at this beach?

B. I'm not really sure. Why don't you ask the lifeguard?

SHE can tell you { if / whether } surfing is allowed at this beach.

A. Do you know { if / whether } anybody here found a cell phone?

B. I'm not really sure. Why don't you ask the cashier?

HE can tell you { if / whether } anybody here found a cell phone.

1. *Do you by any chance know . . . ?*
   ask Mr. Blake

2. *Could you please tell me . . . ?*
   ask the bus driver

3. *Can you tell me . . . ?*
   check with the librarian

4. *Do you know . . . ?*
   speak with Dr. Bell

5. *Do you by any chance know . . . ?*
   talk to our supervisor

6. *Do you have any idea . . . ?*
   ask the usher

7. *Do you know . . . ?*
   speak to the flight attendant

8. *Do you by any chance know . . . ?*
   check with the conductor

9. *Can you tell me . . . ?*
   ask those people over there

10.

READING

AT THE MIDTOWN MEDICAL CLINIC

It's a busy afternoon at the Midtown Medical Clinic. Lots of people are sitting in the waiting room and thinking about the questions they're going to ask the doctor.

Frank wants to know if he broke his arm. Mrs. Wilkins needs to know if she has lost too much weight. Arnold wants to find out whether he should go on a diet. Mrs. Parker is wondering whether her children have the measles. Dan is hoping to find out if he'll be able to play in the soccer match next week. Linda is going to ask the doctor whether she has to have her tonsils taken out. Edward expects to find out whether he needs glasses. And Vicki is anxious to know if she's pregnant.

Everybody is waiting patiently, but they hope they don't have to wait too long. They're all anxious to hear the answers to their questions.

✔ READING *CHECK-UP*

Q & A

The people in the story are registering with the receptionist at the Midtown Medical Clinic. Using this model, create dialogs based on the story.

   A. I'd like to see the doctor, please.
   B. What seems to be the problem?
   A. I'm wondering (if/whether) *I broke my arm.*
   B. All right. Please take a seat in the waiting room. The doctor will see you shortly.

CHOOSE

1. Do you know if _____?
   a. is it going to rain
   b. it's going to rain

2. I'm not really sure whether _____.
   a. the bus will be late
   b. will the bus be late

3. The teacher can tell us _____.
   a. if we'll have a test
   b. whether will we have a test

4. Can you tell me _____?
   a. whether have they moved
   b. whether they have moved

5. I'm anxious to know _____.
   a. how did I do on the exam
   b. how I did on the exam

6. Jackie is wondering _____.
   a. whether she got the job
   b. did she get the job

LISTENING

Listen and decide where the conversation is taking place.

1. a. a book store   b. a library
2. a. a kitchen   b. a supermarket
3. a. a laundromat   b. a department store
4. a. a concert hall   b. a museum

5. a. an airport   b. an airplane
6. a. a school   b. a doctor's office
7. a. a clinic   b. a hospital
8. a. a bus station   b. a bus stop

INTERACTIONS

Practice with another student. Read about each situation. Brainstorm more questions.
Then create a conversation, using the following expressions:

Do you know . . . ?	Could you please tell me . . . ?	Do you by any chance know . . . ?
Can you tell me . . . ?	Could you possibly tell me . . . ?	I'd like to know . . . .
Could you tell me . . . ?	Do you have any idea . . . ?	I'm wondering . . . .

Melinda wants to buy a house. She's visiting a house right now and talking with a real estate agent.

How old is this house?
Does the roof leak?

_____ ?
_____ ?
_____ ?

Do you know how old this house is?
Can you tell me if the roof leaks?

_____
_____
_____

Michael is planning to go to college next year. He's visiting a college right now and talking with a person in the admissions office.

What courses do students
   have to take?
Does the school have a good
   library?

_____ ?
_____ ?
_____ ?

Could you please tell me what courses
   students have to take?
I'd like to know whether the school has
   a good library.

_____
_____

**Police Department
Missing Person Information Sheet**

1. What is your name?

2. What is the missing person's name?

3. What is his/her address?

4. How old is he/she?

5. How tall is he/she?

6. How much does he/she weigh?

7. Does this person have any scars, birthmarks, or other special characteristics?

8. Where was he/she the last time you saw him/her?

9. What was he/she wearing at that time?

10. What was he/she doing?

11. What is your relationship to the missing person?

12. What is your telephone number?

13. When can we reach you at that number?

A student in your class is missing! Call the police!

I want to report a missing person!

1.  Please tell me what your name is.

2.  And can you tell me what the missing person's name is?

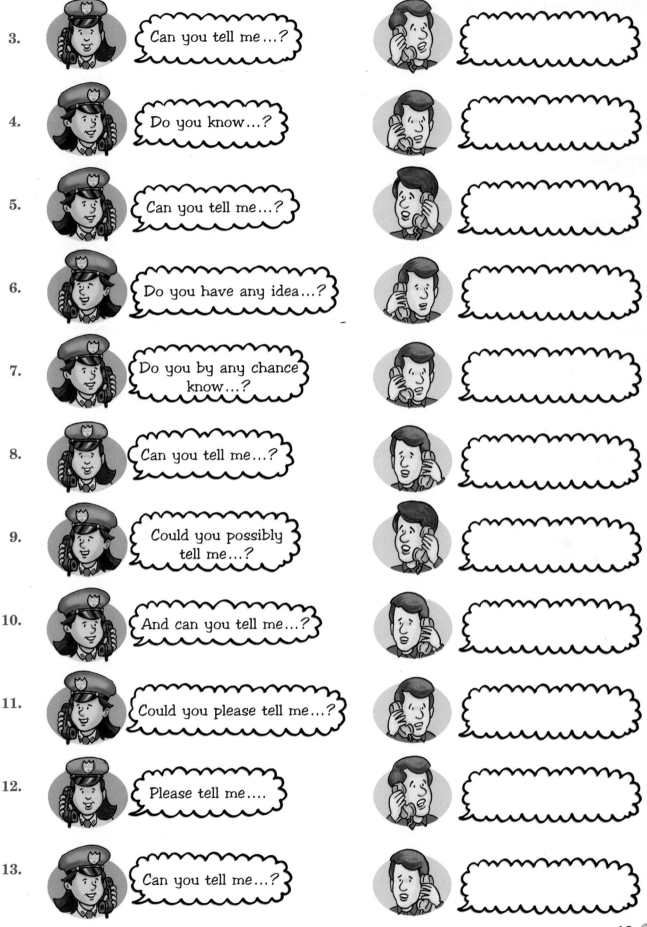

PRONUNCIATION Reduced *you*

Listen. Then say it.

Do you know where the bank is?

Do you have any idea how much this costs?

Can you tell me if the train will arrive on time?

Say it. Then listen.

Do you know if I have the flu?

Do you have any idea if we're almost there?

Can you tell me whose dog this is?

SIDE by SIDE JOURNAL

Some people wonder a lot about the future. They wonder where they will live. They wonder what they will do. They wonder if they will be happy. What do **you** wonder about? What questions do you ask yourself about the future? Write about it in your journal.

GRAMMAR FOCUS

EMBEDDED QUESTIONS:

WH-QUESTIONS WITH BE

Where is the bank?
Do you know where the bank is?
I don't know where the bank is.

What is he doing?
Do you know what he's doing?
I don't know what he's doing.

Why were they crying?
Do you know why they were crying?
I don't know why they were crying.

WH-QUESTIONS WITH DO/DOES/DID

Where does he live?
Do you know where he lives?
I don't know where he lives.

How often do they come here?
Do you know how often they come here?
I don't know how often they come here.

How did she break her leg?
Do you know how she broke her leg?
I don't know how she broke her leg.

YES/NO QUESTIONS

Is Tom in school today?

Do you know { if / whether } Tom is in school today?

I don't know { if / whether } Tom is in school today.

Does Mary work here?

Do you know { if / whether } Mary works here?

I don't know { if / whether } Mary works here.

Complete the sentences.

1. Where's the dog? I have no idea ____ ____ ____ .

2. When does the train arrive? I'm not sure ____ ____ ____ ____ .

3. How did Sally twist her ankle? Ask her brother. He can tell you ____ ____ ____ ____ ____ .

4. Did anyone here find a wallet? Ask the manager. She can tell you ____ ____ ____ ____ a wallet.

5. Is talking allowed in the library? Ask the librarian. He can tell you ____ ____ ____ ____ in the library.

1 CONVERSATION RETURNING & EXCHANGING DEFECTIVE PRODUCTS

Practice conversations between a customer and a store employee.

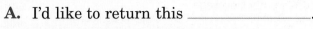

A. I'd like to return this _____.
B. What's the matter with it?
A. _____
B. Would you like to exchange it?
A. No, thanks. I'd like a refund, please.
B. All right. Do you have your receipt?
A. Yes. Here you are.

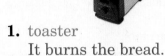

1. toaster
   It burns the bread.

2. iron
   The water leaks out.

3. vacuum cleaner
   The hose is broken.

4. blender
   The motor gets very hot and smells like it's burning.

5. electric toothbrush
   The on-off switch doesn't work.

6. clock radio
   It receives AM stations, but it doesn't receive FM stations.

TEAMWORK Work with a classmate. Make a list of items you buy in a store and the reasons you might return them. Practice conversations about these items.

2 CONVERSATION REQUESTING PRODUCT REPAIR SERVICES

Practice conversations between a store employee and a customer.

A. May I help you?
B. Yes. I bought this _____ here, and it's broken.
A. What seems to be the problem?
B. _____
A. I see. Do you have your receipt?
B. Yes. Here it is. Will there be a charge for the repair?
A. ⎰ No. It's still under warranty because you bought it less than a year ago.
   ⎱ Yes. The warranty has expired because you bought it more than a year ago.

1. notebook computer
   Some of the keys get stuck.

2. cell phone
   The "Send" button doesn't work.

3. printer
   The paper always jams in the machine.

THINK & SHARE What are the repair policies at different stores in your community?

64a

Ultrasonic DVD Video Player
Limited Warranty

Limited Warranty Coverage

Ultrasonic warrants this product and its parts against defects in materials or workmanship for a period of ninety (90) days after the date of original purchase.

During this period Ultrasonic will exchange a defective product for a new one without charge to you.

During the period that begins ninety-one (91) days after the date of original purchase and ends one (1) year after the date of original purchase, Ultrasonic will exchange a defective product for a new one for a fee.

THE ABOVE WARRANTIES ARE SUBJECT TO THE FOLLOWING CONDITIONS:

1. You must keep your bill of sale or provide other proof of purchase.
2. Warranties do not cover any damage to the product caused by fires, misuse, accident, improper installation, or improper maintenance.

How to Obtain Warranty Services

For instructions on how to obtain warranty service, call our toll-free customer service number 1-800-769-5400. They will give you the address of the nearest Ultrasonic Warranty Exchange Center.

When shipping the product, include proof of date of purchase. You are responsible for all transportation and insurance charges.

Edison 25-inch LCD Television
Limited Warranty

What Is Covered:

If your product does not work properly because of a defect in materials or workmanship, Edison Electronics Company will for the length of the period indicated on the chart below, either repair or replace your product. This period starts with the date of original purchase.

PARTS	LABOR
ONE YEAR	90 DAYS

During the "Labor" Limited Warranty period, there will be no charge for labor. During the "Parts" Limited Warranty, there will be no charge for parts.

What Is Excluded:

Your warranty does not cover

- labor charges for installation or setup of the product
- product repair because of misuse or accident
- reception problems caused by inadequate antenna systems

To Get Warranty Service

Contact an Edison factory service center (see enclosed list) to arrange repair. This product must be carried in for service. You must show proof of purchase to receive warranty service.

LIMITED WARRANTY for Miller Vacuum Cleaners

What the Warranty Covers and for What Period

Miller Appliances warrants to the original purchaser of this product:

a. that this product will be free from defects in material and workmanship for a period of one (1) year from the date of original purchase.

b. that this product's motor will be free from defects in material and workmanship for a period of five (5) years from the date of original purchase.

Miller Appliances will repair or replace, free of charge, to the original purchaser any part which is found to be defective in material or workmanship during the period of the limited warranty if the product is returned together with proof of purchase to Miller Appliances or to a Miller Service Center.

Warranty Restriction

Under no circumstances will Miller guarantee the appliance unless it has been bought from a Miller vacuum cleaner dealer.

What Is Not Covered by this Warranty

This limited warranty does not cover the replacement of belts, brushes, bulbs, and disposable bags unless they are defective in material or workmanship.

This limited warranty does not cover damage resulting from repairs, service, or alterations to the product that have been made by repairpeople at service centers other than Miller service centers.

This limited warranty does not cover damage caused by accident or improper use or maintenance of the product.

Problems with Products

1. You bought an Ultrasonic DVD player last week, but it doesn't work. The unit won't play DVDs. What will Ultrasonic do?

2. You just bought an Edison 25-inch LCD television. There's a problem with the sound. What should you do?

3. You bought a Miller vacuum cleaner four years ago. The motor isn't working. What should you do?

4. You bought an Edison 25-inch LCD television six months ago. It isn't working. What will your warranty pay for?

5. The Ultrasonic DVD player you bought two months ago is broken. What should you do? What, if anything, will you have to pay?

6. The Miller vacuum cleaner you bought last month hasn't been working since you dropped it. Will the warranty cover it? Why, or why not?

7. The Ultrasonic DVD player you bought nine months ago has stopped working. Can you still exchange it? If so, what will you have to pay?

((((((((● Know Your Consumer Rights! ●))))))))

Don't be afraid to speak up when you have a problem with something you've bought. You can solve most consumer problems by speaking with a customer service representative or a store manager or by writing a letter of complaint. Sometimes, however, you need to do more. Fortunately, there are a number of organizations that can help you, including consumer hotlines at radio and TV stations, the Better Business Bureau, and your local government's consumer affairs department.

Timothy Chang learned how helpful a consumer hotline could be when he tried to return a television. Mr. Chang had ordered a large flat-screen plasma television online from Big Buy Electronics. When it arrived at his home and he opened the box, he saw that the screen was cracked. He called the store to complain and was told to contact the Internet Sales department. However, the person in that department insisted that the television was in good condition when it was sent from the factory. She told him to call National Parcel Service, the shipping company. National Parcel Service refused to take responsibility for the damage because Mr. Chang had signed for the box. (The box hadn't looked damaged.) Mr. Chang finally called the consumer hotline at a local TV station. A consumer affairs reporter investigated the problem, and a week later Big Buy Electronics sent Mr. Chang a new television.

Julia Cruz also had a problem with an electronics store. She bought a desktop computer from Electronics City, but it didn't work. She brought it back to the store the next week, and they agreed to repair it. But two weeks later, when the repairs were completed, the computer still didn't work. This time, Ms. Cruz asked for a new computer. The manager refused her request. Once again, she left her computer with the repair department. It took another two weeks before she got her computer back, and it still didn't work. This time Electronics City refused to replace her computer because the 30-day return period had expired. She was told to send the computer to the manufacturer for repairs under the one-year warranty. Ms. Cruz was tired of arguing with Electronics City. She called the Better Business Bureau for help. She found out that there were more than 100 complaints filed against Electronics City, and the store had promised the Bureau that it would improve its customer service. She went back to the store with this information and finally convinced the store manager to give her a new computer. (Most companies will resolve your complaint when they hear from the Better Business Bureau. If they don't, the Bureau can bring in a mediator to solve the problem.)

Tamara Nelson had a frustrating experience with a health club and turned to a local consumer affairs agency for help. Ms. Nelson joined Gould's Health Club when she received a special offer in the mail. She signed a contract and paid the membership fee ($50) and the first month's dues ($75) with her credit card. She was told that the club would automatically deduct her dues from her credit card each month, and she could cancel her membership at any time. At the end of the first month, Ms. Nelson decided to cancel her membership. The membership clerk gave her a form to fill out and explained that the club would keep her $50 membership fee. Ms. Nelson thought that was fair. At least she wouldn't have to pay any more dues. But two weeks later her credit card statement arrived, and she saw that she had been billed $75 for a second month's dues. She called the club and was told that they billed in advance but she would receive a $75 credit on her next credit card bill. The next credit card statement arrived with no credit and another $75 charge for the third month's dues. She called the local Department of Consumer Affairs for advice. They told her to follow the instructions for disputing a charge on the back of her credit card statement and the credit card company would get her money back. Ms. Nelson sent the information to her credit card company, and the next month there was a $150 credit on her bill.

Tell the class about a consumer problem you had. If you solved the problem, describe how. If not, what could you have done to solve it? Discuss with the class.

Choose the correct answer.

1. Can we _____ you at that telephone number?
   A. require
   B. receive
   C. run into
   D. reach

2. Natasha _____ to find out soon if she's going to get a raise.
   A. wonders
   B. expects
   C. invents
   D. results

3. Your _____ has expired because you bought the printer more than a year ago.
   A. alteration
   B. restriction
   C. warranty
   D. workmanship

4. If you want to exchange this, you'll need to show proof of _____.
   A. purchase
   B. circumstance
   C. protection
   D. maintenance

5. According to the warranty, the customer is _____ for all transportation costs.
   A. reliable
   B. responsible
   C. disposable
   D. limited

6. If the CD player is defective, the manufacturer will replace it free of _____.
   A. damage
   B. change
   C. charge
   D. condition

7. A mediator can help you _____ the problem you're having.
   A. provide
   B. result
   C. cause
   D. solve

8. It's important to know your consumer _____.
   A. rights
   B. bills
   C. service
   D. instructions

9. The warranty for this product does not _____ repair due to misuse or accident.
   A. resolve
   B. contact
   C. cover
   D. obtain

10. If you're unhappy with your purchase, you can write a letter of _____.
    A. condition
    B. complaint
    C. coverage
    D. contract

SKILLS CHECK ✓

Words:

- □ cover
- □ deduct
- □ dispute
- □ exchange
- □ expire
- □ guarantee
- □ improve
- □ insist
- □ investigate
- □ obtain
- □ repair
- □ replace
- □ resolve
- □ result
- □ return
- □ warrant

- □ Better Business Bureau
- □ bill of sale
- □ consumer affairs agency
- □ complaint
- □ consumer hotline
- □ coverage
- □ customer service representative
- □ damage
- □ defect
- □ labor
- □ letter of complaint
- □ limited warranty

- □ manufacturer
- □ mediator
- □ parts
- □ policy
- □ proof of purchase
- □ receipt
- □ refund
- □ replacement
- □ restriction
- □ return period
- □ service center
- □ warranty
- □ workmanship

I can ask questions using:

- □ Do you know . . . ?
- □ Can you tell me . . . ?
- □ Could you tell me . . . ?
- □ Could you please tell me . . . ?
- □ Could you possibly tell me . . . ?
- □ Do you have any idea . . . ?
- □ Do you by any chance know . . . ?
- □ I'd like to know . . . .
- □ I'm wondering . . . .

I can answer questions using:

- □ I don't know . . . .
- □ I don't remember . . . .
- □ I can't remember . . . .
- □ I've forgotten . . . .
- □ I'm not sure . . . .
- □ I have no idea . . . .

I can:

- □ explain problems to store personnel
- □ return & exchange defective products
- □ request product repair services
- □ interpret product warranties
- □ identify consumer rights

I can write about:

- □ things I wonder about the future

5

Conditional:
Present Real (If _____ Will)
Present Unreal (If _____ Would)
Hope-Clauses

- Describing Plans and Intentions
- Consequences of Actions
- Discussing Future Events
- Expressing Hopes
- Asking for and Giving Reasons
- Making Deductions

- Emergencies
- Reporting an Emergency
- Responding to Directions of Emergency Personnel
- Home Fire Safety
- Smoke Detectors

VOCABULARY PREVIEW

1. coin
2. pollution
3. report card
4. representative
5. wishing well
6. drop in
7. encourage
8. hold hands
9. increase
10. sneeze
11. aggressive
12. burnt
13. carsick
14. dressed up
15. missing

They Aren't Sure

| if _____ will _____ |

A. How is Angela going to get to work tomorrow?

B. She isn't sure.
If the weather is good, she'll probably ride her bicycle.
If the weather is bad, she'll probably take the bus.

1. What's Ben going to do this Saturday?
If it's sunny, _____.
If it rains, _____.

2. What are you going to do tomorrow?
If I still have a cold, _____.
If I feel better, _____.

3. What are Mr. and Mrs. Taylor going to do tonight?
If they're tired, _____.
If they feel energetic, _____.

4. Where is Roy going to have lunch today?
If he's busy, _____.
If he isn't busy, _____.

5. Where is Lisa going to go after school today?
If she has a lot of homework, _____.
If she doesn't have a lot of homework, _____.

6. What's Alan going to have for dessert this evening?
If he decides to stay on his diet, _____.
If he decides to forget about his diet, _____.

Do You Think . . . ?

if _____ might _____

A. Do you think Rover should come to the beach with us today?

B. No, I don't. If he comes to the beach with us today, he might get carsick.

1. Do you think Abigail should go to school today?

give her cold to the other children

2. Do you think I should skip my history class today?

miss something important

3. Do you think Roger should quit his job?

have trouble finding another one

4. Do you think I should put some more salt in the soup?

spoil it

5. Do you think we should try to break up that fight?

get hurt

6. Do you think Ricky should stay up and watch TV with us?

have trouble getting up in the morning

7. Do you think I should marry Norman?

regret it for the rest of your life

8.

I hope it rains tomorrow.
I hope it doesn't rain tomorrow.

Will our team win the game tomorrow?
I hope so.

A. I hope our team wins the game tomorrow.

B. I hope so, too.

Will the teacher give a quiz today?
I hope not.

A. I hope the teacher doesn't give a quiz today.

B. I hope not, too.

Will I get the job?
I hope so.

1.

Will the cake be burnt?
I hope not.

2.

Will the weather be nice this weekend?
I hope so.

3.

Will our dinner guests be late?
I hope not.

4.

Will it rain tomorrow?
I hope not.

5.

Will our new boss be friendly?
I hope so.

6.

Will Dad be laid off again?
I hope not.

7.

Will we be invited to our English teacher's birthday party? I hope so.

8.

I Hope

A. Do you think the train will be crowded?

B. I hope not.
If the train is crowded, we'll have to stand.
And if we have to stand, we'll be exhausted by the time we get to work!

A. You're right. I hope the train isn't crowded.

1.

A. Do you think the boss will retire this year?

B. I hope not.
If _____, his son will take his place.
And if _____, everybody will quit!

A. You're right. I hope _____.

2.

A. Do you think the economy will get worse this year?

B. I hope not.
If _____, I'll have to get a second job.
And if _____, my family will be very upset!

A. You're right. I hope _____.

3.

A. Do you think Mr. Mudge will increase our rent this year?

B. I hope not.
If _____, we won't be able to pay it.
And if _____, we'll have to move!

A. You're right. I hope _____.

4.

A. Do you think our computer will be at the repair shop for a long time?

B. I hope not.
If _____, we won't have access to the Internet.
And if _____, we won't be able to read our e-mail!

A. You're right. I hope _____.

THE WISHING WELL

There's a park in the center of Danville, and in the park there's a wishing well. It's a very popular spot with the people of Danville. Every day people pass by the wishing well, drop in a coin, and make a wish. Some people make wishes about their jobs, others make wishes about the weather, and lots of people make wishes about their families and friends.

Today is a particularly busy day at the wishing well. Many people are coming by and making wishes about their hopes for the future.

Ralph hopes he sells a lot of used cars this month. If he sells a lot of used cars, he'll receive a large year-end bonus.

Patricia hopes she gets a raise soon. If she gets a raise, her family will be able to take a vacation.

Andy hopes it snows tomorrow. If it snows, his school might be closed.

Nancy and Paul hope they find a cheap apartment soon. If they find a cheap apartment, they won't have to live with Paul's parents anymore.

Claudia hopes her next movie is a big success. If it's a big success, she'll be rich and famous.

John hopes he gets good grades on his next report card. If he gets good grades, his parents will buy him the CD player he has wanted for a long time.

Mr. and Mrs. Clark hope they live to be a hundred. If they live to be a hundred, they'll be able to watch their grandchildren and great-grandchildren grow up.

J.P. Morgan hopes the nation's economy improves next year. If the economy improves, his company's profits will increase.

And Wendy hopes she gets accepted to medical school. If she gets accepted to medical school, she'll become a doctor, just like her mother and grandfather.

You can see why the wishing well is a very popular spot with the people of Danville. Day after day, people pass by, drop in their coins, and hope that their wishes come true.

✔ READING *CHECK-UP*

Q & A

You're talking with the people in the story. Using this model, create dialogs based on the story.

A. I hope *I sell a lot of used cars this month*.
B. Oh?
A. Yes. If *I sell a lot of used cars, I'll receive a large year-end bonus*.
B. Well, good luck! I hope *you sell a lot of used cars*!
A. Thanks.

CHOOSE

1. We hope our landlord doesn't ____ our rent.
   a. increase
   b. improve

2. Jennifer is very smart. She gets good ____ in all her subjects.
   a. cards
   b. grades

3. People go to the wishing well and make ____ about the future.
   a. profits
   b. wishes

4. Have you ____ today's mail yet?
   a. received
   b. accepted

5. Arthur hopes his new Broadway play is a big ____.
   a. access
   b. success

6. The company couldn't increase my salary this year, but they gave me a very nice ____.
   a. raise
   b. bonus

If They Lived Closer, They'd Visit Us More Often

if _____ would _____

(I would)	I'**d**	
(He would)	He'**d**	
(She would)	She'**d**	
It would		} work.
(We would)	We'**d**	
(You would)	You'**d**	
(They would)	They'**d**	

A. Why don't our grandchildren visit us more often?

B. They don't live close enough.
If they lived closer, they'd visit us more often.

A. Why isn't Alexander able to lift weights?

B. He isn't strong enough.
If he were* stronger, he'd be able to lift weights.

* If [I, he, she, it, we, you, they] were . . .

1. Why don't I feel energetic?
You don't sleep enough.
If _____ .

2. Why isn't Sally a good driver?
She isn't careful enough.
If _____ .

3. Why doesn't Brian get good grades?

He doesn't study enough.

If _____ .

4. Why aren't you satisfied with your job?

I don't get paid enough.

If _____ .

5. Why doesn't Amy have friends at school?

She isn't outgoing enough.

If _____ .

6. Why doesn't Stan have a yearly checkup?

He doesn't care enough about his health.

If _____ .

7. Why aren't most Americans in good physical condition?

They don't exercise enough.

If _____ .

8. Why isn't Melvin a good salesman?

He isn't aggressive enough.

If _____ .

9. Why doesn't my car get better gas mileage?

You don't tune up your engine often enough.

If _____ .

10. Why don't you and Janet get along with each other?

We don't have enough in common.

If _____ .

11. Why don't our representatives in Congress do something about pollution?

They aren't concerned enough about the environment.

If _____ .

12. Why doesn't our English teacher buy a new pair of shoes?

He doesn't make enough money.

If _____ .

73

if _____ wouldn't (would not) _____

A. I wonder why Olivia works so hard.

B. She must like her job.

A. You're probably right.
If she didn't like her job, she wouldn't work so hard.

A. I wonder why Paul is so dressed up.

B. He must have a job interview.

A. You're probably right.
If he didn't have a job interview, he wouldn't be so dressed up.

1. I wonder why Gary is so nervous.
He must have an exam today.

2. I wonder why our supervisor is shouting at us today.
She must be in a bad mood.

3. I wonder why Rover is barking at the door.
He must want to go outside.

4. I wonder why Melanie wants to be a schoolteacher.
She must like children.

5. I wonder why Gregory makes so many mistakes.
He must be careless.

6. I wonder why Beth is home tonight.
She must have to take care of her little brother.

7. I wonder why Donald gets into so many fights.
He must like to argue with people.

8. I wonder why my brother and his girlfriend hold hands all the time.
They must be in love.

9. I wonder why I'm sneezing so much.
You must be allergic to my perfume.

10.

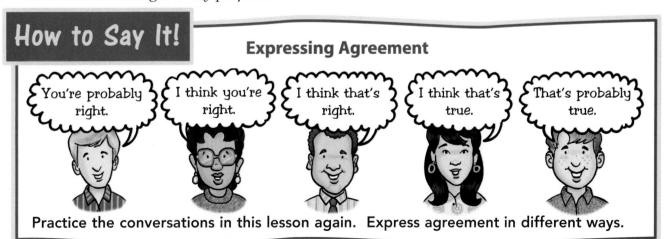

How to Say It!

Expressing Agreement

You're probably right.

I think you're right.

I think that's right.

I think that's true.

That's probably true.

Practice the conversations in this lesson again. Express agreement in different ways.

READING

THEY WOULD BE WILLING TO IF . . .

For several months, Frederick has been pressuring his wife, Doris, to go to the dentist, but she refuses to go. The reason is that she can't stand the sound of the dentist's drill. Doris says that if the dentist's drill didn't bother her so much, she would be willing to go to the dentist. Frederick hopes his wife changes her mind and goes to the dentist soon.

For several months, Barry's family has been encouraging him to ask his boss for a raise, but Barry refuses to do it. The reason is that he's afraid his boss might get angry and say "No." Barry says that if he weren't afraid of his boss's reaction, he would be willing to ask for a raise. Barry's family hopes he changes his mind and asks for a raise soon.

✔ READING CHECK-UP

TRUE, FALSE, OR MAYBE?

Answer True, False, or Maybe (if the answer isn't in the story).

1. Frederick refuses to go to the dentist.
2. Doris is going to find a different dentist.
3. Doris would be willing to go to the dentist if the sound of the drill didn't bother her.
4. Barry isn't willing to ask for a raise right now.
5. If Barry asked for a raise, his boss would say "No."
6. Barry's family began to encourage him to ask for a raise one month ago.

LISTENING

Listen and choose the statement that is true based on what you hear.

1. a. It's raining today.
   b. It isn't raining today.

2. a. We have enough money.
   b. We don't have enough money.

3. a. Mrs. Carter isn't her English teacher.
   b. Mrs. Carter is her English teacher.

4. a. They might receive bonuses.
   b. The company's profits didn't increase.

5. a. He isn't allergic to trees.
   b. He isn't going hiking this weekend.

6. a. He isn't going to the movies tonight.
   b. He doesn't have to work tonight.

Talk with other students about these emergencies.

1. What would you do if you saw a bad accident?

2. What would you do if you saw someone having a heart attack?

3. What would you do if somebody in your family were missing?

4. What would you do if you were bitten by a dog?

5. What would you do if you were at the beach and you saw someone drowning?

6. What would you do if somebody came up to you on the street and tried to rob you?

7. What would you do if a fire broke out in your house or apartment?

8. What would you do if you were lying in bed and you heard someone trying to break into your house or apartment?

Think of some other emergencies and talk with other students about what you would do.

SIDE by SIDE JOURNAL

What would you do with the money if you won a million dollars on a TV game show? Write about it in your journal.

PRONUNCIATION Contractions with *would*

Listen. Then say it.

If I got paid more, I'd be satisfied with my job.

If she were more outgoing, she'd have friends at school.

Say it. Then listen.

If we had more in common, we'd get along better.

If you tuned up your car more often, it'd get better gas mileage.

GRAMMAR FOCUS

PRESENT REAL CONDITIONAL (IF ___ WILL)

If	I we you they	feel	better,	I'll we'll you'll they'll	eat dinner.
	he she it	feels		he'll she'll it'll	

PRESENT UNREAL CONDITIONAL (IF ___ WOULD)

If	I he she we you they	had more time,	I'd he'd she'd we'd you'd they'd	study more.

If	I he she we you they	didn't have an exam,	I he she we you they	**wouldn't** be nervous.

If	I he she we you they	were stronger,	I'd he'd she'd we'd you'd they'd	be able to do that.

If	I he she we you they	weren't careless,	I he she we you they	**wouldn't** make mistakes.

HOPE-CLAUSES

I We You They	hope	I we you they	get	a raise soon.
He She	hopes	he she	gets	

I hope it rains tomorrow.
I hope it doesn't rain tomorrow.

I hope the weather is nice this weekend.
I hope the weather isn't bad this weekend.

Complete the sentences.

1. Alan doesn't get good grades because he doesn't study enough. If ____ ____ more, ____ get good grades.

2. I'm not a good dancer because I'm not graceful. If ____ ____ graceful, ____ ____ a good dancer.

3. Alexandra is nervous today. She must have a big exam. If ____ ____ ____ a big exam, ____ ____ ____ nervous.

4. I hope the bus ____ on time today. If ____ ____ on time, ____ get to work late. And if ____ ____ to work late, my supervisor ____ ____ angry.

1 CONVERSATION GIVING AND FOLLOWING EMERGENCY PROCEDURES

The **Heimlich maneuver** is an important emergency procedure. When a person chokes on a piece of food, the food blocks the person's airway. The person can't breathe. In just four minutes a choking person can die or have brain damage. The Heimlich maneuver forces the piece of food out of the airway. It uses the air in the person's lungs to push out the food. This procedure can save the person's life.

Practice with a classmate.

A. Emergency Operator.

B. My brother is choking on a piece of food!

A. Is he coughing, or is he able to speak?

B. No. He can't breathe.

A. The food is blocking his airway. Do you know how to perform the Heimlich maneuver?

B. No.

A. Okay. Follow my instructions carefully. Are you ready?

B. Yes.

A. Stand behind your brother. Make a fist with one hand, and put the thumb side of the fist just below the rib cage. Do you understand?

B. Yes.

A. Then grab the fist with your other hand. Press into his abdomen with four quick inward and upward thrusts. You may have to repeat this several times until the object comes out.

B. He just coughed out the food. He's okay now. Thank you very much.

> **Important!**
> If you act out this conversation, don't do the thrusts. This can injure the other person.

2 TEAMWORK CPR (CARDIOPULMONARY RESUSCITATION)

With a classmate, find out the basic procedures to follow for CPR (cardiopulmonary resuscitation). Then practice giving and following the directions.

COMMUNITY CONNECTIONS Where can you take a course in CPR and other first-aid procedures in your community? (The Red Cross, hospitals, and other institutions often offer these courses.) Share the information as a class.

Prevent Fires at Home!
Keep your home and family safe—
Prepare, Plan, Practice!

Keep a fire extinguisher in the kitchen.

Store flammable products away from heat.

Put new batteries in smoke detectors every six months.

Keep space heaters at least three feet away from clothing, furniture, and other flammable materials.

Plan an escape route in case of fire.

When a home fire starts, people inside only have a few minutes to get out safely. Do you know how to escape from any place in your home or apartment? Do you have an emergency escape route in case doors are blocked? Do you have an outside meeting place? Make an escape plan and practice it twice a year.

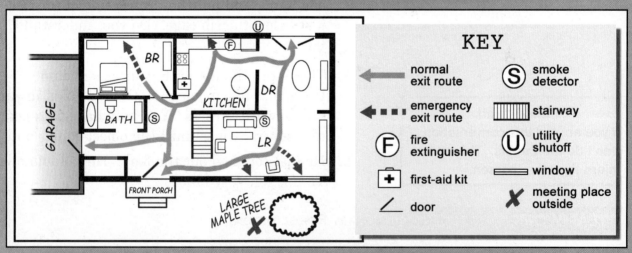

KEY

GARAGE — BR — DR — KITCHEN — BATH — LR — FRONT PORCH — LARGE MAPLE TREE

← normal exit route

◄ ••• emergency exit route

Ⓕ fire extinguisher

➕ first-aid kit

╱ door

Ⓢ smoke detector

▥ stairway

Ⓤ utility shutoff

▭ window

✗ meeting place outside

TEAMWORK Work with a classmate. What other fire safety practices can you think of? Make a list. Then share with the class.

DRAW YOUR ESCAPE PLAN Draw an escape plan for your apartment or home. Show the rooms, your fire safety equipment, and your escape routes.

Alarm-First
Smoke Detector

OWNER'S MANUAL

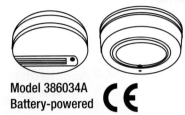

Model 386034A
Battery-powered CE

Thank you for purchasing an *Alarm-First* smoke detector. It is an important part of your family's home safety plan. You can trust this product to provide the highest quality safety protection.

IMPORTANT: Read all instructions before installation and keep this manual for future reference.

CONTENTS
1. **WHERE TO INSTALL SMOKE DETECTORS**
2. **HOW TO INSTALL**
3. **MAINTENANCE**

1. WHERE TO INSTALL SMOKE DETECTORS
For minimum protection:
- In the hallway outside each sleeping area.
- On each level of a home with more than one floor.
   In the basement, at the *bottom* of the basement stairway.
   On the second floor, at the *top* of the stairway to the second floor.

For maximum protection:
- Inside each bedroom.
- In the living room, dining room, storage room, and other rooms.

IMPORTANT: Do *NOT* install smoke detectors in the kitchen, bathrooms, attic, or garage. Install heat detectors in the kitchen and garage.

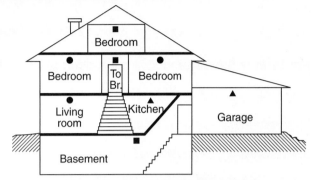

- ■ Smoke Detectors For Minimum Protection
- ● Smoke Detectors For Additional Protection
- ▲ Heat-Activated Detectors

2. HOW TO INSTALL
- Put detectors as close to the center of the ceiling as possible.
- Measure the distance between the holes in the detector. Drill holes in the ceiling at that same distance.
- Use screws to attach the detector to the ceiling.

3. MAINTENANCE
- Test smoke detectors once a month. You can use a broom handle or stick to press the test button. Never use an open flame to test a detector.
- Replace batteries twice a year. When you change your clocks in the spring and fall, change your batteries.
- If the low-battery signal begins to chirp or beep, replace the batteries immediately.

⚠ **WARNING!** If the alarm sounds, do not ignore it! Get everyone out immediately!

---

1. For minimum protection, where should you install detectors?
2. For the best protection, where else should you have detectors?
3. Why is it important to have detectors on every level of the house?
4. Where should you *not* install smoke detectors?
5. What kind of detector should you install in a kitchen?
6. How often should you check detectors?
7. How often should you change the batteries?
8. What does a beeping sound mean?

Draw a floor plan of your home. Draw circles to show where you currently have smoke detectors. Draw an 'X' to show where you should add detectors. How many smoke detectors do you need in your home?

Choose the correct answer.

1. My doctor says it's important to be in good physical _____.
   A. reaction
   B. reason
   C. access
   D. condition

2. My friends have been _____ me to look for a better job.
   A. accepting
   B. improving
   C. encouraging
   D. wishing

3. Do you know how to _____ the Heimlich maneuver?
   A. perform
   B. prevent
   C. ignore
   D. press

4. That man is choking on a piece of food! He can't _____!
   A. block
   B. breathe
   C. beep
   D. grab

5. You need to know how to _____ from any place in your home in case of fire.
   A. evict
   B. expect
   C. escape
   D. attach

6. Remember to _____ flammable products away from heat.
   A. measure
   B. press
   C. sound
   D. store

7. It's essential to have an outside meeting _____ if you have a fire in your home.
   A. step
   B. place
   C. practice
   D. shutoff

8. Be sure to purchase a smoke detector that will give you the highest quality _____.
   A. protection
   B. installation
   C. reference
   D. contents

9. Instructions for maintenance of this product can be found in the owner's _____.
   A. plan
   B. area
   C. manual
   D. equipment

10. You should _____ twice a year.
    A. install new smoke detectors
    B. replace smoke detectors
    C. replace batteries in clocks
    D. change smoke detector batteries

SKILLS CHECK ✔

Words:
- ☐ attach
- ☐ block
- ☐ breathe
- ☐ choke
- ☐ drill
- ☐ escape
- ☐ force
- ☐ grab
- ☐ press
- ☐ prevent
- ☐ sound
- ☐ store
- ☐ test
- ☐ trust

- ☐ CPR
- ☐ emergency operator
- ☐ emergency procedure
- ☐ escape plan
- ☐ escape route
- ☐ fire extinguisher
- ☐ first-aid kit
- ☐ first-aid procedure
- ☐ floor plan
- ☐ heat detector
- ☐ Heimlich maneuver
- ☐ meeting place
- ☐ smoke detector
- ☐ utility shutoff

I can say:
- ☐ If I'm *tired*, I'll probably *read*.
- ☐ If I *quit*, I might *be sorry*.
- ☐ I hope *I get the job*.
- ☐ I hope *it doesn't rain*.
- ☐ I hope so, too./I hope not, too.
- ☐ If I *lived closer*, I'd *visit you*.
- ☐ If I were *stronger*, I'd *be able to lift it*.
- ☐ If I didn't *like it*, I wouldn't *buy it*.
- ☐ If I weren't *allergic*, I wouldn't *be sneezing*.

I can write about:
- ☐ what I would do if I won a lot of money

I can:
- ☐ report an emergency
- ☐ respond to directions of emergency personnel
- ☐ give and follow instructions for CPR
- ☐ identify home fire safety procedures
- ☐ draw an escape plan for my home
- ☐ follow instructions for installing a smoke detector
- ☐ draw a floor plan indicating smoke detectors in my home

I can express agreement:
- ☐ You're probably right./I think you're right./ I think that's right./I think that's true./ That's probably true.

Feature Article
Fact File
Around the World
Interview
We've Got Mail!

SIDE by SIDE Gazette

Global Exchange
Listening
Fun with Idioms
What Are They
Saying?

Volume 4   Number 2

The Music of Wishes and Hopes

Songwriters often express wishes and hopes through their music. Their songs are filled with lyrics such as "If I could . . . ," "If I had . . . ," "If I were. . . ," I wish . . . ," and "I hope . . . ." Here are some favorite songs about wishes and hopes from the worlds of popular, folk, Broadway, country, and rock music.

"If I Had a Hammer": This famous folk song was originally written as a poem by Lee Hays, then put to music by Pete Seeger. The singer sings about what he would do to bring peace all over the land.
He sings that if he had a hammer, he'd hammer in the morning. If he had a bell, he'd ring it. If he had a song, he'd sing it. This popular tune was made famous by the folk singers Peter, Paul, and Mary.

"(If I Could Save) Time in a Bottle": In this song written by Jim Croce, the singer wishes he had more time to spend with his girlfriend. If it were possible, he would save time the way people save money. He would save the days in a bottle and then spend all the time with the one he loves.

"If I Had a Million Dollars": In this popular song sung by the Canadian group Barenaked Ladies, the leader of the group sings about what he would do if he had a million dollars. He would buy
the woman he loves a house, furniture, a car, an exotic pet, a green dress, and other things.

"I Hope You Dance": This song of hope is sung by the popular country music singer Lee Ann Womack. She sings about her hopes for the people she loves. She hopes they never go hungry or without love. She hopes they find joy in simple pleasures like the ocean. She hopes they appreciate what they have.

"If I Were a Bell": In this song from the musical *Guys and Dolls*, Sarah Brown sings about her feelings for the man she loves, a gambler named Sky Masterson. She is so happy that if she were a bell, she'd be ringing. If she were a gate, she'd be swinging.

"If I Were a Rich Man": In the musical *Fiddler on the Roof*, Tevye, a poor dairyman, sings that he wishes he were rich. If he were a rich man, he wouldn't have to work
hard, and he would build a big house for his family.

"(If I Could) Change the World": Singer Eric Clapton won a Grammy Award for this song from the movie *Phenomenon*. In this song, the singer wishes he could change the world and be with the girl he loves. If he could, he would be the center of her universe. He would be a king, and she would be a queen. But for now, he realizes it's impossible.

Try to find some of these songs and listen to them. Do you know other songs about wishes and hopes?

FACT FILE

Song Search

Word	Number of Songs with Word in Title
"if"	1130
"hope"	41
"wish"	149

Making Wishes

There are many different traditions and customs for making wishes around the world.

If you find a four-leaf clover, make a wish and then throw the clover away. (Ireland)

When you see a new moon, hold a coin up to the moon and wish for money. As the moon increases, your money will increase. (Jamaica)

If you make a wish as you throw a coin or a pebble into a wishing well, your wish may come true. (Many countries)

Make a wish before you blow out the candles on a birthday cake. (The United States and other countries)

If you open a nutshell and find two nuts instead of one, give one to a friend. Each of you should make a wish. If you're the person who remembers to say "lucky nut" the next morning, you will get your wish. (Russia)

At midnight on New Year's Eve, eat one grape for each of the twelve chimes of the clock. Make the same wish as you eat each grape and your wish will come true. (Spain, Portugal, and Venezuela)

If you catch a falling leaf, make a wish. (Japan)

When you see lightning, make a wish. (The Philippines)

Hold one end of a wishbone (from a chicken or turkey) while someone else holds the other end. Make a wish, then break the wishbone. If you get the longer piece, your wish will come true. (The United States)

When you see the first full moon of the year, make a wish. (Korea)

Stand with your back to a fountain. Throw three coins, one at a time, over your shoulder into the water. Each time make the same wish. If you hear the coins splash into the water three times, your wish will come true. (Europe)

When you see the first star in the evening sky, say this poem and make a wish:

Star light, star bright,
First star I see tonight.
I wish I may, I wish I might
Have the wish I wish tonight.

(Many countries with similar poems in different languages)

Which of these traditions for wishing did you know about? What are some traditions that you know?

Interview

A Side by Side Gazette
reporter asked these people:

Q: What would you do if you won a million dollars?

A: I don't know. I wouldn't quit my job, that's for sure! I wouldn't know what to do if I had so much free time.

A: I'd pay all my bills, and I'd pay off all my debts. I'd put the rest of the money in the bank.

A: I think I would quit my job and travel around the world.

A: I'd invest some money, and I'd save the rest for my children's college education.

A: I'd help my parents. They don't have a lot of money. I'd buy them a house in a nice neighborhood.

A: I'd give most of the money to charities that help people. I'd really feel good if I could do that.

A: All my life I've dreamed about starting my own business. I'd open up a flower shop, and my dream would come true.

FUN with IDIOMS

Do You Know These Expressions?

_____ 1. You're breaking my heart.

_____ 2. You light up my life.

_____ 3. You're a heel!

_____ 4. You've got me wrapped around your little finger.

a. I'm very happy.

b. I'll do anything for you.

c. I'm very sad.

d. You aren't a nice person.

We've Got Mail!

Dear Side by Side,

I'm confused about the correct tense to use with the word "hope." It seems to me that the future tense should be used when someone expresses hope about the future. For example, I think a person should say, "I hope the weather will be nice tomorrow." But according to my teacher, the present tense should be used: "I hope the weather is nice tomorrow." And I'm sure I've heard English speakers use the future tense after the word "hope." Are these people making a grammar mistake?

Sincerely,

"Hoping for an Answer"

Dear "Hoping for an Answer,"

Yes, those people are making a very common grammar mistake. We understand why you think the future tense should be used to express hope about the future. It seems to make sense. Unfortunately, grammar rules in English don't always make sense! In this case, the rule is that the present tense should be used. We hope this answers your question.

Sincerely,

Side by Side

Dear Side by Side,

I have a question about the words "were" and "was" in conditional sentences. According to your book, the following sentences are correct:

If he **were** stronger, he'd be able to lift weights.

If I **were** bitten by a dog, I'd call the doctor.

If she **weren't** in a bad mood, she wouldn't be shouting.

But I think it's better to use the word "was" instead of "were" in these sentences. Plus, I hear people use "was" in sentences like these all the time! Can you explain this?

Sincerely,

"Confused About Conditionals"

Dear "Confused About Conditionals,"

Your question is wonderful because it shows the difference between grammatically correct English and the informal English people use every day. "Were" is the grammatically correct verb in these conditional sentences. However, it is indeed very common in informal speech for people to say "was." If you were a student in our classroom, we would encourage you to use "were." That's the correct form, and after all, you're studying the rules of the language!

Sincerely,

Side by Side

Global Exchange

Sari4: Hi! It's Friday afternoon, and I just got home from school. I'm really looking forward to the weekend. I'm not sure yet what I'm going to do. If the weather is nice tomorrow, I might go bicycling with some friends. If the weather is bad, we might go bowling or see a movie. On Sunday, if my cousins from Toronto visit us, my family will probably make a big dinner at home. If they don't visit, we'll probably have a picnic in the park. What are YOUR plans for the weekend?

Send a message to a keypal. Tell about your plans for the weekend.

LISTENING

Tempo Airlines

Press

_e_	①	**a.** to plan a vacation
___	②	**b.** to repeat the menu
___	③	**c.** to fly in the U.S. or Canada
___	④	**d.** to speak to a representative
___	⑤	**e.** to find out about today's flights
___	⑥	**f.** to fly overseas
___	⑦	**g.** to get travel awards
___	⑧	**h.** to listen to airport check-in rules

What Are They Saying?

	Questions with *To Be*	Questions with *Do/Does/Did*
Information Questions	Where is the library? Can you tell me where the library is?	What does this word mean? Can you tell me what this word means?
Yes/No Questions	Is swimming allowed here? Do you know if/whether swimming is allowed here?	Do your children have the flu? Do you know if/whether your children have the flu?

Practice these conversations with a classmate.

What is the homework assignment?

A. What's the question?

B. *What is the homework assignment?*

A. Can you make it into an embedded question?

B. Yes. *Can you tell me what the homework assignment is?*

How much does this cell phone cost?

A. What's the question?

B. *How much does this cell phone cost?*

A. Can you make it into an embedded question?

B. Yes. *Could you tell me how much this cell phone costs?*

Are the smoke detectors working?

A. What's the question?

B. *Are the smoke detectors working?*

A. Can you make it into an embedded question?

B. Yes. *Do you know if the smoke detectors are working?*

Do we have a first-aid kit?

A. What's the question?

B. *Do we have a first-aid kit?*

A. Can you make it into an embedded question?

B. Yes. *Does anyone know whether we have a first-aid kit?*

Use these expressions to make the following questions into embedded questions. Then practice new conversations about these questions.

Do you know . . . ?	Could you tell me . . . ?	Can you tell me . . . ?
Do you have any idea . . . ?	Does anyone know . . . ?	Can anybody tell me . . . ?

1. Where are the fire exits in our school?
2. Is there a fire extinguisher on this floor?
3. How did Mr. Carter sprain his ankle?
4. Does this bus go to the shopping mall?
5. Are we going to get a raise this year?
6. Why does our dog always get carsick?
7. When is our English teacher's birthday?
8. Did the students get good grades on last month's tests?

SAFETY FIRST!

PERSONAL PROTECTIVE EQUIPMENT (PPE)

Gloves • Safety Glasses • Shoes • Earplugs • Hard Hats •
Respirators • Overalls • Body Suits . . . only work if you wear them!

Remember:
- Know what equipment you need for your job.
- Put on your PPE correctly, and adjust it so it fits well and is comfortable.
- Take care of your PPE. Keep it clean!
- Remember to wear it!

EYE PROTECTION

Protect your eyes and face against:
- <u>Impact</u> from flying pieces, sand, and dirt
- <u>Heat</u> from extreme temperatures
- <u>Chemicals</u> that may have fumes or splash
- <u>Dust</u> from woodworking and polishing
- <u>Intense light</u> from welding and laser work

Emergency Eye Wash Station

Know the location of your nearest emergency eye wash station.

Memorize the eye first-aid instructions posted there.

If an accident happens, go to the eye wash station immediately to rinse your eyes!

- Push the button to start the flow of water.
- Take off your contact lenses or glasses if you wear them.
- Put your head into the basin so that the water flows into both eyes. Hold each eye open with your thumbs and index fingers.
- Without moving your head, move your eyes around from side to side and up and down while you rinse. Rinsing will remove dust, dirt, or chemicals that can hurt your eyes.
- Keep rinsing your eyes for at least 15 minutes or until a doctor or EMT arrives.

TOXIC CHEMICALS

Whether gas, liquid, or solid, toxic chemicals are dangerous! They are poisonous! They can burn your eyes and skin, and hurt your lungs!

If there is a toxic chemical spill, or other emergency, follow these safety procedures:
- Leave the area quickly!
- Don't go through the spill area!
- Use the emergency escape route!
- Look for shelter and wait for the danger to pass!

MACHINE SAFETY

- Know the location of your machine's emergency shut-off button.
- Wear eye and ear protection while operating machines.
- Make sure safety guards are working at all times.
- Beware of machines that start automatically.
- Keep your hands and fingers out of all machinery.
- Don't open a machine while it is operating.
- Don't oil or repair a machine while it is operating.
- If a machine is not operating properly, notify a supervisor immediately.

KNOW THE SIGNS OF A HEART ATTACK!

If you see someone who . . .

- has suddenly collapsed or passed out
- is unresponsive and doesn't answer when you call his or her name
- isn't breathing or has irregular breathing
- doesn't have a pulse
- has dark or bluish skin

. . . that person may be having a heart attack!

Call for help! Then look for the nearest AED (Automated External Defibrillator). The AED will give an electrical shock to restore the person's heartbeat.

HOW TO USE AN AED *It's easy! No training is needed! You can save a life!*

1. Call 911 or have someone else call.
2. Be sure the person is having a heart attack. Check for breathing and pulse. If the person is breathing and the heart is beating, you do not need to use the AED.
3. If there is no pulse and the person isn't breathing, you need to use the AED.
4. Tilt the person's head back and lift up the chin to open the airway.
5. Press the power button to turn on the AED. Listen to the AED voice instructions.
6. Unbutton or take off the person's shirt or sweater. Make sure the skin is dry.
7. Put the pads on the person's chest, following the voice instructions. Make sure the wire from the pads is plugged into the AED.

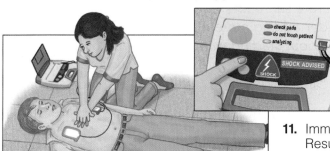

8. Press the Analyze button. Wait while the AED checks the person's pulse.
9. If you get a No Shock Advised message, do *not* push the Shock button.
10. If you get a Shock Advised message, have everyone stand away from the patient. Don't touch the patient. Push the Shock button.
11. Immediately after the shock, give CPR (Cardiopulmonary Resuscitation) for 2 minutes. Do not remove the AED pads.
12. Check for breathing. The AED will again check for a pulse. Follow the voice instructions.

Be careful!

- Only use an AED on a person who is unresponsive and isn't breathing.
- Never use an AED on a person who is not having a heart attack.
- Don't use an AED on a person who has collapsed because of alcohol or drugs.
- The AED chest pads must be on the skin . . . and the skin must be completely dry.

DID YOU UNDERSTAND?

1. What is PPE? What can it include?
2. Why do workers need to use PPE?
3. What are the five things that workers need to protect their eyes against?
4. Why is it important to go to the eye wash station right away?
5. How long should a person rinse his or her eyes?
6. Why are toxic chemicals dangerous?
7. What safety equipment is important for using machines?
8. What should you do if you think someone is having a heart attack?
9. How does an AED help someone who is having a heart attack?
10. What should you do after the AED delivers a shock?
11. When should you *not* use an AED?

Think & Share

1. Why is it important to call 911 before you start using the AED?
2. What safety equipment have you used at work or at home? Why did you need to use it?
3. What companies in your area may have toxic chemicals?
4. Most large companies and public buildings now have AEDs. What other places should also have them? Why do you think so?

Revising is an important step in the writing process. After you write a first draft, you need to revise your writing. When you revise, you reread and rethink your writing, and you make changes to improve it.

First, read your writing to yourself silently, or read it aloud. Think about your purpose and your audience. Does your writing do what you want it to do? Will your readers like it? Will they understand it? What should you add or delete? What should you move to a different place? Do you have a strong beginning? Do you have a good ending? What changes should you make?

Next, have a **peer conference**. Read your writing aloud to a classmate, or have your classmate read it silently. Then ask for *feedback*—suggestions. Does your classmate understand your writing? What does your classmate like about it? How can you improve it?

Peer Conference Questions	Peer Conference Suggestions*
Is the purpose of my writing clear?	I suggest *shortening this very long paragraph.*
Did I accomplish my purpose?	I recommend *breaking this long sentence into two*
What do you like about it?	*separate sentences.*
Will my audience understand it?	Consider *adding more information in this paragraph.*
Are any parts of the writing unclear?	Think about *starting with a stronger introduction.*
What should I add?	Try *moving this sentence from your first paragraph to*
What should I delete?	*the last paragraph.*
What should I move?	
Do I have a strong beginning?	* "You should" is very direct advice. It's like an instruction.
Do I have a good ending?	Instead, use these expressions with "softer" verbs followed
What other changes should I make?	by gerund forms.

If–Would **essay:** In an *If–Would* essay, the writer describes what would happen if some situation occurred. The conditional tense and the words *if*, *would*, and *might* are commonly used in an *If–Would* essay.

Write an *If–Would* essay.

Write: Choose one of these topics, brainstorm ideas, and write a first draft.
- If you could invite three important people from the past to have dinner with you, who would you invite? Why? What would you ask them? What would you tell them?
- If you could go back in time to any year and place in history, where would you go? What year would it be? What would you do there?
- If you were the mayor, the governor, or the president, what would you do? What would you change? How would life be different?

Revise: Reread and rethink your first draft. Make some changes to improve it, or wait until after the peer conference.

Peer conference: Discuss your writing with a classmate. Use the Peer Conference Questions above to ask about your writing. Your classmate can use the Peer Conference Suggestions as examples of how to give feedback. After the peer conference, make more changes to improve your writing.

6

Present Unreal Conditional (continued)
Wish-Clauses

- Advice
- Expressing Wishes
- Job Satisfaction
- Expressing Ability
- Asking for and Giving Reasons

- Life in Cities and Suburbs
- Requesting Bank Services
- Opening a Bank Account
- Bank Brochures
- Budget-Planning Strategies

VOCABULARY PREVIEW

1. classified ad
2. day shift
3. night shift
4. full-time job
5. part-time job

6. baby food
7. baby picture
8. beard
9. driver's ed
10. fan

11. foreign language
12. obituary
13. pronunciation
14. taxes
15. voter

If I Were You

A. Do you think the boss would be angry if I went home early?

B. Yes, I do. I think she'd be VERY angry.

A. Do you really think so?

B. Yes. I'm positive. I wouldn't go home early if I were you.

A. I suppose you're right.

1. Do you think Ted would be disappointed if I missed his birthday party?

2. Do you think Mom would be angry if I drove her new car?

3. Do you think the neighbors would be annoyed if I practiced the drums now?

4. Do you think Mrs. Riley would be upset if I skipped English class tomorrow?

5. Do you think the owners of the building would be upset if I painted the kitchen purple?

6. Do you think my parents would be disappointed if I dropped out of medical school?

7. Do you think Roy would be jealous if I went out with his girlfriend?

8. Do you think Dad would be mad if I borrowed his cell phone?

9. Do you think the voters would be upset if I raised taxes?

10. Do you think my fans would be unhappy if I got a haircut?

11. Do you think Matt would be embarrassed if I showed his baby pictures to his girlfriend?

12.

To Tell the Truth

A. I'm thinking of **growing a beard**. What do you think?

B. To tell the truth, I wouldn't **grow a beard** if I were you.

A. Why do you say that?

B. If you **grew a beard**, you'd probably **look very funny**.

A. Hmm. You might be right.

1. *buy a used car from Ralph Jones*
   spend a lot of money on repairs

2. *get a dog*
   be evicted from your apartment building

3. *start an Internet company*
   "lose your shirt"

4.

How to Say It!

Giving a Personal Opinion

To tell the truth,
To tell you the truth,
To be honest,   } *I wouldn't grow a beard.*
To be honest with you,
If you ask me,

Practice the conversations on this page again. Use different expressions for giving a personal opinion.

Wishes

Tom **lives** in Boston. He **wishes** he **lived** in New York.

A. Do you enjoy driving a taxi?

B. Not really. I wish I drove a school bus.

A. Does Mr. Miller enjoy being a teacher?

B. Not really. He wishes he were an actor.

1. Does Alice enjoy living in the suburbs?
in the city

2. Does Barry enjoy being single?
married

3. Does Mrs. Dexter enjoy teaching music?
something else

4. Do you enjoy working the night shift?
the day shift

5. Does Vincent enjoy painting houses?
portraits

6. Does Ann enjoy having two part-time jobs?
one good full-time job

7. Do you enjoy being the vice president?
the president

8. Does Albert enjoy having a cat?
a dog

9.

"SICK AND TIRED"

Frank is "sick and tired" of selling used cars! He has been doing that for twenty-eight years. Frank wishes he sold something else. In fact, at this point in his life, he would be willing to sell ANYTHING as long as it wasn't used cars!

Peggy is "sick and tired" of writing classified ads and obituaries for the Midville Times! She has been doing that since 1989. Peggy wishes she wrote something else. In fact, at this point in her life, she'd be willing to write ANYTHING as long as it wasn't classified ads and obituaries!

Mr. Dellasandro is "sick and tired" of teaching driver's ed! He has been teaching that for the past twenty-one years. "Mr. D" wishes he taught something else. In fact, at this point in his life, he would be willing to teach ANYTHING as long as it wasn't driver's ed!

Patty and Jimmy are "sick and tired" of eating tuna fish sandwiches for lunch. They have been eating them for lunch every day for the past four years. Patty and Jimmy wish their parents would give them something else for lunch. In fact, at this point in their lives, they would be willing to eat ANYTHING for lunch as long as it wasn't tuna fish sandwiches!

✓ READING CHECK-UP

CHOOSE

1. Tom found his job through the ____.
   a. classified ads
   b. obituaries

2. If you don't visit Aunt Nellie in the hospital, she'll be very ____.
   a. disappointed
   b. sick and tired

3. I was ____ when my driver's ed teacher shouted at me in front of the other students.
   a. jealous
   b. embarrassed

4. I enjoy working the ____.
   a. night shift
   b. full time

5. Howard ____ the meeting because he had to go to the dentist.
   a. dropped out of
   b. skipped

6. This is a ____ of me that was painted when I was three years old.
   a. portrait
   b. photograph

They Wish They Could

A. Can Jeffrey cook?

B. No, he can't . . . but he wishes he could. If he could cook, he'd **invite his friends over for dinner**.

1. Can Brian dance?
go dancing every night

2. Can Cheryl type fast?
be able to leave work on time

3. Can Steve speak a foreign language?
be able to get a better job

4. Can Martha knit?
make sweaters for her grandchildren

5. Can Gary fix his car by himself?
save a lot of money

6. Can Mr. and Mrs. Bradley ski?
take their children skiing in Colorado

7. Can Abby play a musical instrument?
be able to march in the town parade

8. Can Jessica talk?
tell her parents she doesn't like her baby food

9. Can Richard roll his "Rs"?
have better pronunciation in Spanish

10.

Why Do You Say That?

if _____ { could / would be able to } _____

My TV is fixed. ☹

A. You know, I wish my TV weren't fixed.

B. Why do you say that?

A. If it weren't fixed, { I could / I'd be able to } talk with my children.

My son wants to be a dentist. ☹

A. You know, I wish my son didn't want to be a dentist.

B. Why do you say that?

A. If he didn't want to be a dentist, { I could / I'd be able to } convince him

to manage my shoe store when I retire.

1. *wear my new raincoat this Saturday*

2. *go to the beach*

3. *have a garden*

4. *see her more often*

5. *concentrate more on my work*

6. *go away for the weekend*

7. *invite my friends over to watch the Super Bowl*

8. *have some "peace and quiet" around the house*

READING

Mr. Anderson
Mrs. Anderson
Michael
Jennifer
Steven

THEY WISH THEY LIVED IN THE CITY

The Anderson family lives in the suburbs, but they wish they lived in the city. If they lived in the city, Mr. Anderson wouldn't have to spend all his spare time mowing the lawn and working around the house. Mrs. Anderson wouldn't have to spend two hours commuting to work every day. Their son Michael would be able to take the bus to the baseball stadium. Their daughter, Jennifer, would be living close to all of her favorite book stores. And their other son, Steven, could visit the zoo more often. It would be very difficult for the Anderson family to move to the city now, but perhaps some day they'll be able to. They certainly hope so.

COMPLETE THE STORY

THEY WISH THEY LIVED IN THE SUBURBS

The Burton family lives in the city, but they _____ ^{1} they lived in the suburbs. If they _____ ^{2} in the suburbs, Mrs. Burton _____ ^{3} be able to plant a garden and grow vegetables. Mr. Burton _____ ^{4} have to listen to noisy city traffic all the time. Their son, Ken, _____ ^{5} have a backyard to play in. Their daughters, Betsy and Kathy, _____ ^{6} have to share a room. And their cat, Tiger, _____ ^{7} be able to go outside and play with the other cats. It _____ ^{8} be very difficult for the Burton family to move to the suburbs now, but perhaps some day they'll be _____ ^{9} to. They certainly hope so.

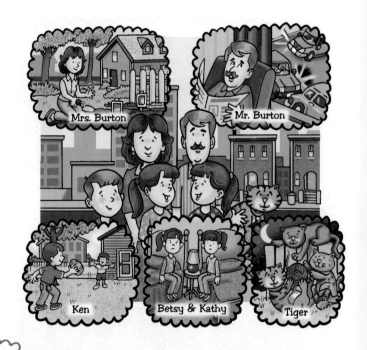

Mrs. Burton
Mr. Burton
Ken
Betsy & Kathy
Tiger

How About You?

Do you wish you lived someplace else? Where? Why?

Compare life in the city and life in the suburbs. What are the advantages and disadvantages of each?

92

"ALL THUMBS"

Ethel can never fix anything around the house. In fact, everybody tells her she's "all thumbs." She wishes she were more mechanically inclined. If she were more mechanically inclined, she would be able to repair things around the house by herself.

Robert can't dance very well. In fact, all the girls he goes out with tell him he has "two left feet." Robert wishes he could dance better. If he could dance better, he wouldn't feel so self-conscious when he goes dancing.

Maria is having a hard time learning English. She's having a lot of trouble with English grammar and pronunciation. Maria wishes she had a "better ear" for languages. If she had a "better ear" for languages, she probably wouldn't be having so much trouble in her English class.

 READING *CHECK-UP*

MATCHING: *Do You Know These Expressions?*

_____ **1.** He's *all thumbs*.	a.	very kind
_____ **2.** She's *handy* around the house.	b.	doesn't know how to fix things
_____ **3.** He has *a green thumb*.	c.	optimistic
_____ **4.** He's *all heart*.	d.	knows how to fix things
_____ **5.** He's very *nosey*.	e.	has many responsibilities
_____ **6.** She's got *a lot on her shoulders*.	f.	good at gardening
_____ **7.** She always *keeps her chin up*.	g.	very angry
_____ **8.** He's *up in arms*.	h.	asks about other people

How About You?

Are you "all thumbs"? Do you have "two left feet"? Everybody has a few things he or she would like to do better. What do you wish you could do better? Why?

LISTENING

Listen and choose the statement that is true based on what you hear.

1. a. He has a dog.
  b. He doesn't have a dog.

2. a. She works the night shift.
  b. She works the day shift.

3. a. She's a musician.
  b. She's a teacher.

4. a. He doesn't have to take biology.
  b. He has to take biology.

5. a. She can't type fast.
  b. She can type fast.

6. a. They don't have a car.
  b. They don't live in the city.

PRONUNCIATION Reduced *would*

Listen. Then say it.

Do you think the boss would be angry?

Do you think the neighbors would be annoyed?

Do you think Roy would be jealous?

Do you think Ted would be disappointed?

Say it. Then listen.

Do you think my parents would be disappointed?

Do you think the voters would be upset?

Do you think Julie would be mad?

Do you think Matt would be embarrassed?

Write in your journal about something in your life you wish for. What do you wish? How would your life be different if your wish came true?

GRAMMAR FOCUS

PRESENT UNREAL CONDITIONAL (IF ___ WOULD)

Do you think the boss **would** be angry **if** I went home early?
I **wouldn't** go home early **if** I were you.

If	I he she we you they	could dance,	I'd he'd she'd we'd you'd they'd	go dancing.

If my TV weren't fixed,	I **could** I'**d be able to**	talk with my children.

WISH-CLAUSES

I We You They	wish	I we you they	lived in New York. were more athletic. could dance. didn't live here. weren't sick.
He She	wishes	he she	

Complete the sentences.

1. I don't enjoy working the night shift. I wish I _____ the day shift.

2. Gregory doesn't enjoy being a salesperson. He wishes he _____ the store manager.

3. If I _____ you, I _____ skip class tomorrow. I'm sure the teacher _____ _____ upset.

4. I wish I _____ fix my car by myself. If I _____ do that, _____ save a lot of money on repairs.

5. If I _____ you, I _____ order the spicy stew. If you _____ it, _____ probably get a bad stomachache.

6. We're busy tomorrow night. If we _____ busy, _____ be happy to see a movie with you.

7. I have a meeting this afternoon. If I _____ have a meeting, _____ be able to drive you to the airport.

8. I _____ buy a TV at Al's Discount Store if I _____ you. If you _____ a TV at Al's, _____ probably regret it.

1 CONVERSATION REQUESTING BANK SERVICES

Practice conversations between a bank teller and a customer.

A. How may I help you?

B. I'd like to _____, please.

A. All right.

1. cash this check

2. make a deposit

3. make a withdrawal

4. order more checks

5. get a certified check

6. send money overseas

2 TEAMWORK OPENING A BANK ACCOUNT

Practice conversations with a classmate.

A. How may I help you?

B. I want to open a savings account.

A. Okay. Your name, please?

B. _____

A. And what's your address, including city, state, and zip code?

B. _____

A. How much would you like to deposit today to open the account?

B. _____ dollars.

A. All right. Please read this information. Then sign at the bottom.

COMMUNITY CONNECTIONS What banks are there in your community? Which bank do you use? What kind of bank account do you have—a savings account? a checking account? Share information with the class.

Midtown Bank | We offer savings and checking accounts designed to meet everyone's needs.

- The **Statement Savings Account** is a good choice for people just starting to save. You can open this account with a deposit of $10. You earn interest, and you can avoid paying a monthly fee. If your daily balance is $100 or more, we will waive the $5 monthly fee.

- The **Passbook Savings Account**, our most popular savings account, can earn you a higher interest rate. Because its interest rates are *tiered*, customers with higher balances receive higher interest rates. The Passbook Savings Account also offers the convenience of a passbook for easy record keeping. There is a $10 monthly fee if your daily balance falls below $1,000.

- The **Money Market Savings Account** offers our highest interest rates plus the convenience of check writing. Customers can write three checks a month on this account. There is a $20 monthly fee if your balance falls below $1,500.

- Three different **Checking Accounts** are available. See the chart below.

	Basic Checking	Regular Checking	Checking Plus
Minimum Opening Deposit	$10	$25	$100
Monthly Fee	None	$7	$20
How to Avoid a Monthly Fee	N/A	No fee with direct deposit	No fee when you maintain a minimum balance of $1,000
Check Writing	No fee for first 8 checks each month. $1 per check fee for each additional check.	Unlimited check writing	Unlimited check writing
Earns Interest	No	No	Yes. See rate sheet to check current interest rates.
Other Features	• Free introductory order of checks • No-fee ATM card • Free online banking	• Free checks including reorders • No-fee ATM card • No-fee traveler's checks • Free online banking	• Free checks including reorders • No-fee ATM card • No-fee traveler's checks • Free online banking • 50% discount on safe deposit box if available

1. When you have $100 in a Passbook Savings Account, you _____.
   A. don't pay a monthly fee
   B. pay a $5 monthly fee
   C. pay a $10 monthly fee
   D. pay a $20 monthly fee

2. To open a Regular Checking Account, you have to _____.
   A. have direct deposit
   B. deposit $7 or more in the account
   C. deposit $10 or more in the account
   D. deposit $25 or more in the account

3. With a Basic Checking Account, you have to _____.
   A. pay a monthly fee
   B. pay to order more checks
   C. pay when you do banking on the Internet
   D. pay for an ATM card

4. You don't pay a monthly fee for a Checking Plus Account _____.
   A. if you have direct deposit
   B. if you pay $20
   C. if you have $1,000 or more in your account
   D. if you have an ATM card

5. When the bank *waives* the monthly fee for the Statement Savings Account, you _____.
   A. pay a higher fee
   B. pay a lower fee
   C. pay $5
   D. don't pay the fee

6. We can infer that *tiered* interest rates _____.
   A. depend on the balance in an account
   B. are bargains
   C. are always the same
   D. are always high

Making a Monthly Budget Changed Their Lives

Last year Eduardo and Isabel Soriano decided to do something about their financial situation. They often ran out of money at the end of the month, and they kept asking themselves, "Where did the money go?" The problem was that they didn't really keep track of what they were spending. As a result, they often didn't have enough money for their expenses, and their monthly bill payments were sometimes overdue. They finally decided to take control of their finances by setting up a budget to help them manage their money, pay their bills on time, and save for the future.

The Sorianos knew the amount of their monthly take-home pay, but they needed to make a list of their expenses. So for two months, they wrote down everything they spent. It wasn't difficult keeping a record of their *fixed* expenses, such as rent and car payments, because these expenses were the same every month. But they needed to collect receipts to help them keep track of their *variable* expenses—expenses that change from month to month—such as groceries and clothing. They made sure to include insurance, taxes, repairs, and other expenses that occur less frequently. They figured out how much they spent on each of these items in a year, and then they divided this amount by twelve for a monthly average.

According to Isabel, setting up a budget wasn't very difficult. "We compared our monthly expenses with our monthly take-home pay to make sure we weren't spending more than we earned. We looked at all our expenses carefully to see how we could reduce our spending and cut out waste. For example, one month our grocery bills were high, so we decided to save money by using coupons and shopping at wholesale stores. We also realized that we were spending money on certain things we didn't really need, such as premium cable TV channels and fast-food lunches near our workplaces. Now we just have basic cable service, and we take lunches to work from home."

Eduardo adds, "Once we figured out how to trim costs, we wrote a new budget based on these amounts. We made room in our budget for an emergency fund. We try to put 5% to 10% of our income into this fund each month so we're prepared in case one of us loses our job or there's an illness in the family."

The Sorianos also decided that it was important for them to make room in their budget for a family vacation. For years their children had been saying, "We wish we could go to Disney World!" The Sorianos have kept to their budget because they know how much this trip means to their children. This July, the family will finally travel to Disney World. "We all have dreams," says Isabel, "and budgeting wisely can help to make them come true."

1. _____ is a fixed expense.
   A. Clothing
   B. Food
   C. A vacation
   D. Rent

2. *Overdue* in paragraph 1 means _____.
   A. late
   B. too many
   C. expensive
   D. paid

3. In the past, the Sorianos ran out of money because _____.
   A. they had a budget
   B. they had overdue bills
   C. they didn't keep track of their expenses
   D. they didn't have any take-home pay

4. *Waste* in paragraph 3 refers to _____.
   A. recycling
   B. unnecessary purchases
   C. necessary expenses
   D. paper

5. You can save money if you _____.
   A. trim costs
   B. spend more than you earn
   C. divide your expenses by twelve
   D. don't have an emergency fund

6. According to the Sorianos, you can do the things you like if you _____.
   A. spend money on things you don't need
   B. collect receipts
   C. compare your monthly expenses
   D. budget carefully

94c

Choose the correct answer.

1. I hope my son doesn't _____ out of law school.
   A. go
   B. lose
   C. drop
   D. skip

2. I live in the suburbs and have to _____ into the city for work every day.
   A. concentrate
   B. convince
   C. move
   D. commute

3. Good morning. I'd like to cash this _____, please.
   A. money
   B. check
   C. fee
   D. account

4. Making a budget has helped our family _____ our money.
   A. manage
   B. avoid
   C. receive
   D. pay

5. If you keep a balance of $200 in your account, the bank will _____ the monthly fee.
   A. offer
   B. earn
   C. waive
   D. weigh

6. You can open an account at this bank with a _____ of just $10.
   A. deposit
   B. withdrawal
   C. discount
   D. passbook

7. I always compare my monthly expenses with my monthly _____ pay.
   A. overdue
   B. variable
   C. tiered
   D. take-home

8. Our family needs to figure out ways we can _____ costs.
   A. run out of
   B. trim
   C. spend
   D. collect

9. If your bill payments are sometimes overdue, you need to _____ your finances.
   A. receive
   B. compare
   C. take control of
   D. run out of

10. My husband and I have _____ fund in case one of us loses our job or someone in our family gets sick.
    A. a no-fee
    B. a minimum
    C. an introductory
    D. an emergency

SKILLS CHECK ✓

Words:

☐ budget (n)
☐ checking account
☐ daily balance
☐ direct deposit
☐ emergency fund
☐ finances
☐ fixed expenses
☐ interest rate
☐ minimum balance
☐ monthly fee
☐ online banking
☐ passbook
☐ safe deposit box
☐ savings account
☐ take-home pay

☐ budget (v)
☐ collect
☐ compare
☐ cut out
☐ earn
☐ figure out
☐ keep track of
☐ maintain
☐ make room
☐ manage
☐ reduce
☐ run out of
☐ take control of
☐ trim
☐ waive

☐ certain
☐ current
☐ financial
☐ free
☐ introductory
☐ minimum
☐ monthly
☐ no-fee
☐ overdue
☐ popular
☐ prepared
☐ same
☐ tiered
☐ unlimited
☐ variable

I can say:
☐ I wouldn't *leave* if I were you.
☐ If you *did that*, you'd probably *be sorry*.
☐ I wish I *lived in the city*.
☐ I wish I were *there*.
☐ If I could *fix it*, I'd *save some money*.
☐ If I *didn't have to work*, I could/I'd be able to *go*.

I can give a personal opinion:
☐ To tell the truth,/To tell you the truth,/To be honest,/To be honest with you,/If you ask me,

I can:
☐ request bank services
☐ open a bank account
☐ identify features of different kinds of bank accounts
☐ identify budget-planning strategies

I can write:
☐ a monthly budget

I can write about:
☐ something I wish for

Past Unreal Conditional (If _____ Would Have)

Wish-Clauses (continued)

- Asking for and Giving Reasons
- Making Deductions
- Discussing Unexpected Events
- Expressing Wishes and Hopes
- Empathizing
- Consequences of Actions
- Rumors

- Describing Symptoms
- Following Medical Advice
- Community Health Care Services
- Nutrition and Food Labels
- Over-the-Counter Medicine
- Medicine Labels
- Safety Procedures at Work

VOCABULARY PREVIEW

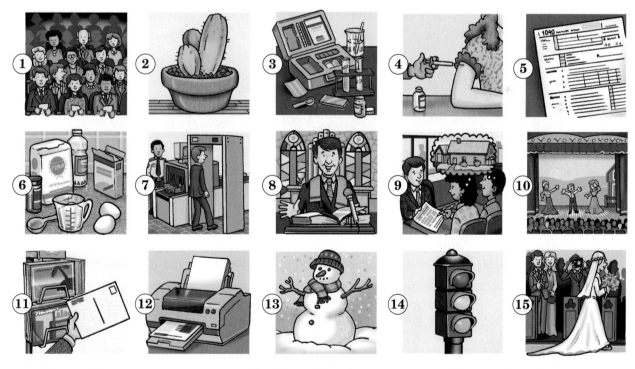

1. audience
2. cactus plant
3. chemistry set
4. flu shot
5. income tax form
6. ingredients
7. metal detector
8. minister
9. mortgage
10. performance
11. postcard
12. printer
13. snowman
14. traffic light
15. wedding dress

If She Had Known . . .

if _____ would have _____

| I He She It We You They | would have eaten. |

A. Why didn't Brenda take her umbrella to work today?

B. She didn't know it was going to rain.
If she had known it was going to rain, she would have taken her umbrella to work today.

A. Why weren't you in class yesterday?

B. I wasn't feeling well.
If I had been feeling well, I would have been in class yesterday.

1. Why didn't Jason stop at the traffic light?
He didn't notice it.
If _____.

2. Why didn't you go to the movies last night?
I wasn't in the mood to see a film.
If _____.

3. Why wasn't Mark on time for work today?
His alarm clock didn't ring.
If _____.

4. Why didn't you hand in your paper today?
My printer wasn't working last night.
If _____.

5. Why didn't the Kramers buy the house on Pine Street?
Their mortgage wasn't approved.
If _____.

6. Why didn't Mr. and Mrs. Park enjoy their ski vacation?
There wasn't enough snow.
If _____.

7. Why didn't you send us a postcard?
We didn't remember your address.
If _____.

8. Why didn't you go to the party last night?
I wasn't invited.
If _____.

9. Why didn't Mr. and Mrs. Sanchez enjoy the play last night?
They didn't have good seats.
If _____.

10. Why wasn't Senator Harrington re-elected?
The people didn't trust him.
If _____.

11. Why didn't Mr. Kelly's students give him a birthday present?
He didn't tell them it was his birthday.
If _____.

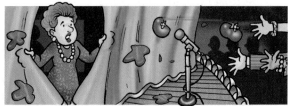

12. Why wasn't Sophia asked to sing an encore last night?
The audience wasn't pleased with her performance.
If _____.

I Wonder Why

A. I wonder why Charles ran by without saying hello.

B. He must have been in a hurry.

A. You're probably right. If he hadn't been in a hurry, he wouldn't have run by without saying hello.

1. I wonder why the boss was so irritable today.
be upset about something

2. I wonder why Pamela arrived late for work.
miss the bus

3. I wonder why Larry quit.
find a better job

4. I wonder why Donna went home early today.
be feeling "under the weather"

5. I wonder why Rover got sick last night.
eat something he shouldn't have

6. I wonder why Jill prepared so much food.
expect a lot of people to come to her party

7. I wonder why Diane went to sleep so early.
have a hard day at the office

8. I wonder why my shirt shrank* so much.
be 100 percent cotton

9. I wonder why my computer shut down.
run out of power

10. I wonder why my cactus plant died.
have a rare disease

11. I wonder why Mom got stopped by a police officer.
be driving too fast

12. I wonder why Dad got searched by the security person.
set off the metal detector

13. I wonder why the minister arrived late for the wedding.
get lost

14.

*shrink - shrank - shrunk

UNEXPECTED GUESTS

Melba had a very difficult situation at her house a few days ago. Her relatives from Minneapolis arrived unexpectedly, without any advance notice whatsoever, and they stayed for the entire weekend.

Needless to say, Melba was very upset. If she had known that her relatives from Minneapolis were going to arrive and stay for the entire weekend, she would have been prepared for their visit. She would have bought a lot of food. She would have cleaned the house. And she certainly wouldn't have invited all her daughter's friends from nursery school to come over and play.

Poor Melba! She really wishes her relatives had called in advance to say they were coming.

✔ READING CHECK-UP

TRUE, FALSE, OR MAYBE?

Answer True, False, or Maybe (if the answer isn't in the story).

1. Melba lives in Minneapolis.
2. Her relatives didn't call to say they were coming.
3. If Melba's relatives hadn't arrived unexpectedly, she would have been prepared for their visit.
4. When her relatives arrived, Melba was upset, but she didn't say so.
5. If her house had been clean and she had had more food, Melba would have been more prepared for her relatives' unexpected visit.
6. Melba's relatives realized they should have called in advance to say they were coming.

WHAT'S THE WORD?

Complete these sentences using *would have* or *wouldn't have* and the correct form of the verb.

1. If the plane had arrived on time, I (*be*) _____ late for the meeting.
2. If the weather had been nice yesterday, we (*go*) _____ to the beach.
3. If I hadn't been out of town, I (*miss*) _____ my daughter's soccer game.
4. If I had seen that stop sign, Officer, I certainly (*drive*) _____ through it.
5. If the president hadn't been in a hurry, he (*give*) _____ a longer speech.
6. If I had known you were a vegetarian, I (*make*) _____ beef stew.

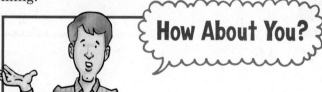

How About You?

Have you ever had a difficult situation when something unexpected happened and you weren't prepared? Tell about it.

WISHING IT HAD HAPPENED DIFFERENTLY

Andrew didn't save his work on his computer yesterday. He really wishes he had saved it. If he had saved it, he wouldn't have lost his history paper. And if he hadn't lost his history paper, he would have been able to hand it in on time today.

Marilyn's alarm clock didn't ring this morning. She really wishes it had rung. If it had rung, she wouldn't have been late for work this morning. And if she hadn't been late, her supervisor wouldn't have scolded her.

Stan filled out his income tax form very quickly this year. He really wishes he had filled it out more carefully. If he had filled it out more carefully, he wouldn't have made so many mistakes. And if he hadn't made so many mistakes, he wouldn't have gotten into trouble with the Internal Revenue Service.

Mr. and Mrs. Carson didn't follow the directions on the box when they baked cookies yesterday. They really wish they had. If they had followed the directions, they would have used the right ingredients. And if they had used the right ingredients, the cookies wouldn't have been as hard as rocks!

 READING *CHECK-UP*

TRUE, FALSE, OR MAYBE?

Answer True, False, or Maybe (if the answer isn't in the story).

1. Andrew handed in his history paper on time.
2. He wishes he had saved his work on his computer.
3. Marilyn's supervisor didn't scold her.
4. If Stan hadn't completed the form quickly, he wouldn't have made any mistakes.
5. Mr. and Mrs. Carson's cookies would have been softer if they hadn't used the wrong ingredients.

How About You?

Have you ever done something and then regretted it? Tell about something you wish you had done differently, and why.

I Wish

I **live** in Boston. I **wish** I **lived** in New York.	I **lived** in Boston. I **wish** I **had lived** in New York.

A. I wish I knew my neighbors.

B. Why do you say that?

A. If I knew my neighbors, I wouldn't be so lonely.

B. I know what you mean.

A. I wish I had known how to get around town when I moved here.

B. Why do you say that?

A. If I had known how to get around town when I moved here, I wouldn't have been so confused.

B. I know what you mean.

1. I don't drive to work. ☹
I have to wait for the train every morning.

2. I didn't drive to work today. ☹
I had to wait an hour for the bus.

102

3. I don't do daily exercises. ☹
I have to go on a diet.

4. I didn't do my homework last night. ☹
I had to do it early this morning.

5. I don't have a good job. ☹
I'm concerned about my future.

6. I didn't have a flu shot last fall. ☹
I was sick all winter.

7. I'm not an optimist. ☹
I get depressed so often.

8. I wasn't prepared for my math test. ☹
I got a low grade.

9. My husband and I don't take dance lessons. ☹
We feel "out of place" at parties.

10. I didn't take medicine when my tooth began to hurt. ☹
I felt miserable all day.

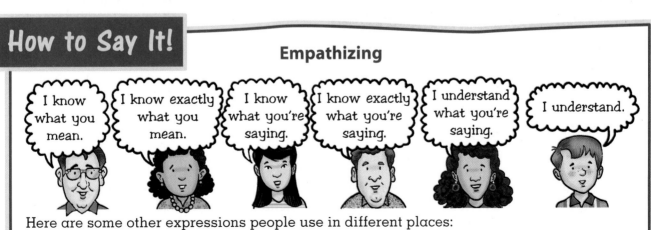

How to Say It!

Empathizing

I know what you mean.

I know *exactly* what you mean.

I know what you're saying.

I know *exactly* what you're saying.

I understand what you're saying.

I understand.

Here are some other expressions people use in different places:
I hear you. I hear what you're saying. I can relate (to that).

Practice the conversations in this lesson again. Use different expressions for empathizing.

RUMORS

All the people at the office are talking about Samantha these days. There's a rumor that Samantha is going to be transferred to the company's office in Paris, and everybody is convinced that the rumor is true. After all, if she weren't going to be transferred to the company's office in Paris, she wouldn't have put her condo up for sale. She wouldn't have started taking French lessons. And she DEFINITELY wouldn't have broken up with her boyfriend.

Of course, the people at the office don't know for sure whether Samantha is going to be transferred to the company's office in Paris. It's only a rumor. They'll just have to wait and see.

All the assembly-line workers at the National Motors automobile company are worrying about the future these days. There's a rumor that the factory is going to close down soon, and everybody is convinced that the rumor is true. After all, if the factory weren't going to close down soon, everybody on the night shift wouldn't have been laid off. The managers wouldn't all be reading the want ads and working on their resumes. And the boss DEFINITELY wouldn't have canceled the annual company picnic!

Of course, the assembly-line workers at National Motors don't know for sure whether the factory is going to close down soon. It's only a rumor. They'll just have to wait and see.

✔ READING *CHECK-UP*

TRUE, FALSE, OR MAYBE?

Answer True, False, or Maybe (if the answer isn't in the story).

1. Samantha is going to be transferred to the company's office in Paris.
2. Samantha hasn't put her condo up for sale.
3. The people at the office think Samantha wouldn't have broken up with her boyfriend if she weren't going to be transferred.
4. There's a rumor that workers on the night shift at the National Motors factory are going to lose their jobs.
5. There isn't going to be a company picnic this year.
6. The factory is going to close down soon.

CHOOSE

1. The students in our class were upset when our teacher quit last week.
   a. We won't be upset if she doesn't quit.
   b. We wouldn't be upset if she didn't quit.
   c. We wouldn't have been upset if she hadn't quit.

2. I didn't come over to your table and have lunch with you because I didn't see you in the cafeteria.
   a. If I saw you, I would have come over and had lunch with you.
   b. If I had seen you, I would have come over and had lunch with you.
   c. If I had seen you, I would come over and have lunch with you.

3. I'm afraid I can't help you type those letters because I'm going to leave work early today.
   a. If I weren't going to leave work early, I'd help you type those letters.
   b. If I were going to leave work early, I'd help you type those letters.
   c. If I were going to leave work early, I wouldn't help you type those letters.

4. Betsy didn't take her umbrella to work today. She got wet on the way home.
   a. If she hadn't taken her umbrella to work, she wouldn't have gotten wet.
   b. If she had taken her umbrella to work, she wouldn't have gotten wet.
   c. If she hadn't taken her umbrella to work, she would have gotten wet.

LISTENING

Listen and choose the statement that is true based on what you hear.

1. a. She's rich.
   b. She isn't rich.

2. a. He remembered her e-mail address.
   b. He didn't remember her e-mail address.

3. a. They would have enjoyed the game more if they had had better seats.
   b. They wouldn't have enjoyed the game more if they had had better seats.

4. a. The boys in the hallway aren't the landlord's children.
   b. The boys in the hallway are the landlord's children.

5. a. He wasn't hired for the job.
   b. He was hired for the job.

6. a. Johnny's grandparents are at his party.
   b. Johnny's grandparents couldn't come to his party.

IN YOUR OWN WORDS

FOR WRITING AND DISCUSSION

Have you heard any rumors lately at school or at work? Tell a story about a rumor.

What's the rumor?
Do you think the rumor is true?
Why or why not?

I hope it's sunny tomorrow.	(It might be sunny.)
I wish it were sunny.	(It isn't sunny.)
I wish it had been sunny during our picnic.	(It wasn't sunny.)

Practice these conversations.

1.

A. I hope it's a nice day tomorrow.

B. Why?

A. If it's a nice day tomorrow, we'll be able to go to the beach.

2.

A. I wish I were taller.

B. How come?

A. If I were taller, I'd be able to play on the basketball team.

3.

A. I wish I had saved my wedding dress.

B. Why do you say that?

A. If I had saved my wedding dress, you could have worn it today at your wedding.

What do **you** hope? What do **you** wish? Share your thoughts with other students.

PRONUNCIATION   Reduced *have*

Listen. Then say it.

They would have enjoyed their vacation.

He wouldn't have arrived late.

She would have taken her umbrella.

I wouldn't have quit.

Say it. Then listen.

We would have used the right ingredients.

They wouldn't have invited so many people.

He would have been on time.

It wouldn't have shrunk.

SIDE by SIDE JOURNAL

Write in your journal about something in your life that you wish you had done, but didn't. What do you wish you had done? Why? What would have happened in your life if you had done that?

GRAMMAR FOCUS

PAST UNREAL CONDITIONAL (IF___ WOULD HAVE)

If	I he she we you they	had known,	I he she we you they	**would have** told them.

If	I he she we you they	hadn't missed the bus,	I he she we you they	**wouldn't have** been late.

WISH-CLAUSES

I We You They	wish	I we you they	had gone there. hadn't gone there.
He She	wishes	he she	

I live in New York.
I wish I lived in California.

I don't know my neighbors.
I wish I knew my neighbors.

I lived in Boston.
I wish I had lived in Miami.

I didn't do that.
I wish I had done that.

Choose the correct word.

1. Rita worked twelve hours yesterday and fell asleep at 9 P.M. If she (**hadn't worked**   didn't work) so many hours, she probably (wouldn't fall   **wouldn't have fallen**) asleep so early.

2. I didn't enjoy the play because I didn't have a good seat. If I (**had**   had had) a good seat, I (**would have enjoyed**   would enjoy) the play.

3. Susan didn't come to my party last Friday because she had to work overtime. If she (hasn't had   **hadn't had**) to work overtime, she (**would have come**   would come) to my party.

4. I arrived late for the meeting because I got lost. If I (didn't get   **hadn't gotten**) lost, I (didn't arrive   **wouldn't have arrived**) late.

5. George is lonely because he doesn't know his neighbors. He wishes he (had known   **knew**) them. If he (didn't know   **knew**) them, he (**wouldn't be**   wouldn't have been) so lonely.

6. I got a low grade on my history exam because I wasn't prepared for it. I really wish I (was   **had been**) prepared for it. If I (**had been**   weren't) prepared for the exam, I (wouldn't get   **wouldn't have gotten**) a low grade.

LIFE SKILLS

- Describing symptoms
- Following medical advice
- Community health care services

1 CONVERSATION DESCRIBING SYMPTOMS

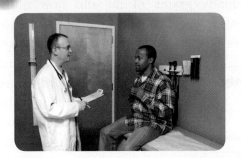

Practice conversations between a doctor and a patient.

A. What seems to be the problem?

B. _____

A. I see. Do you have any idea what might have caused this?

B. Yes. _____

1. My back has been hurting for more than a week. I lifted a very heavy box at work, and I think I pulled a muscle in my back.

2. My wrist is very swollen, and I can't move it. I fell on my arm while I was playing basketball a few days ago.

3. It hurts when I try to bend my right leg at the knee. I got kicked hard in the leg during a soccer game last weekend.

4. I have a really big bump on my head, and it hurts when I touch it. I walked into a swinging door at the restaurant where I work.

Now practice new conversations. Describe your symptoms and what caused them.

2 CONVERSATION FOLLOWING MEDICAL ADVICE

Practice conversations between a doctor and a patient.

A. I want you to _____.

B. _____?

A. Yes. If you do that, I think you'll be a lot healthier.

1. exercise regularly

2. drink several glasses of water every day

3. eat more yogurt and other low-fat dairy products

Now work with a classmate. Make a list of other ways to stay healthy and practice conversations about them.

3 COMMUNITY CONNECTIONS HEALTH CARE PROVIDERS

As a class project, make a list of health care providers in your community. Include their addresses and telephone numbers, and describe the health care services they offer.

Before you purchase packaged food, check the nutrition facts section on the label. It gives important information about the nutrients and calories in the food.

The label always starts with the serving size—the amount people usually eat—for example, a cup or a piece. In the soup label on the right, the serving size is a cup (or 236 grams). The label also tells you how many servings there are in the container. There are two servings in this can of soup.

In addition, the label lists the number of calories and calories from fat in one serving. There are 120 calories in one serving of this soup; 31 of those calories come from fat. The calorie information on the label can help you control your weight. Calories measure the amount of energy in the food. If you eat more calories than you need for energy, you gain weight.

It is important to limit the amount of fat (especially saturated fat and trans fat), cholesterol, and sodium in your diet. Eating too much of these nutrients can raise your blood cholesterol and blood pressure and lead to heart disease. The label tells how many grams of fat and how many milligrams of cholesterol and sodium are contained in each serving. When shopping, compare products and choose the ones with the least saturated fat, trans fat, cholesterol, and sodium. You can also use the percent daily values on the label as a guide: 5% or less is low, and 20% or more is high. 100% is the maximum amount of each nutrient that you should eat in one day. The percentages on this label indicate that the vegetable soup is low in fat and cholesterol but very high in sodium.

Fats, carbohydrates, and proteins provide the body with energy. Choose carbohydrates that are high in dietary fiber and low in sugar. Look at the percentages. A serving of the soup supplies 5% of the carbohydrates and 12% of the fiber you need in a day. (There is no percent daily value for protein since most Americans get all the protein they need.) Fiber and the vitamins and minerals listed at the bottom of the label help prevent disease, so it is important to get 100% or more of the recommended daily amount of each of these nutrients.

Farm Fresh Vegetable Soup

Nutrition Facts

Serving Size 1 cup (236.0g)
Servings per Container 2

Amount per Serving	
Calories 120	Calories from Fat 31

	% Daily Value*
Total Fat 3.5g	5%
Saturated Fat 0.5g	2%
Trans Fat 0g	0%
Cholesterol 15mg	5%
Sodium 870mg	36%
Total Carbohydrate 16.0g	5%
Dietary Fiber 3.0g	12%
Sugars 2.0g	
Protein 6.0g	

Vitamin A 15%	•	Vitamin C	0%
Calcium 2%	•	Iron	6%

*Percent Daily Values are based on a 2,000 calorie diet.

DID YOU UNDERSTAND?

1. How many servings are there in the can of vegetable soup?
2. How many calories are there in a serving?
3. How many calories are there in half a cup of the soup?
4. What nutrients are there in the soup?
5. What vitamins and minerals are there?
6. Which nutrients should you limit?
7. Which nutrients provide energy?
8. How can you tell from the label if a food is high in a nutrient?
9. How can you tell if a food is low in a nutrient?
10. How much fat is there in a serving of the vegetable soup?
11. How much fiber is there in a serving?

APPLYING YOUR KNOWLEDGE

1. What makes this vegetable soup healthy?
2. What makes this soup unhealthy?

Peter's Peanut Butter

Nutrition Facts
Serving Size 2 Tbsp (32g)
Servings per Container 12

Amount per Serving

Calories 190	Calories from Fat 108

	% Daily Value*
Total Fat 12g	18%
Saturated Fat 2.5g	12%
Trans Fat 0g	0%
Cholesterol 0mg	0%
Sodium 130mg	5%
Total Carbohydrate 15g	5%
Dietary Fiber 2g	8%
Sugars 5g	
Protein 7g	

Vitamin A 0%	•	Vitamin C 0%
Calcium 0%	•	Iron 4%

*Percent Daily Values are based on a 2,000 calorie diet.

Sunny's Peanut Butter

Nutrition Facts
Serving Size 2 Tbsp (32g)
Servings per Container 14

Amount per Serving

Calories 190	Calories from Fat 144

	% Daily Value*
Total Fat 16g	25%
Saturated Fat 3g	15%
Trans Fat 0g	0%
Cholesterol 15mg	5%
Sodium 190mg	8%
Total Carbohydrate 15g	5%
Dietary Fiber 2g	8%
Sugars 2g	
Protein 8g	

Vitamin A 0%	•	Vitamin C 0%
Calcium 0%	•	Iron 4%

*Percent Daily Values are based on a 2,000 calorie diet.

Benson Farm White Bread

Nutrition Facts
Serving Size 1 slice (35g)
Servings per Package 19

Amount per Serving

Calories 120	Calories from Fat 14

	% Daily Value*
Total Fat 0.5g	2%
Saturated Fat 0.5g	2%
Trans Fat 0g	0%
Cholesterol 0mg	0%
Sodium 250mg	10%
Total Carbohydrate 22g	7%
Dietary Fiber 1g	4%
Sugars 4g	
Protein 4g	

Vitamin A 0%	•	Vitamin C 0%
Calcium 4%	•	Iron 6%
Thiamine 10%	•	Niacin 8%
Riboflavin 8%	•	Folic Acid 10%

*Percent Daily Values are based on a 2,000 calorie diet.

David's Whole Wheat Bread

Nutrition Facts
Serving Size 1 slice (43g)
Servings per Package 16

Amount per Serving

Calories 110	Calories from Fat 20

	% Daily Value*
Total Fat 2g	3%
Saturated Fat 0g	0%
Trans Fat 0g	0%
Cholesterol 0mg	0%
Sodium 250mg	10%
Total Carbohydrate 21g	7%
Dietary Fiber 3g	12%
Sugars 3g	
Protein 5g	

Vitamin A 0%	•	Vitamin C 0%
Calcium 0%	•	Iron 4%
Thiamine 15%	•	Niacin 6%
Riboflavin 2%	•	Folic Acid 4%

*Percent Daily Values are based on a 2,000 calorie diet.

1. Which peanut butter has less fat?

2. Which peanut butter has less sugar?

3. Which peanut butter has less sodium?

4. Which peanut butter has more protein?

5. How many calories are there in a serving of peanut butter?

6. How many calories are there in one tablespoon of peanut butter?

7. How much sugar is there in one tablespoon of Sunny's Peanut Butter?

8. Which bread has more calories?

9. Which bread has less saturated fat?

10. Which bread has more fiber?

11. How much fiber is there in a sandwich made with 2 tablespoons of Peter's Peanut Butter and 2 slices of Benson Farm White Bread?

12. How many calories are there in a sandwich made with 2 tablespoons of Sunny's Peanut Butter and 2 slices of David's Whole Wheat Bread?

Read the article and answer the questions.

Health Safety Tips: Using Over-the-Counter Drugs Carefully

Each year there are more and more over-the-counter medications that you can buy. These non-prescription drugs can relieve your symptoms and help you feel better, but they can also send you to the emergency room if you ignore the directions, warnings, and other information on the label. Be sure to read the label carefully before you buy medicine, and read it again each time you use it.

The label begins with a list of the active ingredients—the ingredients that treat your ailment—and the amount of these ingredients in a dose. It also tells you the purpose of the medicine—whether it's a pain reliever or an antacid, for example—and what symptoms or ailments you should use the medicine for. Choose medications that treat only the symptoms that you have. If you take several medicines at the same time, check the active ingredients to make sure you don't take too much of an ingredient.

Read the warning on the label carefully to find out whether it's safe for you to take the medication or if you should talk to a doctor first. People react differently to the same drug. Learn about possible side effects, such as dizziness, and when to stop taking the medication and contact a doctor.

Follow the directions on the label. Don't take more than the recommended dose. If the symptoms don't go away, that's a sign you should call the doctor, not increase the dose. Use the correct measuring spoon or a dosage cup with liquid medicine. Be especially careful not to give children too high a dose. An overdose can be very serious.

Check the expiration date on all your medications frequently and throw out any that have expired. If you have allergies, pay close attention to the inactive ingredients in medications, such as food coloring and flavors.

Keep all drugs away from young children. Make sure they can't see or reach them. And be aware that many teenagers take large doses of over-the-counter cough and cold medicines to *get high*. If you have teenagers at home, talk with them about the dangers of drug abuse and check the amounts of these medications regularly to make sure teens aren't abusing these drugs.

[Bottle label: Extra Strength Acetaminophen, 200 Capsules, 500 mg. each]

1. When should you read the medicine label?
2. What are the active ingredients in a medication?
3. When is it especially important to check them?
4. What does the warning on the label tell you?
5. If your symptoms continue, what should you do?
6. How should you take a dose of cough syrup?
7. Why should you check the inactive ingredients?
8. How can you tell if a medicine is too old to use?
9. What should parents do to protect young children and teenagers from an overdose?

Read the warnings on the medicine labels and answer the questions.

Sleep-Well Cold Medicine
Warnings: Do not use with other medications containing acetaminophen.

Ask a doctor before use if you have
- heart disease
- diabetes
- thyroid disease
- high blood pressure

When using this product
- be careful when driving a vehicle.
- avoid alcoholic drinks.
- drowsiness may occur.

Stop use and ask a doctor if
- you get nervous, dizzy, or sleepless.
- cough lasts more than 7 days.

AMAREX PAIN RELIEVER
Warnings: Do not use
- if you have ever had an allergic reaction to any other pain reliever.
- right before or after heart surgery.

Ask a doctor before use if you have
- bleeding problems.
- heart or kidney disease.

When using this product
- long-term use may increase the risk of heart attack.

Stop use and ask a doctor if
- pain lasts more than 10 days.

Lomart Antacid
Warnings: Do not use if you have a bleeding problem.

Ask a doctor before use if you
+ have a fever.
+ are taking any drug for arthritis.

Stop use and ask a doctor if
+ ringing in the ears occurs.
+ diarrhea lasts more than 2 days.

Keep out of reach of children. In case of overdose, get medical help or contact a Poison Control Center right away.

1. When should you stop using Amarex?
2. Who should NOT use Lomart Antacid?
3. What side effect may occur with Sleep-Well?
4. Who should talk to a doctor before taking Amarex?
5. If your child takes too much Lomart, what should you do?
6. Why shouldn't you use Amarex for a long time?
7. If you're allergic to aspirin, which product shouldn't you take?

Be alert! Don't get hurt! Be safe at work!

Be safe around machinery!

- Keep machine guards in place when you operate a machine.
- Shut down your machine before cleaning or repairing and when leaving work.
- Don't wear jewelry or loose clothing around machinery.

Good housekeeping prevents accidents!

- Keep your work area clean and neat.
- Clean up spills promptly.
- Don't eat or drink in your work area.

Obey all safety signs and warnings!

Beware high voltage. Avoid an electric shock.

Don't swallow or inhale poisonous substances.

Avoid skin and eye contact with corrosive materials.

Be careful with flammable materials to prevent a fire.

Be careful with combustible materials to prevent an explosion.

Use your safety equipment!

- Helmets, safety glasses, gloves, respirators, and other safety items prevent injuries and save lives.
- Know the location of fire extinguishers and first-aid kits.

Exit the building quickly and safely in an emergency!

- Know the two exits closest to your work area.
- Know where to assemble outside in case of an evacuation.

Report safety hazards, injuries, and accidents to your supervisor immediately!

1. Why shouldn't workers wear jewelry or loose clothing around machinery?
2. What is "good housekeeping" at the workplace?
3. How can you avoid an electric shock?
4. What might happen with flammable materials? with combustible materials?
5. What does this safety equipment protect: helmet? safety glasses? gloves? respirator?
6. Where are fire extinguishers in your school?
7. Where is the building exit closest to your classroom?

WORK CONNECTIONS What safety procedures do employees follow in a workplace you know? What safety equipment do they use? What safety signs are there in the workplace? Share with the class.

Choose the correct answer.

1. My parents are very _____ about my future.
   A. advanced
   B. approved
   C. concerned
   D. prepared

2. I got _____ by a security person after I went through the metal detector.
   A. shrunk
   B. transferred
   C. put up
   D. searched

3. Do you have any idea what might have _____ your injury?
   A. hurt
   B. caused
   C. composed
   D. pulled

4. To stay healthy, you need to _____ the amount of saturated fat in your diet.
   A. limit
   B. consume
   C. supply
   D. ignore

5. Following safety rules at work will _____ accidents.
   A. report
   B. prevent
   C. provide
   D. shut down

6. A food label provides important _____ information.
   A. location
   B. prescription
   C. nutrition
   D. treatment

7. You should never take more than the recommended _____ of a medicine.
   A. expiration date
   B. ingredients
   C. directions
   D. dose

8. Different people can _____ differently to the same drug.
   A. react
   B. relieve
   C. treat
   D. contact

9. It's important to _____ all safety signs and warnings in the workplace.
   A. avoid
   B. obey
   C. choose
   D. exit

10. You should try to eat foods that are high in _____ and low in _____.
    A. fat . . . servings
    B. calories . . . nutrients
    C. fiber . . . sugar
    D. sugar . . . energy

SKILLS CHECK ✓

Words:
- ☐ abuse
- ☐ cause
- ☐ contact
- ☐ control
- ☐ exit
- ☐ ignore
- ☐ increase
- ☐ indicate
- ☐ inhale
- ☐ limit
- ☐ obey
- ☐ react
- ☐ relieve
- ☐ swallow
- ☐ treat
- ☐ daily amount
- ☐ danger
- ☐ dose
- ☐ emergency
- ☐ food label
- ☐ injury
- ☐ machinery
- ☐ medical help
- ☐ medicine label
- ☐ nutrition
- ☐ reaction
- ☐ safety hazard
- ☐ safety procedure
- ☐ side effect
- ☐ warning

I can ask & answer:
- ☐ What seems to be the problem?
- ☐ Do you have any idea what might have caused this?

I can say:
- ☐ If I had *known*, I would have *told you*.
- ☐ If I hadn't *gotten lost*, I wouldn't have *been late*.
- ☐ I wish I *knew my neighbors*.
- ☐ I wish I had *known how to get around*.

I can write about:
- ☐ something I wish I had done, but didn't

I can:
- ☐ describe symptoms
- ☐ follow medical advice
- ☐ identify community health care providers
- ☐ identify nutrition information on food labels
- ☐ interpret instructions & warnings on medicine labels
- ☐ identify workplace safety procedures

I can empathize:
- ☐ I know what you mean.
- ☐ I know exactly what you mean.
- ☐ I know what you're saying.
- ☐ I know exactly what you're saying.
- ☐ I understand what you're saying.
- ☐ I understand.

Reported Speech
Sequence of Tenses

- **Reporting What People Have Said**
- **Reporting Information**
- **Expressing Surprise**
- **Leaving, Taking, and Conveying Messages**
- **Advice**

- **Job Interviews:**
  Talking About Personal Qualities
  Asking Appropriate Questions
  Answering Difficult Questions
- **Help Wanted Ads**
- **Resumes**

VOCABULARY PREVIEW

1. bride	6. college entrance exam	11. navy
2. groom	7. dictionary	12. pipe
3. interviewer	8. engine	13. puppy
4. movie star	9. lion	14. radiator
5. school-bus driver	10. message	15. robbery

What Did She Say?

"**I'm** busy."		**he was** busy.
"**I'm working** hard."		**he was working** hard.
"**I like** jazz."		**he liked** jazz.
"**I'm going to** buy a new car."		**he was going to** buy a new car.
"**I went** to Paris last year."	He said (that)*	**he had gone** to Paris last year.
"**I was** in London last week."		**he had been** in London last week.
"**I've seen** the movie."		**he had seen** the movie.
"**I'll call** the doctor."		**he would call** the doctor.
"**I can** help you."		**he could** help me.

A. I forgot to tell you. Grandma called yesterday.

B. Really? What did she say?

A. She said (that)* **she was sick**.

A. I forgot to tell you. _____ called yesterday.

B. Really? What did _____ say?

A. _____ said (that)*_____ .

1. *Miguel and Maria*

2. *Robert*

* Or: "He / She / They told me (that)"

110

3. *Aunt Margaret*

4. *our upstairs neighbors*

5. *our niece Terry*

6. *Uncle Ted*

7. *your brother in Detroit*

8. *your sister in Seattle*

9. *the woman from the furniture store*

10. *the TV repairman*

11. *my boss*

12. *our nephew Paul*

13. *the little girl down the street*

14. *the auto mechanic*

15. *my boyfriend*

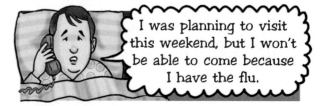

16. *Uncle Frank*

Haven't You Heard?

John **is** sick. $\left.\begin{array}{l}\text{I knew}\\\text{I didn't know}\end{array}\right\}$ (that) John **was** sick.

Our English teacher is in the hospital!

A. What's everybody talking about?

B. Haven't you heard? Our English teacher is in the hospital!

A. You're kidding! I didn't know (that) our English teacher was in the hospital.

B. You didn't?! I thought EVERYBODY knew (that) our English teacher was in the hospital!

A. What's everybody _____ about?

B. Haven't you heard? _____ !

A. You're kidding! I didn't know (that) _____ .

B. You didn't?! I thought EVERYBODY knew (that) _____ !

Jack is going to be a father!

Our landlord wants to sell the building!

1. What's everybody talking about?

2. What's everybody so upset about?

3. What's everybody so happy about?

4. What's everybody so nervous about?

5. What's everybody so angry about?

6. What's everybody so happy about?

7. What's everybody so anxious about?

8. What's everybody so excited about?

9. What's everybody talking about?

10.

How to Say It!

Expressing Surprise

You're kidding! No kidding! You've got to be kidding! I can't believe it!

Practice the conversations in this lesson again. Express surprise in different ways.

113

READING

A LOT OF MESSAGES

Sally was home alone this afternoon while her parents were at work. There were a lot of phone calls, and Sally wrote down a lot of messages.

Grandpa is feeling much better today.

Grandma

I haven't received this month's rent yet.

the landlord

I'll call back later.

Uncle Harry

We were robbed last night.

the neighbors across the street

I won't be able to fix the bathtub today because I'm sick.

the plumber

We fixed the radiator, but we've found something wrong with the engine.

Joe's Auto Repair Shop

Grandma called. She said Grandpa was feeling much better today.

The landlord called. He said he hadn't received this month's rent yet.

Uncle Harry called. He said he would call back later.

The neighbors across the street called. They said they had been robbed last night.

The plumber called. He said he wouldn't be able to fix the bathtub today because he was sick.

Joe's Auto Repair Shop called. They said they had fixed the radiator, but they had found something wrong with the engine.

✔ READING CHECK-UP

Q & A

The next day, Sally was home alone again. Her mother called from the office. Create dialogs based on the following model and information.

> **A.** Tell me, have there been any calls?
> **B.** Yes. _____ called.
> **A.** Oh? What did ___ say?
> **B.** ___ said _____.

1. Grandma • "Grandpa isn't feeling very well and wants me to call the doctor."
2. The landlord • "I received your check this morning."
3. Uncle Harry • "I'm getting married next month, and I want all of you to come to my wedding."
4. The neighbors across the street • "The police caught the man who robbed our house."
5. The plumber • "I'm still sick, and I can't get there today."
6. Joe's Auto Repair Shop • "We've finished working on the engine, and the car is ready to be picked up."

COMPLETE THE STORY

Well, . . .

Your brother got engaged.

Your sister and brother-in-law are going to have a baby.

Your father is planning to retire next month.

There was a big fire at the high school.

The dog had six puppies.

And your high school sweetheart married a movie star and moved to Hollywood.

Aside from that, not much else happened.

Hi, Mom! What's new?

HOME FROM THE NAVY

Bill serves as a lieutenant in the navy. He returned home last weekend after being at sea for several months. Since he hadn't been in touch with his family for a long time, he was very surprised at all the things that had happened while he was away.

He didn't know his brother __had gotten__ [1] engaged. He also didn't know his sister and brother-in-law _____ [2] have a baby. And he was unaware that his father _____ [3] retire next month.

In addition, he didn't know there _____ [4] a big fire at the high school. He hadn't heard that the dog _____ [5] six puppies. And he had no idea that his high school sweetheart _____ [6] a movie star and _____ [7] to Hollywood.

A lot of things certainly had changed while Bill was away.

TRUE, FALSE, OR MAYBE?

Answer True, False, or Maybe (if the answer isn't in the story).

1. Bill has been on a ship for the past several months.
2. His sister had a baby while he was away.
3. His father has retired.

4. Bill's high school was very large.
5. Bill's former girlfriend lives in Hollywood now.

LISTENING

Listen and choose the statement that is true based on what you hear.

1. a. It snowed.
   b. It's still snowing.

2. a. He didn't know that his supervisor had been in the hospital.
   b. He didn't know that his supervisor was in the hospital.

3. a. She wasn't aware that jackets were on sale.
   b. She wasn't aware that jackets had been on sale.

4. a. He didn't know she had to work on Saturday.
   b. He didn't know she had worked on Saturday.

5. a. She was aware that Sherman had been thinking of leaving.
   b. She was unaware that Sherman had been thinking of leaving.

6. a. Her friends hadn't told her they were going to move.
   b. Her friends had told her they were going to move.

What Did They Ask?

"Where is the bank?"

"When are you going to visit me?"

"Do you speak English?"

"Have you seen Mary?"

He asked me
{
where the bank was.
when I was going to visit him.
{ if / whether } I spoke English.
{ if / whether } I had seen Mary.
}

Why is there a Santa Claus in every department store in town?

A. You won't believe what a three-year-old boy asked me today!

B. What did he ask you?

A. He asked me why there was a Santa Claus in every department store in town.

B. I can't believe he asked you that!

A. I can't either.

Do you want to receive a raise this year?

A. You won't believe what my boss asked me today!

B. What did she ask you?

A. She asked me { if / whether } I wanted to receive a raise this year.

B. I can't believe she asked you that!

A. I can't either.

A. You won't believe what _____ asked me today!

B. What did _____ ask you?

A. _____ asked me_____.

B. I can't believe _____ asked you that!

A. I can't either.

1. *my history teacher*

2. *my boyfriend*

3. *my nine-year-old nephew*

4. *the woman at my job interview*

5. *my students*

6. *my parents*

(continued)

7. *my philosophy professor*

8. *my daughter*

9. *my basketball coach*

10. *my son*

11. *a taxi driver*

12. *the patient in Room 12*

13. *Grandma*

14.

THE JOB INTERVIEW

Where did you go to school?

Have you had any special training?

Where have you worked?

Are you willing to move to another city?

Can you work overtime and weekends?

How is your health?

Have you ever been fired?

Why did you have four different jobs last year?

Why do you think you're more qualified for the position than the other sixty-two people who have applied?

Charles had a job interview a few days ago at the United Insurance Company. The interview lasted almost an hour, and Charles had to answer a lot of questions.

First, the interviewer asked Charles where he had gone to school. Then she asked if he had had any special training. She asked where he had worked. She also asked whether he was willing to move to another city. She wanted to know if he could work overtime and weekends. She asked him how his health was. She asked him whether he had ever been fired. She wanted to know why he had had four different jobs last year.

And finally, the interviewer asked the most difficult question. She wanted to know why Charles thought he was more qualified for the position than the other sixty-two people who had applied.

Charles had never been asked so many questions at a job interview before. He doesn't know how well he did, but he tried his best.

✔ READING *CHECK-UP*

ROLE PLAY

You're applying for a job at the United Insurance Company. Role-play a job interview with another student, using the questions in the illustration as a guide.

How About You?

Tell about a job interview you had.
 Where was the interview?
 How long did it last?
 What questions did the interviewer ask?
 What were your answers?
 What was the most difficult question, and how did you answer it?
 Did you get the job?

Job interviewers sometimes like to ask difficult questions. Why do you think they do this? What are some difficult questions interviewers might ask? Make a list, and think of answers to those questions.

What Did They Tell You?

"Call me after five o'clock."
"Stop complaining!"

"Don't worry!"
"Don't call me before nine o'clock."

He told me

to call him after five o'clock.
to stop complaining.

not to worry.
not to call him before nine o'clock.

A. I'm a little annoyed at the mailman.

B. How come?

A. He told me to keep my dog in the house.

B. Why did he tell you that?

A. He said (that) he was afraid to deliver my mail.

Keep your dog in the house! I'm afraid to deliver your mail!

A. I'm a little annoyed at my neighbors.

B. How come?

A. They told me not to play my music so loud.

B. Why did they tell you that?

A. They said (that) I was bothering them.

Don't play your music so loud! You're bothering us!

A. I'm a little annoyed at _____.

B. How come?

A. _____ told me _____.

B. Why did _____ tell you that?

A. _____ said (that) _____.

1. *my doctor*

2. *my dentist*

3. *my math teacher*

4. *the school-bus driver*

5. *my girlfriend*

6. *my parents*

7. *my boss*

8. *my landlord*

9. *my seven-year-old son*

How About You?

Do you remember the last time someone said something that really annoyed you?

What did the person say? (*He/She told me . . .*)

Why do you think he/she said that?

Did you say anything back?

121

GOOD ADVICE

Margaret had a bad stomachache yesterday afternoon. She called her doctor and asked him what she should do. Her doctor told her to rest in bed. He also told her not to eat too much for dinner. And he told her to call him in the morning if she was still sick. Margaret felt better after speaking with her doctor. She's glad she can always depend on him for good advice.

Eric went out on his first date yesterday evening. Before he left the house, he asked his parents if they had any advice. They told him to be polite when he met the girl's mother and father. They also told him not to drive too fast. And they told him not to bring his date home later than ten o'clock. Eric felt more prepared for his date after speaking to his parents. He's glad he can always depend on them for good advice.

Mrs. Tanaka's students are going to take the college entrance examination this Saturday, and they're very nervous. They asked Mrs. Tanaka if she had any helpful advice. She told them to answer the questions carefully. She also told them not to spend too much time on a question that was too difficult. And she told them to get a good night's sleep the night before the examination. Mrs. Tanaka's students felt more confident after speaking with her. They're glad they can always depend on her for good advice.

Mr. and Mrs. Pratt are going away on vacation soon, and they're concerned because there have been several robberies in their neighborhood recently. They called the police and asked them what they could do to prevent their house from being broken into while they were away. The police told them to lock all the windows and leave on a few lights. They also advised them to ask the neighbors to pick up the mail. And they warned them not to tell too many people that they would be away. Mr. and Mrs. Pratt felt reassured after speaking with the police. They're glad they can always depend on them for good advice.

✔ READING CHECK-UP

True, False, or Maybe?

Answer True, False, or Maybe (if the answer isn't in the story).

1. Margaret told her doctor to rest in bed.
2. Margaret didn't eat very much for dinner yesterday.
3. Eric hadn't gone out on a date before yesterday.
4. Eric brought his date home by ten o'clock.
5. Mrs. Tanaka teaches at a college.
6. Mrs. Tanaka got a good night's sleep the night before the examination.
7. Locking windows and leaving on lights are two ways to prevent robberies.
8. The Pratts' house was broken into while they were away.

Choose

1. Eric's parents told him _____.
   a. not to drive too fast
   b. don't drive too fast

2. Mrs. Tanaka told her students _____.
   a. answer the questions carefully
   b. to answer the questions carefully

3. She told him _____.
   a. don't worry
   b. not to worry

4. She asked _____ a vegetarian.
   a. if I was
   b. whether are you

5. My friends said that _____.
   a. they will be here
   b. they would be here

6. We _____ them to call us.
   a. said
   b. told

PRONUNCIATION Reduced *to*

Listen. Then say it.

He told me to sit down.

She told me not to call her.

She asked me where I went to school.

They said they wouldn't be able to come to the party.

Say it. Then listen.

She told me to lose some weight.

He told me not to eat candy.

He asked me if I wanted to get married.

She said I didn't have to work overtime.

Write in your journal about a time when you needed advice. Why did you need advice? (What was the situation?) Who did you ask for advice? What did you ask? What did the person tell you? Did you follow the person's advice? Was it good advice or bad advice? Why?

GRAMMAR FOCUS

REPORTED SPEECH
SEQUENCE OF TENSES

"I'm busy."		he was busy.
"I like jazz."		he liked jazz.
"I'm going to buy a new car."		he was going to buy a new car.
"I went to Paris last year."	He said (that)	he had gone to Paris last year.
"I was in London last week."		he had been in London last week.
"I've seen the movie."		he had seen the movie.
"I'll call the doctor."		he would call the doctor.
"I can help you."		he could help me.

John **is** sick.			John **was** sick.
Jack **is** going to be a father.	I knew (that)		Jack **was** going to be a father.
Our landlord **wants** to sell the building.	I didn't know (that)		our landlord **wanted** to sell the building.
We **can't** use our dictionaries.			we **couldn't** use our dictionaries.

"Where is the bank?"		where the bank was.
"When are you going to visit me?"		when I was going to visit him.
"Do you speak English?"	He asked me	{ if / whether } I spoke English.
"Have you seen Mary?"		{ if / whether } I had seen Mary.

"Call me after five o'clock."		to call him after five o'clock.
"Stop complaining!"		to stop complaining.
"Don't worry!"	He told me	not to worry.
"Don't call me before nine o'clock."		not to call him before nine o'clock.

Choose the correct word.

1. Jessica called. She told me (if she likes   she liked) her new job very much.

2. Richard said (he was   if he's) sorry he (wouldn't   won't) be able to help us move.

3. Did Uncle Walter (tell   ask) you (did he get   he had gotten) fired from his job?

4. Ms. Chen called. She told me (she couldn't   if she can) come to the meeting tomorrow.

5. I didn't know (we didn't   don't we) have to come to work early tomorrow morning.

6. I just spoke to Marta. She told me (has she been   she had been) promoted again.

7. My secretary said he (was   is) sorry he (hasn't   hadn't) finished the report on time.

8. My parents asked me (when are my exams   when my exams were).

9. The interviewer asked me where (I had gone   did I go) to school.

10. My doctor is concerned. She told me (to lose   must I lose) fifteen pounds.

11. Our landlord told us (to don't play   not to play) loud music after midnight.

12. The waiter (asked   told) me (do I want   if I wanted) to order dessert.

13. The nurse (told   asked) me (if I had ever   have I ever) had a flu shot.

1 CONVERSATION JOB INTERVIEW QUESTIONS

Practice conversations between an interviewer and a job applicant.

A. What do you consider your greatest strengths?

B. _____, and
_____

A. Do you know about what we do here?

B. Yes. _____

A. Do you have any questions for me?

B. Yes. _____

I'm hardworking.

I'm dependable.

I'm a good communicator.

I get along well with people.

I have a very positive attitude.

I'm always enthusiastic about my work.

I learn quickly.

I always try to improve my skills.

_____
(other)

I've read a lot about the company in the newspaper.

I've looked closely at the information on your website.

I'm familiar with your work because my friend/relative _____(name)_____ is employed here.

_____
(other)

Can you tell me more about the specific job responsibilities?

I'd be interested to know more about the company's history and its work.

When do you plan to fill the position?

Are there opportunities for promotion and advancement?

_____
(other)

THINK & SHARE

Work with a classmate. Answer these questions. Then practice more conversations.

What other personal qualities can a job applicant talk about during an interview?

What other ways can an applicant learn about a company before a job interview?

What additional questions are appropriate to ask during an interview?

2 TEAMWORK ANSWERING DIFFICULT JOB INTERVIEW QUESTIONS

Work with a classmate. How would each of you answer the following questions at a job interview? Compare your answers. Then share with the class. Discuss the best ways to answer these questions.

1. Why do you want to work here?

2. We have many applicants for this position. Why should we hire *you*?

3. What do you consider your greatest weakness?

4. What are your long-term goals for the future?

ADMINISTRATIVE ASSISTANT FT opening for qualified person in large insurance agency. General ofc. duties. Must have gd. computer skills w/ exper. in Word, Excel, & PowerPoint. H.S. dipl. req. 2 yrs. ofc. exper. min. Excel. bnfts. incl. health and dental ins. Fax cover letter, resume, & refs. to 323-578-2769.	**HOME HEALTH AIDES** Looking for cert. home health aides to work in L.A. area. Must have car. Bilingual skills (Span., Viet.) a plus. Refs. req. Call Los Angeles Home Healthcare Services at 323-764-5092.
BILINGUAL SECY (Spanish) FT position in law office. Exc. keyboarding skills nec. 60 wpm or more. Must be able to work well in a fast-paced environment. 2 yrs. exp. pref. Oppty. for advancement. Call Carol at 323-479-1462.	**MAINTENANCE SUPERVISOR** The Holiday Hotel is looking for a FT maintenance supervisor. All candidates should have plumbing, carpentry, and elec. exper. Computer skills helpful. Must be avail. wknds. Email resume to holidayhotel.com.
BOOKKEEPER Growing co. seeks FT bookkeeper for our accounting dept. Exp. w/ Word, Excel, and QuickBooks programs a must. Assoc. degree or equiv. and 3 yrs. exp. in bkkpg./acctg. field req. Send resume to Lee Associates, 2519 Pacific Drive, Los Angeles, CA 90074.	**MEDICAL ASSISTANT** Dr's office has an opening for cert. medical asst. w/ at least 1 yr. exper. Duties incl. taking blood pressure & other vitals and giving injections. Some recep. duties also req'd. Must have excel. interpersonal skills. Fax resume to 323-764-0984.
DENTAL ASSISTANT Busy dental practice in need of PT dental asst. Grad. of approved dental assisting program w/ 2 yrs. exp. X-ray & CPR cert. req. Computer skills a plus. Must work some Sats. Fax resume to 323-764-9871.	**PAINTERS NEEDED** FT temp. position (6 mo.). Start immed. Must have own transp. Will train. Call Ronald at 323-578-2874.
DRIVER Assemble and deliver furniture. Co. vehicle provided. Must have valid CA driv. lic., clean DMV record, and be able to lift & carry 75 lbs. No prev. exp. req. Drug testing employer. Call George at 323-764-1900.	**SOFTWARE ENGINEER** Lead team of 5 software developers in design & development of web-based applications. The right person will have a B.S in Comp. Sci. or a related field & 5 yrs. exp. in software dvlpmt. incl. project mgmt. Fax resume to 323-684-0047.

1. You must have your own car if you want to work as a home health aide or a _____.
   - A. driver
   - B. school bus driver
   - C. bilingual secretary
   - D. painter

2. The home health aide and the medical assistant both must have _____.
   - A. high school diplomas
   - B. associate degrees
   - C. certificates
   - D. bilingual skills

3. Maria has been a secretary for 3 years and is familiar with office software. She types 40 words per minute. She should apply for the job as _____.
   - A. a bilingual secretary
   - B. an administrative assistant
   - C. a bookkeeper
   - D. a medical assistant

4. Victor is looking for an entry-level position. He should answer the ad for _____.
   - A. a bookkeeper
   - B. a medical assistant
   - C. a dental assistant
   - D. a driver

5. The _____ position requires a person to work during the weekend.
   - A. bookkeeper
   - B. home health aide
   - C. software engineer
   - D. dental assistant

6. We can infer that the medical assistant sometimes has to _____.
   - A. answer telephones
   - B. lift heavy objects
   - C. use PowerPoint
   - D. make repairs

TEAMWORK Work with a classmate. Make a list of all the abbreviations in the help wanted ads above. Then write the full word for each abbreviation. (Some words have more than one abbreviation.)

Donna Santos
155 Milton Road
Houston, TX 77043

713-504-6239 (home)   713-504-7732 (cell)   dsantos@usa.com

OBJECTIVE: A position in office management or human resources.

EDUCATION: University of Houston—Downtown, Houston, TX
Bachelor of Arts, Business Administration 2012

Houston Community College, Houston, TX
Associate of Arts, Business Administration 2010

EXPERIENCE:

Sept. 2016–present   **Office Manager**, Green Energy Consultants, Houston, TX
Oversee day-to-day administration of office. Supervise a staff of fifteen employees.
Responsible for hiring, training, and evaluating office staff. Oversee maintenance of
equipment. Plan on-site and off-site meetings.

Sept. 2014–Aug. 2016   **Administrative Assistant**, Green Energy Consultants, Houston, TX
Handled company correspondence. Managed and maintained office filing system.
Responsible for company's newsletter. Made travel arrangements for staff.
Assisted with payroll.

Sept. 2012–Jun. 2014   **Administrative Assistant**, Office of Community Development, Houston, TX
Entered and updated information in database. Ordered supplies. Maintained
records. Scheduled meetings. Assisted in creating newsletter. Translated documents.

Jan. 2011–Jun. 2012   **Office Assistant**, English Department, University of Houston, Houston, TX
Assisted in general clerical duties such as filing, photocopying, proofreading,
data entry, and word processing.

Sept. 2006–Aug. 2008   **Sales Associate**, Texas Outdoor Shop, Houston, TX
Provided customer service. Operated cash register. Set up window displays.

SKILLS: Proficient in Microsoft Word, Microsoft Excel, Microsoft PowerPoint, QuickBooks.
Fluent in Spanish.

OTHER ACTIVITIES: Monument Musical Theater Company: Assistant director.
Houston Community Chorus: I sing in the chorus and serve as business manager.

References Available Upon Request

Read the resume and answer the questions.

1. What kind of job does Donna want?
2. What colleges did she attend?
3. What degrees did she receive?
4. What is her current job?
5. What job did she have while she was in college?
6. What sales experience does she have?
7. When did she start working at Green Energy Consultants?
8. What did she do at the Office of Community Development?
9. How long did she work there?
10. What computer skills does she have?
11. What experience in human resources has she had as an office manager?
12. What musical activities does she enjoy? Why do you think she included them on her resume?

Choose the correct answer.

1. I believe I'm very _____ for the job.
   A. successful
   B. positive
   C. hardworking
   D. qualified

2. I'm looking for a full-time _____ in office management.
   A. position
   B. objective
   C. employer
   D. responsibility

3. For this job, drivers must have a _____ Florida driver's license.
   A. general
   B. vital
   C. valid
   D. fluent

4. I know I need previous experience to apply for this job. The help wanted ad says _____.
   A. exc. bnfts.
   B. 3 yrs. exp. req.
   C. no prev. exper. req.
   D. assoc. degree or equiv.

5. The administrative assistant position requires good computer skills and experience with _____.
   A. CPR
   B. DMV
   C. X-rays
   D. Excel and PowerPoint

6. _____ I consider that my greatest strength.
   A. I've read a lot about your company.
   B. I've looked closely at your website.
   C. I'm very dependable.
   D. I'm familiar with your company's history.

7. I'm an office assistant. I help with general clerical duties, such as _____.
   A. filing and photocopying
   B. hiring and training
   C. evaluating office staff
   D. planning on-site and off-site meetings

8. Our company needs a software engineer with experience in the development of _____.
   A. plumbing and carpentry
   B. web-based applications
   C. company correspondence
   D. human resources

9. I have a Bachelor of Arts degree from _____.
   A. Green Energy Consultants
   B. Plainville High School
   C. Microsoft Word
   D. the University of Houston

10. The Paxton Company offers its employees excellent benefits. These benefits include _____.
    A. a cover letter, a resume, and references
    B. Word and QuickBooks
    C. health and dental insurance
    D. keyboarding skills

SKILLS CHECK ✔

Words:

☐ assist
☐ evaluate
☐ handle
☐ maintain
☐ manage
☐ operate
☐ order
☐ oversee
☐ photocopy
☐ proofread
☐ schedule
☐ set up
☐ supervise
☐ translate
☐ update

☐ administration
☐ advancement
☐ application
☐ attitude
☐ development
☐ duties
☐ goal
☐ management
☐ objective
☐ opportunity
☐ promotion
☐ quality
☐ responsibility
☐ strength
☐ weakness

☐ appropriate
☐ approved
☐ certified
☐ clerical
☐ dependable
☐ enthusiastic
☐ fast-paced
☐ fluent
☐ hardworking
☐ interpersonal
☐ long-term
☐ positive
☐ proficient
☐ temporary
☐ valid

I can say:

☐ "I'm *sick*."
☐ I said (that) I was *sick*.
☐ "I like *my new job*."
☐ I said (that) I liked *my new job*.
☐ "I got *a raise*."
☐ I said (that) I had gotten *a raise*.
☐ "I've done *that*."
☐ I said (that) I had done *that*.
☐ "I can do *that*."
☐ I said (that) I could do *that*.
☐ "I'll *call you*."
☐ I said (that) I would *call you*.
☐ "Where is *the bank*?"
☐ I asked you where *the bank* was.

☐ "Do you *live here*?"
☐ I asked you if/whether you *lived here*.

I can speak well during a job interview:

☐ talk about personal qualities
☐ ask appropriate questions
☐ answer difficult questions

I can:

☐ interpret help wanted ads
☐ interpret a resume

I can express surprise:

☐ You're kidding!/No kidding!/You've got to be kidding!/I can't believe it!

I can write about:

☐ a time I needed advice

Volume 4   Number 3

Polish Up Your Interview Skills!

Tips from the experts

Going to a job interview can be a very challenging experience. A lot of people are probably applying for the same job. What can you do to make a good impression and stand out from the crowd?

The experts say, "Be prepared!" Learn about the company before your interview. Find out about the company's products or services. Read about the company in the newspaper, or try to find information on the Internet. (Many companies have their own websites with lots of information.) Also, dress appropriately for the interview. Don't wear casual clothes. Dress neatly and conservatively.

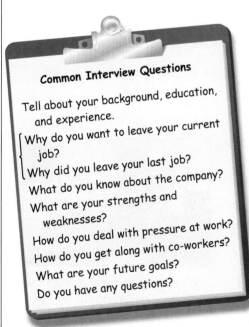

Common Interview Questions

Tell about your background, education, and experience.

Why do you want to leave your current job?

Why did you leave your last job?

What do you know about the company?

What are your strengths and weaknesses?

How do you deal with pressure at work?

How do you get along with co-workers?

What are your future goals?

Do you have any questions?

Prepare in advance for the types of questions you will probably be asked. The interviewer will most likely ask you to tell about your background, education, and experience. If you are employed, the interviewer may ask you why you want to leave your current job. Or, if you aren't employed at the time of the interview, the interviewer might ask why you left your last job. You should be prepared to talk about what you know about the company. Don't be surprised if you are asked what your strengths and weaknesses are. Be ready to answer questions about how you deal with pressure at work. An interviewer will most likely ask you how you get along with co-workers. You may also be asked what your future goals are. And don't forget that the interviewer will probably ask if you have any questions.

Be sure to answer the interviewer's questions honestly. Try to show that you are motivated, responsible, and very interested in the job. Be confident, but don't brag about yourself. (Don't say how great you are. Instead, give examples of things you've done that show your strengths.)

Be prepared for when the interviewer asks if you have any questions. You can ask about the job responsibilities, the company in general, when the position will be filled, and other things. Some experts say that it isn't a good idea to ask too many questions about salary, vacations, or benefits during the first interview. If the company has follow-up interviews for the position, that might be a better time for such questions. Before you leave the interview, make sure you know the names and titles of all the people you met. Write a thank-you letter to the interviewer as soon as possible. Say thank you for the interviewer's time, describe why you think you're the right person for the job, and offer to go back for another interview if they want you to.

FACT FILE

How People Find Jobs

want ads 14%
employment agencies 11%
other 10%
networking 35%
contacting employer directly 30%

Who Got the Job?

Sarah Jones went to a job interview yesterday at a computer software company. First, the interviewer asked her about her background and experience. She told about where she had gone to school, what she had studied, and what kinds of jobs she had had. When the interviewer asked her why she wanted to leave her current job, she said that she was looking for a more challenging position. Then the interviewer asked Sarah what she knew about the company. She answered that she used some of the company's software and she had read articles about the company in the newspaper. Then the interviewer asked what her strengths and weaknesses were. She replied that she worked very hard and got along well with people, but she had some problems writing business letters. She explained that she was now taking a business writing class at a local college. Finally, the interviewer asked Sarah if she had any questions. Sarah asked if the job required a lot of travel, and she asked what the company's plans for the future were. As soon as she got home, Sarah wrote a thank-you note to the interviewer.

Bob Mills went to a job interview yesterday at the same company. First, the interviewer asked him about his background and experience. Bob said he had listed all that information on his resume and the interviewer could find it there. When the interviewer asked him why he wanted to change employers, Bob replied that he was looking for a job with shorter hours and fewer responsibilities. Then the interviewer asked what he knew about the company. Bob said he wasn't really familiar with the company's products, and he asked what they were. When the interviewer asked what his strengths and weaknesses were, Bob said he hadn't really thought about that before, but it was a good question. Finally, the interviewer asked Bob if he had any questions. Bob asked if he could have 25 vacation days during his first year, and he wanted to know whether he would be able to bring his dog to the office every day. Bob went home feeling good about the interview. He thought it had gone well, and he waited for the company to call.

Who do you think got the job? For fun, act out the two interviews!

AROUND THE WORLD

Job Interviews

Job interviews can be very different around the world. An interviewer's questions, the "body language" that should be used, and the formality of an interview vary from country to country.

If you're at a job interview in Japan, don't look directly into the eyes of the interviewer. It is considered rude. But if you're at an interview in the United States, you should definitely make eye contact with the interviewer. If you don't, the interviewer may think you aren't trustworthy or confident.

In the United States and some other countries, interviewers aren't supposed to ask questions about family, marital status, and other personal information. In most countries, however, personal questions are very common during job interviews.

In France, shake hands with the interviewer lightly, not firmly. In many other countries, you should shake hands firmly, because a firm handshake is a sign of confidence. In Germany, your interview might begin with a very short informal conversation followed by a formal interview. In Mexico and many other countries, the informal small talk might take longer, and in some cases the entire interview might be informal.

What are job interviews like in countries you know?

Interview

A Side by Side Gazette reporter recently interviewed Monica Salinas, a Human Resources manager for a large insurance company. As a job interviewer, Ms. Salinas reads thousands of resumes and interviews hundreds of people each year.

Q: Tell us about your job.

A: I'm responsible for interviewing applicants for all the available positions in our company. Our firm is very large, so we receive more than 50 resumes and interview up to ten people each day. It's a lot of work!

Q: What are your favorite interview questions?

A: I like to ask applicants how they think other people would describe them. I also like to ask about weekend activities, hobbies, and other things that help me get to know the applicant as a person.

Q: What was your most memorable interview?

A: It was with a young woman from Brazil. She had only been in this country for four years. When she arrived, she didn't speak a word of English. But at her interview, her English was excellent! She said she had taken English courses and then studied business at a community college. She said she was the first person from her family to go to college. She impressed me so much. I asked her how she could contribute to our company. She said she would be the hardest worker here. Well, she is! I hired her, and last month she was chosen "Employee of the Year" and received a big bonus check. I asked her what she was going to do with the extra money. She said that she had already sent it to her family in Brazil so they could start building a new home.

Q: Have you had any unusual interviews?

A: One applicant said he was hungry. He opened a paper bag, took out a sandwich, and ate during the entire interview! Another time, an applicant was so nervous that she fainted. I got her some water, and I offered to reschedule the interview. She was lying on the floor, but she said that she was okay and wanted to continue. So I sat with her on the floor, and we had a very nice conversation.

Q: What is your best piece of advice for someone going to a job interview?

A: Be yourself! Smile, relax, and be honest. Let the interviewer see who you really are.

FUN with IDIOMS

Do You Know These Expressions?

____ 1. Don't put your foot in your mouth!

____ 2. Don't talk the interviewer's head off!

____ 3. Don't inflate your resume!

____ 4. Don't beat around the bush!

a. Answer questions briefly!

b. Answer questions directly!

c. Don't say the wrong thing!

d. Don't exaggerate your skills or experience!

Dear Side by Side,

I have a question about tenses and reported speech. I understand that this is the correct way to say each of these sentences:

He said (that) he **was** hungry.

She told me (that) she **was** sick.

They said (that) they **were** engaged.

However, I often hear English speakers say:

He said (that) he **is** hungry.

She told me (that) she **is** sick.

They said (that) they **are** engaged.

Are both ways correct? I'm very confused.

Sincerely,

"Tense About Reported Speech"

Dear "Tense About Reported Speech,"

The first way to say these sentences is grammatically correct. However, in informal speech, the second way is also correct, especially when the person is reporting about something that someone has just said. We also "break the rule" when we talk about facts that are always true. For example:

We knew (that) Paris **is** the capital of France.

The teacher said (that) the Amazon **is** the longest river.

We hope this answers your question. Thanks for writing.

Sincerely,

Side by Side

Global Exchange

BillG: You won't believe what my neighbor in the apartment across the hall told me today! She said I was the noisiest person in our building! She told me that I played the drums too loud at night. She said that I had too many parties on weekends. And she asked me if I knew that dogs weren't allowed in the building. I told her that she had made a mistake, and that she had mixed me up with our neighbor down the hall. After all, I don't play the drums, I never have parties, and I don't have a dog! She apologized, and we had a nice conversation after that. I told her that if she wanted, I would go with her to talk to our noisy neighbor. That should be an interesting conversation!

Send a message to a keypal. Tell about an interesting conversation you have had.

What Are They Saying?

LISTENING

You have six messages!

You Have Six Messages!

1
a. Jim Gavin wanted to know why money had been taken out of his paycheck.
b. Jim Gavin wanted to know why money hadn't been taken out of his paycheck.

2
a. Denise said she hadn't been able to go to the meeting.
b. Denise said she wouldn't be able to go to the meeting.

3
a. Patty told Joe that she had ordered more pens.
b. Patty told Joe that she had canceled the order for pens.

4
a. Jane Adams called to say that the painters hadn't arrived yet.
b. Jane Adams called to tell Joe when the painters would arrive.

5
a. George asked Joe if he could go to a doctor's appointment tomorrow morning.
b. George told Joe that he would be at a doctor's appointment tomorrow morning.

6
a. Michelle told Joe she had taken a job with another company.
b. Michelle told Joe that another company had offered her a job.

A **direct quotation** shows a person's exact words. You use **quotation marks** to write a quotation.

A quotation begins with a capital letter. It can be at the beginning or at the end of a sentence. Periods go inside quotations. Question marks and exclamation points go inside quotations if they are part of the quotation.

A **divided quotation** is in two parts. If the second part continues a sentence, it doesn't begin with a capital letter. If the second part is a new sentence, the first word is capitalized.

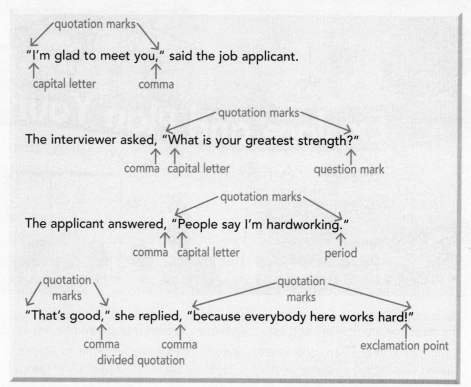

Practice these conversations with a classmate.

The boss said please come to work early tomorrow.

A. What's wrong with this sentence?

B. The quotation isn't punctuated correctly.

A. How should the punctuation be fixed?

B. Put a comma after the word *said*. Put an opening quotation mark before the word *Please*. Capitalize the *P* in *Please*. And put a closing quotation mark after the period at the end of the quotation.

Candy is bad for your teeth warned my dentist.

A. What's wrong with this sentence?

B. The quotation isn't punctuated correctly.

A. How should the punctuation be fixed?

B. Put an opening quotation mark before the word *Candy*. Put a comma after the word *teeth*. And put a closing quotation mark after the comma.

Rewrite each sentence. Fix the punctuation and any capitalization errors. Then practice new conversations about these sentences.

1. The interviewer asked what are your future goals?

2. I want to be a manager I replied.

3. When will you fill the position I asked.

4. His parents said don't drive too fast.

5. The plumber called and asked can I fix your tub tomorrow instead of today?

6. Study hard our teacher warned because I know the test will be difficult.

Explore and Plan Your Career!

Career Pathways—A new way to explore, plan, and learn for your future!

As a student at Lake Community College, you can use Career Pathways to explore a variety of careers, understand the skills that are needed, and take the courses that will prepare you for the job that's right for you.

Educators and business and industry experts have joined together to identify a total of sixteen Career Clusters. A Career Cluster is an industry sector—a large group of occupations that have common skills and knowledge. Within each of the sixteen clusters, there are many Career Pathways. A Career Pathway is a direction that you can take toward specific jobs.

Career Clusters	Description
Agriculture, Food, and Natural Resources	Growing, processing, and selling food, wood, animals, and natural resources
Architecture and Construction	Designing, planning, managing, building and maintaining buildings
Arts, Audio/Visual Technology, and Communications	Designing, performing, writing, and publishing multimedia content including visual and performing arts and design, journalism, and entertainment
Business Management and Administration	Organizing and managing businesses
Education and Training	Teaching and managing courses and training
Finance	Financial planning, banking, and insurance
Government and Public Administration	Planning and managing government services and taxes
Health Science	Providing and managing health services and research
Hospitality and Tourism	Providing services in restaurants, hotels, travel, tourism, and recreation
Human Services	Providing community and mental health services
Information Technology	Designing and managing technology and software
Law, Public Safety, Corrections, and Security	Providing legal, safety, and security services
Manufacturing	Planning and manufacturing
Marketing	Marketing of products and services
Science, Technology, Engineering, and Mathematics	Planning and research in science and technology
Transportation, Distribution, and Logistics	Moving and managing people and products

Our college has identified six Career Clusters that are important in our local economy. Each cluster has many Career Pathways. These six clusters have the most job opportunities in our area. We have worked together with local businesses and companies to develop special programs of study for our students.

| Agriculture, Food, and Natural Resources | Architecture and Construction | Health Science | Hospitality and Tourism | Marketing | Science, Technology, Engineering, and Mathematics |

The Marketing Career Cluster is one of the most popular industry sectors with students. Many jobs in our local economy are part of this Career Cluster. If you like to shop for yourself and others, or if you would be good at selling a product or idea, this is a Career Cluster you should explore. Within the Marketing Career Cluster, there are four different Career Pathways, each preparing students for a variety of jobs, as shown below. These are jobs that are important in our community.

Marketing Career Cluster

Sales and Marketing Pathway	International Commerce Pathway	Internet Marketing Pathway	Entrepreneurship Pathway
marketing managers retail buyers real estate customer service advertising	sales representatives shipping and receiving international commerce specialists	software engineers online marketing specialists customer service representatives	marketing managers business owners event planners

Your Career Pathway

Our counselors at the Career Center can help you explore your interests and your skills. First, you will take a survey to help you decide which Career Cluster interests you. You will also take a skills assessment. Then you will meet with a counselor to discuss your future. Your counselor will explain the variety of Career Pathways that fit your interests and skills.

After you have selected a Career Pathway, your counselor will help you plan your studies at Lake Community College. Your counselor will identify the courses you need to take each semester. Step by step, we will help you learn the skills needed for your Career Pathway.

We work closely with local businesses and services so our students can get valuable work experience while they are in college. We also have many opportunities for special training courses, company visits, job shadowing, and internships. Our career center frequently posts job openings as well, and we help prepare students for the interview process. By building strong connections between our college and the business community, we can offer you the best possible preparation for your career.

DID YOU UNDERSTAND?

1. What is a Career Cluster?
2. How many Career Clusters have been identified?
3. Which Career Cluster includes banking?
4. Which Career Cluster includes recreation?
5. How many Career Clusters are there at Lake Community College?
6. Why did the college select these clusters?
7. How many Career Pathways are there for Marketing?
8. What occupations are in the Sales and Marketing Pathway?
9. What should students do before they meet with a counselor?
10. How does the career center help students get work experience?

Think & Share

1. What are two Career Clusters that are interesting to you?
2. What are three Career Clusters that are important in your local economy?
3. What occupation are you interested in preparing for? How can your courses prepare you? How can you get work experience?

155 Milton Road
Houston, TX 77043 ———— **heading**

June 1, 2016

Ms. Victoria Delgado
Human Resources Director
Infotech Systems ———— **inside address**
3100 South Loop West
Houston, TX 77054

Dear Ms. Delgado: ———— **salutation**

body

I am writing to apply for the position of office manager at Infotech Systems. I saw the job posting in today's issue of the Houston Chronicle.

As you can see from the resume I have included with this letter, I believe that my skills and experience are a good match for the office manager position at your company. I have worked for several years as an office manager and administrative assistant at a major energy company, and I have previous experience in information systems technology.

I have learned about the work of Infotech Systems through the company's web site, and I would look forward to talking with you about how I can be part of this important and interesting work in the future. If I can provide you with any further information on my background and qualifications, please let me know. Thank you for your consideration.

Respectfully yours, ———— **closing**

Donna Santos ——— **signature**

Donna Santos

Business letters are formal. You should always type a business letter. A business letter has six parts:

The **heading** shows the address of the writer and the date. Leave a blank line between the address and the date. Use a comma between the day and the year.

The **inside address** shows the full name (with title), the company, and the address of the person the writer is writing to.

The **salutation** is the greeting. Capitalize the first word of the salutation and use the person's title and the person's last name. (Only use a person's first name if you know the person very well.) Use a colon (:) after the person's name.

The **body** contains the content of the letter. Don't indent the paragraphs of the body. Leave a blank line between each paragraph.

The **closing** comes at the end of the letter. Capitalize only the first word in the closing. Use a comma after the closing.

The **signature** shows the name of the writer. After the closing, leave four blank lines for your signature, and then type your name on the next line. After you print out the letter, sign your name in the space for your signature.

Write a cover letter.

Write a cover letter to apply for a job at a company. In the first paragraph, describe the job you are applying for and how you learned about the position. In the second paragraph, explain why you believe you are qualified for the job – why your skills and experience are a good match. (Don't give too much information or repeat everything in your resume. Just describe your key strengths in two or three sentences.) In the third paragraph, describe how you have learned something about the company's work (through its web site, newspaper articles, or other ways), offer to send more information, say that you look forward to talking to the person about the position, and say thank you. Type your letter, and follow the form of a business letter carefully.

Tag Questions
Emphatic Sentences

- Verifying
- Expressing Surprise
- Reporting Information
- Congratulating
- Expressing Opinions
- Expressing Agreement
- Writing a Personal Letter

- Feedback on Job Performance
- Following Procedures
- Employee Benefits
- Career Advancement
- Work-Related Values
- Writing a Business Memo

VOCABULARY PREVIEW

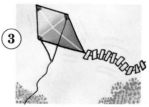
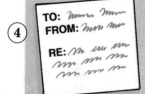

1. couple
2. dolphin
3. kite
4. memo
5. moon
6. spare tire
7. toaster
8. wagon
9. engaged
10. overcooked
11. punctual
12. scary

This Is the Bus to the Zoo, Isn't It?

> Ken **is** here, **isn't** he?
> You **were** sick, **weren't** you?
> Maria **will** be here soon, **won't** she?
> Timmy **has** gone to bed, **hasn't** he?
>
> I **am** on time, **aren't** I?

> You like ice cream, **don't** you?
> Ed worked yesterday, **didn't** he?

A. This is the bus to the zoo, isn't it?

B. Yes, it is.

A. That's what I thought.

1. Neil Armstrong was the first person on the moon, ____?

2. I can skateboard here, ____?

3. Ms. Lee will be on vacation next week, ____?

4. It's going to rain today, ____?

5. We've already seen this movie, ____?

6. I'm on time for my interview, ____?

7. You work in the Shipping Department, ____?

8. You locked the front door, ____?

9. You're a famous movie star, ____?

This TV Isn't On Sale This Week, Is It?

Bill **isn't** here, **is** he?
You **weren't** angry, **were** you?
Nina **won't** be upset, **will** she?
You **haven't** eaten, **have** you?
I'**m not** late, **am** I?

Mark **doesn't** ski, **does** he?
They **didn't** leave, **did** they?

A. This TV isn't on sale this week, is it?

B. No, it isn't.

A. That's what I thought.

1. There weren't any computers when you were young, _____?

2. I can't fish here, _____?

3. Mr. Martinez won't be in the office tomorrow, _____?

4. You aren't really going to go swimming, _____?

5. The mail hasn't come yet, _____?

6. I'm not allowed to park here, _____?

7. The children don't use this old wagon anymore, _____?

8. We didn't have a homework assignment yesterday, _____?

9. I haven't taught "tag questions" before, _____?

I'm Really Surprised!

A. You like spaghetti, don't you?

B. Actually, I don't.

A. You DON'T?! I'm really surprised!
I was SURE you liked spaghetti!

A. This ride isn't scary, is it?

B. Actually, it is.

A. It IS?! I'm really surprised!
I was SURE this ride wasn't scary!

1. It's going to be a nice day tomorrow, _____?

2. I don't have to wear a jacket and tie here, _____?

3. This building has an elevator, _____?

4. You can swim, _____?

5. The bank hasn't closed yet, _____?

6. I did well on the exam, _____?

7. I'm going to play today, _____?

8. Dolphins can't talk, _____?

9. I wasn't going over fifty-five miles per hour, _____?

10. We have a spare tire, _____?

11. You aren't allergic to fish, _____?

12. I'm not a suspect, _____?

How to Say It!

Expressing Surprise

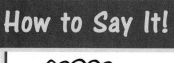

I'm really surprised!

I'm very surprised!

That's very surprising!

I can't believe it!

I don't believe it!

Practice the conversations in this lesson again. Express surprise in different ways.

Congratulations!

A. I have some good news.

B. What is it?

A. My wife and I are celebrating our fiftieth wedding anniversary tomorrow!

B. You ARE?!

A. Yes, we are.

B. I don't believe it! You aren't REALLY celebrating your fiftieth wedding anniversary tomorrow, are you?

A. Yes, it's true. We ARE.

B. Well, congratulations! I'm very glad to hear that.

A. I have some good news.

B. What is it?

A. I just got a big raise!

B. You DID?!

A. Yes, I did.

B. I don't believe it! You didn't REALLY get a big raise, did you?

A. Yes, it's true. I DID.

B. Well, congratulations! I'm very glad to hear that!

1. I'm going to have a baby!

2. We won the basketball championship!

3. I've been promoted!

4. I can tie my shoes by myself!

5. My son is going to be in the Olympics!

6. I got a perfect score on the SAT test!

7. Steven Steelberg wants me to star in his new movie!

8. I've been invited to perform at the White House!

9. I was interviewed by *Time* Magazine yesterday!

10. My daughter has been accepted at Harvard University!

11. I've discovered a cure for the common cold!

12.

You're Right!

George was angry.
I'm late.
They aren't very friendly.
I don't know the answer.

They work hard.
John looks tired.
Janet came late to class.

George WAS angry, wasn't he!
I AM late, aren't I!
They AREN'T very friendly, are they!
I DON'T know the answer, do I!

They DO work hard, don't they!
John DOES look tired, doesn't he!
Janet DID come late to class, didn't she!

A. You know . . . the color blue looks very good on you.

B. You're right! The color blue DOES look very good on me, doesn't it!

A. You know . . . it isn't a very good day to fly a kite.

B. You're right!   It ISN'T a very good day to fly a kite, is it!

1. . . . you work too hard.

2. . . . Charlie is a very talented dog.

3. . . . Aunt Betty hasn't called in a long time.

4. . . . you're playing this song too slowly.

5. . . . this milk tastes sour.

6. . . . these hamburgers are overcooked.

7. . . . you have quite a few gray hairs.

8. . . . you've been online for a long time.

9. . . . we really shouldn't be playing frisbee here.

10. . . . Peter looks just like his father.

11. . . . children these days don't dress very neatly.

12. . . . you missed a few spots.

13. . . . Ms. Taylor gave us a lot of homework yesterday.

14. . . . I won't be able to play in the game tomorrow.

15. . . . your brother and my sister would make a nice couple.

16. . . . this new toaster doesn't work very well.

17. . . . Howard was a very generous person.

18.

A BROKEN ENGAGEMENT

Dear John,

It's been a long time since I've written to you, hasn't it! I'm sorry it has taken me such a long time to write, but I really don't know where to begin this letter. You see, John, things have been very difficult since you took that job overseas several months ago. It has been very difficult for me to be engaged to somebody who is four thousand miles away, so I've decided that things have got to change.

I've decided to move out of my parents' house.

I'm going to get my own apartment.

I've started dating other guys.

I want to break our engagement.

And I gave your mother back the ring you had given me.

I'm sorry things have to end this way. You DO understand why I must do this, don't you?

Sincerely,
Jane

Dear Jane,

I received your letter today, and when I opened it I was shocked. I couldn't believe what you had written.

You haven't really decided to move out of your parents' house, have you?

You aren't really going to get your own apartment, are you?

You haven't really started dating other guys, have you?

You don't really want to break our engagement, do you?

And you didn't really give my mother back the ring I had given you, did you?

Please answer me as soon as possible!

Love,
John

P.S. You DO still love me, don't you?

Dear John,

I HAVE decided to move out of my parents' house.

I AM going to get my own apartment.

I HAVE started dating other guys.

I DO want to break our engagement.

And I DID give your mother back the ring you had given me.

I know this must hurt, but I DO have to be honest with you, don't I! I hope that someday you will understand.

Good-bye,
Jane

 READING *CHECK-UP*

WHAT'S THE ANSWER?

1. Why did Jane decide to break her engagement to John?
2. Where has Jane been living?
3. What did Jane do with the ring that John had given her?
4. How did John feel when he received Jane's first letter?
5. Did Jane realize how John would feel when he received her second letter?

CHOOSE

1. John wanted to know if Jane _____ to break their engagement.
   a. had really decided
   b. has really decided

2. John asked Jane whether she _____ her own apartment.
   a. had really gotten
   b. was really going to get

3. In her first letter, Jane said she _____ break their engagement.
   a. wants to
   b. wanted to

4. John was hoping she _____ him.
   a. still loved
   b. had still loved

5. In Jane's second letter, she told John she really _____ to move out of her parents' house.
   a. has decided
   b. had decided

6. She told him she hoped that someday he _____.
   a. would have understood
   b. would understand

IN YOUR OWN WORDS

FOR WRITING AND DISCUSSION

John is willing to do anything he can to save his relationship with Jane. He has some ideas about how to do this, and he's going to write to her one more time. Write John's letter to Jane.

UNFAIR ACCUSATIONS

```
To:   Michael Parker
From:  Ms. Lewis
Re:   Your performance at work

I'm concerned about your performance at work.

    You have been working too slowly.
    You often get to work late.
    You took too many vacation days last month.
    You aren't very polite to the customers.
    And you don't get along well with the other employees.

I'd like to meet with you as soon as possible to discuss this.
```

Michael's boss, Ms. Lewis, sent him a memo recently about his performance at work. In the memo, she said he had been working too slowly. She also said that he often got to work late. In addition, she observed that he had taken too many vacation days last month. She also mentioned that he wasn't very polite to the customers. And finally, she complained that he didn't get along well with the other employees.

When Michael got the memo, he was very upset. He feels that his boss is making unfair accusations. Michael feels that he HASN'T been working too slowly. He also feels that he DOESN'T often get to work late. In Michael's opinion, he DIDN'T take too many vacation days last month. He thinks he IS very polite to the customers. And he maintains that he DOES get along well with the other employees.

Michael realizes that he and his boss see things VERY differently, and he plans to speak to her about this as soon as possible.

✔ READING *CHECK-UP*

MATCH

Match the descriptions of job performance on the left with their meanings.

____ 1. punctual

____ 2. honest

____ 3. efficient

____ 4. industrious

____ 5. cooperative

____ 6. friendly

____ 7. considerate

____ 8. dedicated

a. pleasant and outgoing

b. easy to work with

c. works quickly and accurately

d. thoughtful of others

e. tells the truth

f. gets to work on time

g. cares about the work

h. works hard

LISTENING

Listen and decide who is speaking.

1. a. student – student
    b. student – teacher

2. a. tenant – tenant
    b. tenant – mail carrier

3. a. employee – employee
    b. student – student

4. a. salesperson – customer
    b. wife – husband

5. a. passenger – driver
    b. police officer – driver

6. a. doctor – nurse
    b. doctor – patient

IN YOUR OWN WORDS

FOR WRITING AND DISCUSSION

```
            MEMO
To:
From:
Re:
```

Mr. Hopper is very pleased with Helen Baxter's performance at work. Using the story below as a guide, write a memo from Mr. Hopper to Helen Baxter.

POSITIVE FEEDBACK

Helen Baxter's boss, Mr. Hopper, sent her a memo recently about her job performance. He said that he was very pleased with her performance at work. He mentioned that she was very efficient and industrious. He observed that she got along well with her co-workers and customers. And he also said that she was very cooperative and considerate. Mr. Hopper wrote that the company had been so pleased with her work that they were going to give her a big raise.

INTERACTIONS

| He's She's It's | late, isn't | he! she! it! | We're You're They're | late, aren't | we! you! they! | I'm late, aren't I! |

A. You're tired, aren't you!

B. Tired? What makes you think I'm tired?

A. Well, you're falling asleep at the wheel.

B. Now that you mention it, I AM falling asleep at the wheel, aren't I!

A. You're nervous, aren't you!

B. Nervous? What makes you think I'm nervous?

A. Well, you haven't stopped pacing back and forth since early this morning.

B. Come to think of it, I HAVEN'T stopped pacing back and forth, have I!

A. You're in a bad mood, aren't you!

B. In a bad mood? What makes you think I'm in a bad mood?

A. Well, you shouted at me for no reason.

B. I guess I DID shout at you for no reason, didn't I!

142

A. You're _____, aren't you!

B. _____? What makes you think I'm _____?

A. Well, _____.

B. Now that you mention it,
Come to think of it,
I guess
} _____, _____ _____!

Practice conversations with other students.

nervous   *angry*   *tired*

frightened   *unhappy*   *bored*

embarrassed   *upset*   *jealous*

How About You?

What do you do when you're nervous? angry? tired? frightened? unhappy? bored? embarrassed? upset? jealous?

PRONUNCIATION Tag Intonation

Listen. Then say it.

Ken is here, isn't he?

You weren't angry, were you?

They DO work hard, don't they!

They AREN'T friendly, are they!

Say it. Then listen.

Timmy has gone to bed, hasn't he?

They didn't leave, did they?

He DOESN'T know the answer, does he!

That WAS an awful movie, wasn't it!

SIDE by SIDE JOURNAL

Have you ever received "positive feedback" about your performance at school, at work, in sports, or in other activities? What did people say? How did you feel after you received the positive feedback?

GRAMMAR FOCUS

TAG QUESTIONS

Ken **is** here, **isn't** he?
You **were** sick, **weren't** you?
Maria **will** be here soon, **won't** she?
Timmy **has** gone to bed, **hasn't** he?

I **am** on time, **aren't** I?

You like ice cream, **don't** you?
Ed worked yesterday, **didn't** he?

Bill **isn't** here, **is** he?
You **weren't** sick, **were** you?
Maria **won't** be here soon, **will** she?
Timmy **hasn't** gone to bed, **has** he?

I**'m not** late, **am** I?

You **don't** like ice cream, **do** you?
Ed **didn't** work yesterday, **did** he?

TAG STATEMENTS

I'm We're You're They're	late,	aren't	I! we! you! they!
He's She's It's		isn't	he! she! it!

Complete the sentences.

1. You were in my class last year, _____ _____?

2. We aren't late, _____ _____?

3. You took the suitcases, _____ _____?

4. I can't take pictures here, _____ _____?

5. She's coming to the party, _____ _____?

6. The movie hasn't begun yet, _____ _____?

7. You live in this building, _____ _____?

8. You won't be late, _____ _____?

9. I'm not disturbing you, _____ _____?

10. I'm late for the meeting, _____ _____!

EMPHATIC SENTENCES

George was angry.	George WAS angry, wasn't he!
I'm late.	I AM late, aren't I!
They aren't very friendly.	They AREN'T very friendly, are they!
I don't know the answer.	I DON'T know the answer, do I!
They work hard.	They DO work hard, don't they!
John looks tired.	John DOES look tired, doesn't he!
Janet came late to class.	Janet DID come late to class, didn't she!

Complete the sentences.

11. These cookies are terrible! You're right. These cookies _____ terrible, _____ _____!

12. Cousin David hasn't called in a long time. You're right. He _____ called in a long time, _____ _____!

13. Our new sofa isn't very comfortable. You're right. Our new sofa _____ very comfortable, _____ _____!

14. Lisa looks like her mother. You're right. Lisa _____ look like her mother, _____ _____!

1 CONVERSATION ASKING FOR & RESPONDING TO FEEDBACK

Practice these workplace conversations with your classmates.

A. Excuse me. Am I labeling the cans correctly?

B. No, you aren't. You're supposed to put the label on the top of the can.

A. Oh, okay. I didn't know that. Thank you for telling me.

A. Excuse me. Am I _____ correctly?

B. No, you aren't. You're supposed to _____ .

A. Oh, okay. I didn't know that. Thank you for telling me.

---

1. filling out my timesheet
list the hours you worked each day separately

2. using the copier
put the original face up in the document feeder

3. attaching this printer
attach it to the USB port on the computer, not the keyboard

2 TEAMWORK FEEDBACK ABOUT FOLLOWING PROCEDURES

Work with a classmate. Think of procedures for doing different things at work or at school. Write down the procedures. Then think of ways someone might do these procedures incorrectly, and practice conversations about them. Present your conversations to the class.

The Shelby Company

Employee Benefits

① **Health Insurance**—Full-time employees have a choice of two medical plans that provide hospital, physician, prescription drug, and vision benefits. The Shelby Company and the employee share the cost of the insurance premiums. The amount the employee pays depends on the plan chosen and the number of family members insured. For more information, contact Human Resources.

② **Dental Insurance**—Full-time employees and their families are eligible for dental insurance. The dental plan pays 100% for preventive care, 80% for other basic services, and 50% for major dental services.

③ **Life Insurance**—The Shelby Company provides all full-time employees with free life insurance equal to twice the employee's annual salary. Additional life insurance may be purchased.

④ **401(k) Plan**—The Shelby Company offers full-time employees a 401(k) retirement savings plan with a wide range of investment choices. This is an excellent way to save money for retirement and to lower taxes. Employees may contribute up to 15% of their salary each month. Taxes on the amount of salary the employee contributes are deferred until the money is withdrawn at retirement. Taxes are also deferred on the earnings in the account. The company will match each dollar that an employee contributes.

⑤ **Employee Assistance Program**—The employee assistance program provides free short-term counseling and legal and financial services for employees and their dependents.

⑥ **Holidays**—Employees are eligible for nine paid holidays in each calendar year.

⑦ **Vacation Time**—Full-time employees earn two weeks of vacation with pay at the end of each of their first five years of employment. Beginning with the sixth year, full-time employees earn three weeks of vacation with pay. After ten years, four weeks of vacation with pay will accrue. Up to five unused vacation days may be carried over to the next year.

⑧ **Personal Days**—Full-time employees are eligible for four paid personal days in a calendar year. Personal days may not be carried over to the next year.

⑨ **Sick Time**—Full-time employees are eligible for five paid days of sick leave a year. Sick days may be carried over from year to year to a maximum of ten days.

1. Jeff earns $40,000 a year. His life insurance policy from the Shelby Company is for _____.
   A. $20,000
   B. $40,000
   C. $60,000
   D. $80,000

2. The company's health insurance does NOT cover _____.
   A. doctor's visits
   B. surgery
   C. over-the-counter drugs
   D. eyeglasses

3. If Rosa contributes $450 to her 401(k) account each month, the Shelby Company _____.
   A. pays the taxes
   B. puts another $450 into her account
   C. contributes 15% to her account
   D. withdraws the money

4. In section 4, *taxes are deferred* means _____.
   A. taxes are paid later
   B. taxes are never paid
   C. taxes are increased
   D. taxes are lowered

5. In section 5, we can infer that *dependents* are _____.
   A. lawyers
   B. co-workers
   C. family members
   D. problems

6. According to the manual, it's possible for an employee to have more than _____ in a year.
   A. 4 paid personal days
   B. 5 paid sick days
   C. 9 paid holidays
   D. 25 paid vacation days

Getting Ahead

Why do some people advance at work while others get left behind? Employees who are "moving up" at their workplaces have some answers.

Carol Chung was recently promoted to office manager at World Wide Travel after working there as a travel agent for two years. "I got the promotion," said Ms. Chung, "because of my hard work and dedication. I was always the first to arrive at the office and the last to leave. I was busier than any of the other agents and made the most sales. Other travel agents had more experience, but the managers knew that they could depend on me. When the office manager was transferred to another office, I replaced him."

Omar Hamdi is the new team leader of the produce department at Food Works. He worked in the produce department for a year and a half before getting the promotion. He was chosen because he gets along well with the members of his team and he has earned their respect. "People like me," he says, "because I try to be considerate and helpful. I listen and share ideas and put the team's needs before my own. Learning to be a good team player prepared me for the job."

Ella Souza, a former trainer at Argosy Software Company, also found that it pays to be friendly. She made friends with an employee in the company's technical writing department who told her about a job opening there. She applied for the position and was hired. Instead of training people to use the company's software programs, now she writes manuals—a job she prefers. "Get to know people in other departments," advises Ms. Souza. "It's an excellent way to network and learn about jobs before they're listed."

Ned Mason owes his success to his flexibility. The organization that he works for, Save the Forests, has a small staff. As a result, he has to perform many different tasks each day—from filing to fund-raising. According to Mr. Mason, "Every day is different from the next, and I have to be ready to adapt. I'm flexible and adaptable. That's why I was given a generous raise."

Rose Curtis became the marketing manager at Hawthorne Books, a chain of bookstores, because of her leadership qualities. She's a problem solver who focuses on *the big picture*. As a marketing associate, she was faced with many challenges. The Internet was cutting into the bookstores' profits and the company was losing money. "I saw each challenge as an opportunity," says Ms. Curtis. "I found ways to save money and to attract customers to the store. When my supervisor left the company, I was offered her job."

If you aren't getting ahead as quickly as you'd like, don't give up. There are many opportunities for advancement for those who are willing to work at it!

1. Omar Hamdi was promoted because _____.
   A. he produces a lot of work
   B. he's flexible
   C. he's efficient
   D. he's cooperative and helpful

2. According to this article, _____ is industrious and punctual.
   A. Ned Mason
   B. Ella Souza
   C. Carol Chung
   D. Rose Curtis

3. Ella Souza _____.
   A. was promoted
   B. was hired by a different company
   C. got a raise
   D. transferred to a different department

4. We can infer that Ned Mason works _____.
   A. alone
   B. seven days a week
   C. in an office
   D. outdoors

5. In paragraph 6, *challenges* refers to _____.
   A. employees
   B. problems
   C. qualities
   D. changes

6. In paragraph 6, to *focus on the big picture* means _____.
   A. to understand what's most important
   B. to pay attention to all the details
   C. to be artistic
   D. to take large photographs

Choose the correct answer.

1. It's important to be ____ when you have an important appointment.
   A. industrious
   B. punctual
   C. efficient
   D. temporary

2. Samantha has advanced in the company because of her outstanding leadership ____.
   A. qualities
   B. ranks
   C. tasks
   D. needs

3. Our company's medical plan provides ____ benefits.
   A. investment
   B. legal
   C. holiday
   D. prescription drug and vision

4. Contributing to a 401(k) plan is an excellent way to ____.
   A. use personal days
   B. advance at work
   C. save money for retirement
   D. make friends at work

5. ____ may be carried over from year to year to a maximum of ten days.
   A. Sick days
   B. Employees
   C. Dependents
   D. Dental insurance

6. After employees work ten years at the Carter Company, ____ will accrue each year.
   A. preventive care
   B. hospital and physician benefits
   C. four weeks of vacation with pay
   D. the Employee Assistance Program

7. Ramon is able to perform many different tasks at work because he is ____.
   A. eligible
   B. flexible
   C. considerate
   D. generous

8. Brenda is a good team player. She ____.
   A. depends on others all the time
   B. advances while others get left behind
   C. arrives at work early and leaves late
   D. works well with the employees in her department

9. Getting to know people in other departments at work is an excellent way to ____.
   A. network
   B. adapt
   C. get a generous raise
   D. replace the manager

10. It's important to ____ on your job performance.
   A. fill out timesheets
   B. ask for feedback
   C. purchase insurance
   D. follow procedures

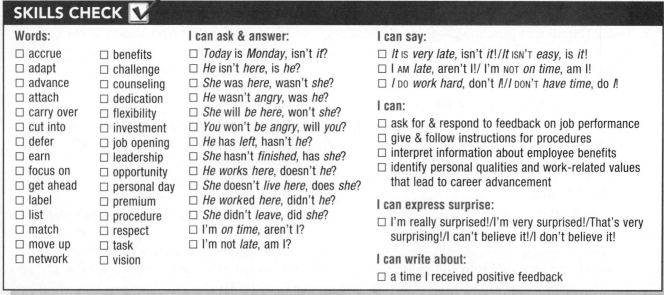

SKILLS CHECK ☑

Words:
- ☐ accrue
- ☐ adapt
- ☐ advance
- ☐ attach
- ☐ carry over
- ☐ cut into
- ☐ defer
- ☐ earn
- ☐ focus on
- ☐ get ahead
- ☐ label
- ☐ list
- ☐ match
- ☐ move up
- ☐ network
- ☐ benefits
- ☐ challenge
- ☐ counseling
- ☐ dedication
- ☐ flexibility
- ☐ investment
- ☐ job opening
- ☐ leadership
- ☐ opportunity
- ☐ personal day
- ☐ premium
- ☐ procedure
- ☐ respect
- ☐ task
- ☐ vision

I can ask & answer:
- ☐ *Today* is *Monday*, isn't *it*?
- ☐ *He* isn't *here*, is *he*?
- ☐ *She* was *here*, wasn't *she*?
- ☐ *He* wasn't *angry*, was *he*?
- ☐ *She* will *be here*, won't *she*?
- ☐ *You* won't *be angry*, will *you*?
- ☐ *He* has *left*, hasn't *he*?
- ☐ *She* hasn't *finished*, has *she*?
- ☐ *He* works *here*, doesn't *he*?
- ☐ *She* doesn't *live here*, does *she*?
- ☐ *He* worked *here*, didn't *he*?
- ☐ *She* didn't *leave*, did *she*?
- ☐ I'm *on time*, aren't I?
- ☐ I'm not *late*, am I?

I can say:
- ☐ *It* IS *very late*, isn't *it*!/*It* ISN'T *easy*, is *it*!
- ☐ I AM *late*, aren't I!/I'm NOT *on time*, am I!
- ☐ I DO *work hard*, don't I!/I DON'T *have time*, do I!

I can:
- ☐ ask for & respond to feedback on job performance
- ☐ give & follow instructions for procedures
- ☐ interpret information about employee benefits
- ☐ identify personal qualities and work-related values that lead to career advancement

I can express surprise:
- ☐ I'm really surprised!/I'm very surprised!/That's very surprising!/I can't believe it!/I don't believe it!

I can write about:
- ☐ a time I received positive feedback

10

Review:
Verb Tenses   Conditionals   Gerunds

- **Invitations**
- **Expressing Disappointment**
- **Calling Attention to People's Actions**
- **Apologizing**
- **Giving Reasons**
- **Decision-Making**

- **Consequences of Actions**
- **Expressing Concern About People**
- **Asking for Assistance**
- **Civics:**
  Civic Rights and Responsibilities
  Community Legal Services

VOCABULARY PREVIEW

1. cast	**6.** hamster	**11.** pet food
2. chicken pox	**7.** income tax return	**12.** satellite dish
3. cockroach	**8.** key	**13.** scrap paper
4. diner	**9.** mess	**14.** wallpaper
5. files	**10.** passport	**15.** wisdom tooth

Would You Like to Go on a Picnic with Me Today?

A. Would you like to **go on a picnic** with me today?

B. I don't think so. To be honest, I really don't feel like **going on a picnic** today. I **went on a picnic** yesterday.

A. That's too bad. I'm disappointed.

B. I hope you understand. If I hadn't **gone on a picnic** yesterday, I'd be very happy to **go on a picnic** with you today.

A. Of course I understand! After all, I suppose you'd get tired of **going on picnics** if you **went on picnics** all the time!

A. Would you like to _____ with me today?

B. I don't think so. To be honest, I really don't feel like _____ ing today. I _____ yesterday.

A. That's too bad. I'm disappointed.

B. I hope you understand. If I hadn't _____ yesterday, I'd be very happy to _____ with you today.

A. Of course I understand! After all, I suppose you'd get tired of _____ ing if you _____ all the time!

1. *see a movie*

2. *go to the mall*

3. *take a walk in the park*

4. *work out at the gym*

5. *go bowling*

6. *have lunch at Dave's Diner*

7. *drive around town*

8.

How to Say It!

Invitations

Would you like to
Do you want to
How would you like to
} go on a picnic with me?

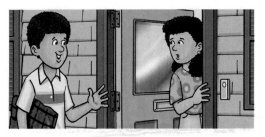

Practice the conversations in this lesson again. Invite people in different ways.

Do You Realize What You Just Did?!

A. Do you realize what you just did?!

B. No. What did I just do?

A. You just **ate both our salads**!

B. I did?

A. Yes, you did.

B. I'm really sorry. I must have **been very hungry**.
If I hadn't **been very hungry**, I NEVER would have **eaten both our salads**!

1. *throw out my homework*
think it was scrap paper

2. *drive past my house*
forget your address

3. *disconnect Aunt Thelma*
press the wrong button

4. *hit me with your umbrella*
be looking the other way

5. *step on my feet*
lose my balance

6. *give bird food to the hamster*
mix up the pet-food boxes

7. *paint the living room window*
have my mind on something else

8. *delete all my files*
hit the wrong key

9. *call me Gloria*
be thinking about somebody else

10. *put tomatoes in the onion soup*
misunderstand the recipe

11. *erase the video of my dance recital*
accidentally rewind the tape

12. *sit on my cat*
think it was a pillow

How About You?

Think of a time when you did something accidentally.
What did you do? When did you realize what you had
done? Why did it happen?

MARCIA'S BAD DAY

Marcia made several bad decisions yesterday.

She decided to drive to work, but she should have taken the train. If she had taken the train, she wouldn't have gotten stuck in a terrible traffic jam.

She decided to have lunch with a friend at a small restaurant far from her office, but she should have gone to a place nearby. If she had gone to a place nearby, she wouldn't have been an hour late for an important afternoon appointment.

She decided not to take the garbage out until after she got home from work that evening, but she should have taken it out in the morning. If she had taken it out in the morning, her cat wouldn't have tipped over the garbage pail and made such a mess in the kitchen.

And finally, that evening she decided to stay up late and watch a scary movie on TV, but she should have turned off the TV and gone to sleep. If she had turned off the TV and gone to sleep, she wouldn't have had terrible nightmares all night.

Marcia certainly didn't have a very good day yesterday. As a matter of fact, she probably shouldn't have gotten out of bed in the first place. If she hadn't gotten out of bed in the first place, none of this would ever have happened!

✔ READING *CHECK-UP*

TRUE, FALSE, OR MAYBE?

Answer True, False, or Maybe (if the answer isn't in the story).

1. Marcia wishes she hadn't taken the train to work yesterday.
2. If Marcia hadn't had lunch far from her office, she would have been on time for her appointment.
3. There aren't any small restaurants near Marcia's office.
4. She decided not to take the garbage out in the morning.
5. If Marcia hadn't watched a scary movie on TV, she probably wouldn't have had nightmares.

How About You?

We all sometimes make decisions we wish we hadn't made. Tell about some bad decisions you have made over the years. What did you decide to do? What should you have done? Why?

CHOOSE

1. If I _____ you were going to be in town, I would have invited you to stay with us.
   a. knew
   b. had known

2. If _____ busy tonight, I'll call you.
   a. I weren't
   b. I'm not

3. If I _____ the plane, I probably would have gotten there faster.
   a. had taken
   b. took

4. I _____ happy to go to the dance with you if you invited me.
   a. would be
   b. would have been

5. If I were you, I _____ that movie.
   a. wouldn't see
   b. won't see

6. I wish I _____ when I was young.
   a. learned to swim
   b. had learned to swim

7. If I had been more careful, I _____ driven through that stop sign.
   a. would have
   b. wouldn't have

8. I suppose you'd get tired of writing reports if you _____ reports all the time.
   a. wrote
   b. write

LISTENING

Listen and choose where the conversation is taking place.

1. a. restaurant
   b. someone's home

2. a. bus
   b. movie theater

3. a. park
   b. shopping mall

4. a. cafeteria
   b. supermarket

5. a. department store
   b. laundromat

6. a. airplane
   b. concert

You Seem Upset. Is Anything Wrong?

A. You seem upset. Is anything wrong?

B. Yes. **My computer is broken.**

A. I'm sorry to hear that. How long **has it been broken**?

B. **For two days.**

A. I know how upset you must be. I remember when MY **computer was broken**. Is there anything I can do to help?

B. Not really. But thanks for asking.

A. You seem upset. Is anything wrong?

B. Yes. _____.

A. I'm sorry to hear that. How long _____?

B. (For/Since) _____.

A. I know how upset you must be. I remember when _____. Is there anything I can do to help?

B. Not really. But thanks for asking.

1. My father is in the hospital.
   a week

2. My children have chicken pox.
   last Friday

3. The elevator in my building is out of order.
two weeks

4. My cat is lost.
three days

5. I'm unemployed.
March 1st

6. I'm having trouble sleeping at night.
a few weeks

7. Mr. Crump refuses to fix our bathtub.
a month

8. My wisdom teeth hurt.
Monday morning

9. My passport is missing.
I took an overnight train last week

10. The air conditioner in my office is broken.
the past week

11. I'm having trouble communicating with my children.
they became teenagers

12. My apartment has cockroaches.
a restaurant opened downstairs

Could You Possibly Come Over and Give Me a Hand?

A. Hello, Carlos? This is Gary.

B. Hi, Gary. How are you?

A. I'm okay. Listen, Carlos, I'm having trouble **putting up my satellite dish**. Could you possibly come over and give me a hand?

B. I'm really sorry, Gary. I'm afraid I can't come over right now. **I'm sick in bed.** If **I weren't sick in bed**, I'd be GLAD to help you put it up.

A. Don't worry about it. If I had known **you were sick in bed**, I wouldn't have called you in the first place!

A. Hello, _____? This is _____.

B. Hi, _____. How are you?

A. I'm okay. Listen, _____, I'm having trouble _____ing. Could you possibly come over and give me a hand?

B. I'm really sorry, _____. I'm afraid I can't come over right now. _____. If _____, I'd be GLAD to help you _____.

A. Don't worry about it. If I had known _____, I wouldn't have called you in the first place!

1. *hook up my DVD player*

2. *figure out the math homework*

3. *move my piano*

4. *assemble my new bookcases*

5. *fill out my income tax return*

6. *set up my new computer*

7. *replace the lock on my front door*

8. *program my new cell phone*

9. *pick out new wallpaper for my kitchen*

10.

DECISIONS

Several years ago, Stanley's friends urged him not to quit his job at the post office. They told him that if he quit his job there, he would never find a better one.

Stanley didn't follow their advice, and he's glad he didn't. He decided to quit his job at the post office, and he found work as a chef at a restaurant downtown. He saved all his money for several years, and then he opened a small restaurant of his own. Now his restaurant is famous, and people from all over town come to eat there.

Stanley is glad he didn't listen to his friends' advice. If he had listened to his friends' advice, he probably never would have opened his restaurant and become such a success.

Kelly's parents thought she was crazy when she bought a used car that had already been driven over two hundred thousand miles. They told her that if she bought that car, she'd probably have lots of problems with it.

Kelly didn't follow her parents' advice, and she's really sorry she didn't. Since she bought the car two months ago, she has had to take it to the garage for repairs seven times.

Kelly wishes she had listened to her parents. If she had listened to them, she never would have bought such a "lemon"!

Jason's ski instructor insisted that Jason wasn't ready to ski down the advanced slopes at the Magic Mountain ski resort. She told him that if he skied down the advanced slopes, he'd probably injure himself.

Jason didn't follow his ski instructor's advice, and he's very sorry he didn't. He skied down an advanced slope, and after just a few seconds, he fell and broke his leg.

Jason wishes he had listened to his ski instructor. If he had listened to her, he wouldn't be lying in the hospital with his leg in a cast.

✔ READING *CHECK-UP*

TRUE, FALSE, OR MAYBE?

Answer True, False, or Maybe (if the answer isn't in the story).

1. Stanley's friends thought he shouldn't continue working at the post office.
2. Stanley is glad he followed his friends' advice.
3. Kelly's mother and father never buy used cars.
4. Kelly's car has been at the garage for repairs for seven months.
5. If Jason had listened to his ski instructor's advice, he wouldn't have skied down an advanced slope.
6. Jason hasn't had his leg in a cast before.

CHOOSE

1. If he _____ to their advice, he wouldn't have gotten hurt.
   a. listened
   b. had listened

2. Since I bought this computer six weeks ago, _____ take it to the repair shop three times.
   a. I've had to
   b. I had to

3. I'm sorry I _____ to my parents' advice.
   a. didn't listen
   b. hadn't listened

4. Sarah wishes _____ bought a used car from Ralph Jones.
   a. she hasn't
   b. she hadn't

5. If I _____ have to work overtime today, I'd be glad to go to the concert with you.
   a. didn't
   b. don't

6. If I _____ sick, I'd be happy to come over and help you.
   a. wasn't
   b. weren't

PRONUNCIATION *Would you & Could you*

Listen. Then say it.

Would you like to see a movie?

How would you like to go dancing?

Could you possibly come over?

Say it. Then listen.

Would you like to have lunch?

How would you like to go bowling?

Could you possibly give me a hand?

Write in your journal about a time when you had to make an important decision and people gave you lots of advice. What was the situation? What did people tell you? Why did they tell you that? Did you follow their advice? What happened? Do you think you made the right decision? Why or why not?

GRAMMAR FOCUS

REVIEW OF VERB TENSES
PRESENT TENSE: TO BE

My computer **is** broken.

PRESENT CONTINUOUS

I**'m** hav**ing** trouble putting up my satellite dish.

SIMPLE PRESENT

I don't feel like going on a picnic today.

SIMPLE PAST

You just **ate** both our salads.

PRESENT PERFECT

How long **has** it **been** broken?
It**'s been** broken for two days.

CONDITIONALS: REVIEW

If I hadn't gone yesterday, I**'d** be very happy to go with you today.
If I hadn't been very hungry, I NEVER **would have** eaten both our salads!
If I had known you were sick in bed, I **wouldn't have** called you.

GERUNDS: REVIEW

I don't feel like **going** on a picnic today.
I suppose you'd get tired of **going** on picnics if you went on picnics all the time!

Choose the correct word.

1. If I (took   had taken) the train today, I (wouldn't have   had) gotten stuck in traffic, and I (would have arrived   would arrive) on time for work.

2. I don't feel like (to go   going) on a picnic today. I (went   have gone) on a picnic yesterday.

3. I'm sure I'd get tired (of jogging   to jog) if I (jog   jogged) all the time.

4. My daughter (has had   had) the measles since last weekend. I remember when I was a child and (have   had) the measles. I (hadn't   wasn't) ever been in bed for such a long time.

The Privileges and Responsibilities of Citizenship

WHAT IS A CITIZEN?

The term *citizen* has a general meaning and a legal meaning in the United States. In a general sense, the term *citizen* refers to anyone living in a city, town, or state, even if the person is not officially a U.S. citizen. Using the legal definition of the term, people are officially citizens if they were born in the United States (*natural-born citizens*) or if they came to the United States and passed the citizenship examination (*naturalized citizens*). There are also many *permanent residents*, individuals who are allowed to live in the country but who do not have official citizenship status. Thus, every person can be considered a citizen of his or her community, even if the person does not have U.S. citizenship.

WHAT ARE THE RESPONSIBILITIES OF A CITIZEN?

Citizens of a city or town enjoy many privileges. They are provided with schools, libraries, community centers, parks, hospitals, highways, and the protection of police and fire departments. Along with these privileges, citizens have duties or responsibilities to their communities and the states they live in. All citizens are expected to obey laws, pay taxes, and keep informed. Responsible citizens are also expected to get involved in community life. In addition, legal U.S. citizens have the responsibility to vote in elections, and along with permanent residents, they are expected to serve on a jury.

Obeying laws

Everyone in the United States must respect and obey local, state, and federal laws. There are many different types of laws, including traffic laws and criminal laws. It is a citizen's responsibility to know, understand, and obey these laws, which are intended to protect everyone's rights and keep people safe.

Paying taxes

Every person who works in the United States must pay income tax. Once a year, employers send each employee a statement of the person's total earnings during the previous year. The employee uses that information to fill in federal and state income tax returns. These forms are available at many government offices, local libraries, and online. They are usually due on April 15th. The person pays taxes based on how much money that person earned during the previous year. Homeowners are also required to pay a property tax to their local government. Local and state governments use the tax money they collect from taxpayers to pay for services such as police, fire, health, education, and local roads. The federal government uses the tax money for national defense, interstate highways, and all the departments and services of the U.S. government.

Keeping informed and getting involved

It is a citizen's responsibility to keep informed about local, state, and national issues and events. Reading the newspaper, watching the news, and talking with local leaders, friends, and neighbors are good ways to stay informed. When people have knowledge about issues that are important to them, they can help find solutions to problems. Attending and speaking at school parent association meetings, school board meetings, city or town council meetings, or neighborhood association meetings are excellent ways for citizens to get involved. When individuals participate in their communities, those communities become stronger.

Voting in elections

One of the most important privileges of U.S. citizenship is the right to vote in elections. Voting gives people a voice in the government. It allows them to participate by electing their leaders and making decisions about policies and laws. In order to vote, an individual must be a legal U.S. citizen who is at least 18 years of age. A person must register to vote in his or her town or city by filling out a voter registration card. As a registered voter, it is important to be informed about current issues and political leaders. The quality of democracy improves when voters are informed and vote in elections.

Serving on a jury

Every person in the United States has the right to have a fair trial for a criminal or civil offense (when the person is accused of breaking the law). In a trial, there is a judge and usually a jury. The twelve members of the jury observe the trial, deliberate, and then reach a verdict about the person's innocence or guilt. Only legal U.S. citizens and permanent residents may serve on a jury. If an individual is called for jury duty, the person is legally required to serve on the jury. It is also the person's civic responsibility to do so. Serving on a jury is an important way of participating in a democracy.

Did You Understand?

1. Citizens have _____ to their communities, such as obeying laws, paying taxes, and keeping informed.
   - A. privileges
   - B. issues
   - C. responsibilities
   - D. rights

2. _____ must pay income tax on any earnings from a job.
   - A. Employers
   - B. Employees
   - C. Only natural-born citizens
   - D. Only naturalized citizens

3. Citizens are well informed when they _____.
   - A. live in a city or town
   - B. register to vote
   - C. understand issues
   - D. enjoy privileges

4. _____ can register to vote.
   - A. All residents
   - B. All citizens
   - C. All people 18 years of age and older
   - D. All citizens 18 years of age and older

5. _____ may serve on a jury.
   - A. All taxpayers
   - B. Permanent residents and legal U.S. citizens
   - C. Only naturalized citizens
   - D. Only natural-born citizens

6. According to this lesson, we can infer that a responsible citizen probably _____.
   - A. speaks at or goes to community meetings
   - B. works as a judge
   - C. has a driver's license
   - D. pays taxes for employees

Have you ever voted before? When and where did you vote?

Why is it important for every working person to pay taxes?

Have you ever served on a jury? What was the trial about?

How do you stay informed about current events and issues? Is being informed important to you? Why or why not?

In your opinion, what are the most important civic responsibilties? Why do you think so?

Community Legal Services
CLS *Serving Our Community Since 1962*

Legal Advice Line: 800-321-4567

Community Legal Services (CLS) provides free legal services to low-income residents in our county. We can help with issues related to housing, immigration, family law, and domestic violence. We have five attorneys, three counselors, and ten assistants to help you with your legal questions.

> CLS can only help with civil legal problems. We do *not* have assistance for criminal issues. If you need assistance with criminal questions, call our Legal Advice Line for a referral to another agency.

Fair Housing and Tenant Rights
345-6000 Extension 12

The Fair Housing office at CLS can advise you on your fair housing rights and responsibilities. We can counsel you on housing conditions, rent, eviction from your home, and discrimination. We can explain what your tenant rights are and what landlords can and cannot do. We provide advice, counseling, and representation in court for all landlord and tenant problems. Remember: "Fair Housing Is Your Right!"

Family Law
345-6000 Extension 14

The Family Law attorneys at CLS are ready to help you with questions about divorce or legal separation and child support.

Domestic Violence
345-6000 Extension 17

Domestic violence is a crime. It occurs when a person tries to control another person by using physical, sexual, or emotional abuse. We provide counseling and legal services. Please call our office or the Legal Advice Line. *Call 9-1-1 if you are in a domestic violence emergency.*

Immigration Services
345-6000 Extension 15

At CLS, our attorneys can help you through the difficult immigration process. For example, we can assist with tourist visas, adjustment of immigration status, work permits, legal residency, and naturalization. Call our office to set up an appointment.

Community Legal Services
CLS *We are here to help you!*

567 First Ave.
Smithtown

Hours: Mon, Wed, Fri   8 A.M.–6 P.M.
       Tues and Thurs 8 A.M.–9 P.M.
Office: (728) 345-6000
Legal Advice Line: 800-321-4567

Look at the brochure and answer these questions.

1. Who can receive free legal services at CLS?
2. What evenings is the office open?
3. What number should a mother call if she hasn't been receiving child support payments?
4. If a tenant is having a legal problem with a landlord, which office should the tenant call?
5. For which service does a person need to make an appointment?

COMMUNITY CONNECTIONS Find out information about a provider of legal services in your community, including the agency's name, phone number, and services offered. Bring the information to class. As a class project, prepare a complete list of community legal services. Organize the list by the types of legal services offered.

Choose the correct answer.

1. I turned left at the light and got completely lost. I must have _____ the directions.
   A. understood
   B. mixed
   C. misunderstood
   D. figured out

2. _____ this button to make a call.
   A. Rewind
   B. Press
   C. Delete
   D. Disconnect

3. People who have come to the United States and have passed the citizenship examination are called _____ citizens.
   A. national
   B. natural-born
   C. registered
   D. naturalized

4. Citizens have many _____ to their communities.
   A. responsibilities
   B. assistance
   C. issues
   D. representation

5. Laws are intended to _____ everyone's rights and keep people safe.
   A. obey
   B. protect
   C. deliberate
   D. control

6. City and town governments use tax money they collect to pay for _____.
   A. national defense
   B. U.S. government services
   C. local roads
   D. interstate highways

7. Citizens should keep informed about national, state, and _____ issues.
   A. newspaper
   B. trial
   C. federal
   D. local

8. The legal service agency's _____ office provides advice about landlord and tenant problems.
   A. fair housing
   B. immigration
   C. family law
   D. domestic violence

9. Domestic violence occurs when a person tries to _____ another person.
   A. help
   B. assist
   C. control
   D. counsel

10. Family law attorneys help with questions about child support, divorce, or legal _____.
    A. association
    B. separation
    C. examination
    D. discrimination

SKILLS CHECK ✔

Words:
- ☐ adjustment
- ☐ agency
- ☐ assistance
- ☐ child support
- ☐ citizenship
- ☐ counseling
- ☐ decision
- ☐ democracy
- ☐ discrimination
- ☐ election
- ☐ eviction
- ☐ family law
- ☐ housing
- ☐ immigration
- ☐ income tax
- ☐ local government
- ☐ national defense
- ☐ naturalization
- ☐ privilege
- ☐ process
- ☐ property tax
- ☐ protection
- ☐ referral
- ☐ representation
- ☐ responsibility
- ☐ services
- ☐ solution
- ☐ tenant rights
- ☐ tourist visa
- ☐ work permit

I can ask & answer:
- ☐ Would you like to *see a movie* with me today?
- ☐ You seem upset. Is anything wrong?
- ☐ I'm having trouble *moving my piano*. Could you possibly come over and give me a hand?

I can say:
- ☐ I don't feel like *playing tennis* today.
- ☐ I *played tennis* yesterday.
- ☐ I must have *forgotten your address*.
- ☐ If I hadn't *forgotten your address*, I never would have *driven past your house*.
- ☐ If I weren't *sick*, I'd be glad to help you.
- ☐ If I had known *you were sick*, I wouldn't have *called you*.

I can:
- ☐ identify civic rights and responsibilities
- ☐ identify community legal services
- ☐ locate legal services in my community

I can extend invitations:
- ☐ Would you like to/Do you want to/ How would you like to _____?

I can write about:
- ☐ a time I had to make an important decision

Feature Article
Fact File
Around the World
Interview
We've Got Mail!

SIDE *by* SIDE **Gazette**

Global Exchange
Listening
Fun with Idioms
What Are They
Saying?

Volume 4

Number 4

Technology in Our Lives

Telephones then and now

Technology plays a role in all aspects of our lives—the way we work, the way we shop, the way we communicate with each other, and the way we live at home. The speed of technological change in the past one hundred years has been incredible.

The early telephones were very large, and they didn't even have dials or buttons. You picked up a receiver and talked to an operator who made the call for you. Nowadays, cellular telephones fit in our pockets, and we can use them to make phone calls from anywhere to anywhere. In grocery stores and supermarkets, cashiers used to punch keys on cash registers to enter the price of each item. These days, scanners read bar codes on product packaging, and the prices are recorded by a computerized cash register. In some supermarkets, customers can even check out by scanning products themselves and paying by credit card, all without the help of a cashier. In the past, we made a trip to the bank to deposit or withdraw money. Now we can use ATMs (automated teller machines) that are found everywhere. And many people now do their bank transactions at home online over the Internet.

Modern technology has dramatically improved our lives. Personal computers enable us to create documents, store information, and analyze data—at work or at home. The Internet allows us to send and receive e-mail messages, connects us to the World Wide Web, and allows us to go shopping online from our homes. Digital cameras enable us to take photographs that we can instantly put on our computers to store, change, and send over the Internet. Satellite communication connects doctors in one country with a patient in another country, bringing medical technology to remote places

around the world. Miniature cameras that patients can swallow permit doctors to diagnose medical conditions without surgery. "Smart homes" operated by computers turn lights on and off as people enter or leave rooms and enable homeowners to "call their houses" to turn on the heat or air conditioning, or even to start the coffeemaker!

What will the future bring? "Smart highways" will carry us to destinations that we program into our cars' computers. Computer chips that are implanted under our skin will hold our medical information in case of an emergency. Household appliances, such as refrigerators and stoves, will have miniature computers that "know" how we like to store or cook our food.

Many people feel, however, that technology has its price. With automated supermarket checkout lines, ATMs and online banking, and Internet shopping, we can meet our daily needs without having contact with other people. Life with technology can be very lonely! Also, many people are concerned about privacy. Technology makes it possible for companies or the government to monitor our use of the Internet. Our credit card numbers, bank account information, medical information, and other personal data are all stored on computers. Protecting that information will be an important issue in the years ahead.

Banking then and now

FACT FILE

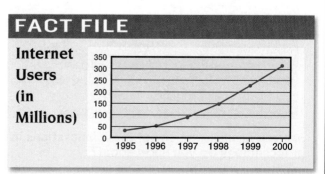

Internet Users (in Millions)

Technology in Action

Innovations in technology are happening throughout the world.

A satellite dish provides television service to a village in Niger in Africa.

Computer technology developed in Tokyo, Japan scans people's eyes to verify their identity.

A new type of scanner screens the baggage of airline passengers at an airport in Washington, D.C.

Solar batteries provide electricity for a hospital in Sudan.

Business people in Sao Paulo, Brazil take part in a video conference with people at another location.

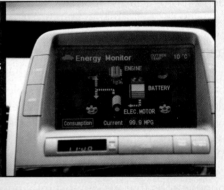
An on-board computer enables the driver of this car to get maps and other information over the Internet.

A doctor uses tele-medicine technology to examine a patient in another country.

A grandmother uses e-mail to keep in touch with her grandchildren who live far away.

Are you familiar with any of these innovations in technology? Which ones? What other innovations in technology do you know about?

Interview

A Side by Side Gazette *reporter asked these people:*

Q. How has technology changed your life?

A: With today's computer and information technology, I don't have to go to my office every day. I "telecommute." I can connect to the computer network at my company and work from home.

A: I love my new game system! The graphics are amazing, and the action is really life-like! When I grow up, I want to develop game system software.

A: I have three children and eight grandchildren, and they all live far away. I keep in touch with them through e-mail. They even send me photos over the Internet. Technology keeps our family together.

A: I use instant messaging all the time to stay in touch with my friends. I can have separate conversations with different friends at the same time over the Internet. It's better and cheaper than talking on the phone!

A: I don't know what I'd do without my cell phone! I'm never home, so I carry it with me everywhere. This way, my family and my friends can always reach me.

A: I have diabetes, so I have to monitor my blood sugar regularly. With my glucometer, I can check my blood sugar reading at any time of the day.

A: With my GPS device, I can navigate using global positioning satellite technology. It tells me the exact location of my boat at any moment.

FUN with IDIOMS

Do You Know These Expressions?

_____ **1.** There's a bug in this software!

_____ **2.** My computer has a virus!

_____ **3.** My computer is frozen!

_____ **4.** My computer is out of memory!

a. The system is infected.

b. There isn't space for more information.

c. The program has a problem.

d. Nothing is happening.

Dear Side by Side,

    I have enjoyed using *Side by Side* in my English classes for the past two years. Now I'd like to ask for your advice. What is the best way for me to improve my English? Should I continue to study in school? Is there more grammar that I need to learn? What are some ways I can practice my English? I look forward to hearing from you.

                  Sincerely,

                  "Love Learning English"

Dear "Love Learning English,"

    We're happy to hear that you have been enjoying your English classes. In our opinion, you should definitely continue studying the language. There is more grammar to learn, and you will also be able to improve your listening, speaking, reading, and writing skills. In addition, try to use English as much as possible outside the classroom. Speak to people in English, watch English-language movies and TV shows, and try to communicate with people in English through letters or over the Internet. Thank you for writing, and good luck as you continue to study English!

                  Sincerely,

                  Side by Side

PEARSON EDUCATION Level 4 Side by Side

Global Exchange

Pop74: Hi, Sally. This is Grandpa. What's new?
CurlyGirl: NMU
Pop74: ?
CurlyGirl: Not much. And you?
Pop74: Grandma and I are fine. We loved the photos you sent us over the Internet of your Halloween party.
CurlyGirl: THX
Pop74: ?
CurlyGirl: Thanks.
Pop74: You looked great in your bee costume. Did you sting anybody?
CurlyGirl: LOL
Pop74: ?
CurlyGirl: Laughing out loud.
Pop74: Grandma says hello.
CurlyGirl: G2G ILU
Pop74: ?
CurlyGirl: Got to go. I love you.
Pop74: ILU2

Have an instant message conversation with a keypal. Talk about anything you'd like. Use some abbreviations in your message.

MORE ABBREVIATIONS

WU? = What's up?	OIC = Oh, I see.
UW = You're welcome.	IMO = In my opinion
L8R = Later.	TTYL = Talk to you later.

LISTENING

Thank You for Calling the Service Department

These people are calling the service department of the Supersonic Electronics store. Which person is going to press each number?

_b_ **1**   a. "When I try to play a video, nothing happens!"

___ **2**   b. "I don't hear any sound in my headphones!"

___ **3**   c. "Whenever I try to save my work, it freezes!"

___ **4**   d. "All my photographs are too dark!"

___ **5**   e. "I don't know how to record a message!"

___ **6**   f. "When I call people, I can hear them, but they can't hear me!"

What Are They Saying?

A **preposition** relates a noun or a pronoun to other words in a sentence.

The **object of a preposition** is the noun or pronoun that follows a preposition.

A **prepositional phrase** is a preposition, its object, and other words that modify the object.

prepositional phrase

Alfreda has been working here for one year.

preposition   object of the preposition

Prepositions

about	down	since
above	during	to
across	for	toward
after	from	under
among	in	until
around	into	up
at	of	with
before	on	within
between	over	without
by		

Practice these conversations with a classmate.

The post office is around the corner.

A. What's the prepositional phrase in this sentence?
B. *Around the corner.*
A. What's the preposition?
B. *Around.*
A. What's the object of the preposition?
B. *Corner.*

I have a meeting today with my boss.

A. What's the prepositional phrase in this sentence?
B. *With my boss.*
A. What's the preposition?
B. *With.*
A. What's the object of the preposition?
B. *Boss.*

Find the prepositional phrase in each sentence. Underline the preposition once and the object of the preposition twice. Then practice new conversations about these sentences.

1. There's an ATM <u>across</u> the <u>street</u>.

2. He's been working here for five years.

3. There will be a meeting during lunch today.

4. My husband has been unemployed since last February.

5. I always go hiking with a GPS device.

6. I don't know what I'd do without my cell phone!

7. We share photographs over the Internet.

8. Can we talk about next week's schedule?

9. My co-workers and I are going to have dinner after work.

10. The employee lounge is down the hall.

Complete each sentence with a prepositional phrase. Then share answers with a classmate and practice more conversations.

1. I was born _____.

2. I've been studying English _____.

3. My home is _____.

4. I've lived here _____.

5. I do my homework _____.

6. I communicate with my friends _____.

Social Media and Today's Citizens

Today's citizens receive important information through both mass media and social media. Mass media—the nation's newspapers, magazines, radio stations, and television channels—reach and influence millions of people throughout the United States. With the popularity of the Internet, mass media is also available on numerous online news websites. Along with mass media, in recent years social media has also become a powerful means of communication. Social media websites and mobile applications such as Facebook, Twitter, and LinkedIn enable large numbers of people to connect with others who have similar interests.

Both mass media and social media help inform people about important topics in their community, their state, and their country. People can get information about news events from mass media and read editorials that present different opinions about topics in the news. However, while mass media provides information to the general public from media companies, social media enables people to receive information from other people and also discuss it. Through social media, people can communicate with others on their computer, tablet, or cell phone about issues that are important to them. Social media is for communicating with smaller groups of people who share similar interests.

Adult Social Media Use in the United States

40% don't use social media

39% use social media for political and civic purposes

21% use social media, but not for political or civic purposes

Source: Pew Research Center's Internet and American Life Project

For this reason, social media is an important tool for civic engagement—the process of individuals and groups working together to improve life in their communities. Social media connects friends and people who have similar interests and allows them to share their ideas, skills, and time in civic engagement. As a result, through social media, people are able to communicate about ways to improve their communities. For example,

many schools use social media to communicate with parents as a way of getting them involved in the school community. A large number of organizations use social media to encourage people to do volunteer work, a very important part of civic engagement. And of course friends can use social media to give their opinions about a variety of topics they can discuss online. Often, friends learn about community issues from other friends on social media and as a result, they may eventually become more active in their community.

Some social media websites are specifically designed to help neighbors communicate and help each other. For example, on the website NextDoor, neighbors can communicate about events, pets, safety issues, crime, and other problems, and they can make recommendations about local stores, household services, and other resources. By using social media, neighbors can very easily and quickly communicate with others about civic issues. NextDoor is an effective social media tool that encourages civic engagement within a neighborhood.

Neighbors Help Fire Victims After Their Home is Destroyed

Posted on July 31, 2016 by Marta Romero

Photo by Neighborhood Watch member Oscar Pedroya

Governments at the local, state, and federal level use social media to provide information and also to ask questions in order to find out what citizens think. The goal is to encourage civic engagement and actively involve citizens in political issues. Well-informed and engaged citizens are important for good government. For example, through social media, a local government can send information about community issues or events to residents who are interested in them. Residents who have already signed onto a local government's social media site are more likely to use the information and get involved.

Of course, not all citizens are on social media. Citizens must sign onto a government or neighborhood social media website in order to participate. As a result, people who use social media for civic engagement are people who are naturally interested and involved. It is difficult to know if social media is really increasing civic engagement. But it is true that social media is making communication faster and easier, and more citizens seem better informed than years ago.

Social media is very important for politicians, too. Through social media, politicians can tell voters what they are doing and what they are thinking. In the same way, politicians can also receive information from voters. Social media helps politicians communicate quickly with voters and find out their opinions. It is also a way for candidates to recruit volunteers to help with political campaigns. Individuals who like a politician can

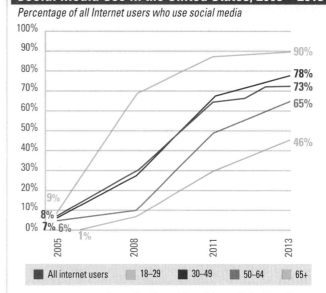

Social Media Use in the United States, 2005 – 2013
Percentage of all Internet users who use social media

All internet users | 18–29 | 30–49 | 50–64 | 65+

Source: Pew Research Center's Internet Project Library Survey

join his or her social media website and connect with others who are also politically active.

Social media does not always result in civic and political engagement. Social media is a tool for communication, but it cannot replace real action. Many people use social media to learn about issues. They may post comments on websites, or they may be part of an online discussion. But true civic engagement means that people are communicating face-to-face. They are discussing issues and helping in their communities. Civic engagement means taking action and doing things. Social media can help people become active, but just using social media by itself does not mean a person is truly engaged in civic life.

DID YOU UNDERSTAND?

1. What are four examples of mass media?
2. What are three social media websites?
3. How is social media different from mass media?
4. How do people receive social media?
5. What is civic engagement?
6. Why do some schools use social media?
7. How do governments use social media?
8. Does using social media always result in more civic engagement? Why, or why not?
9. What percentage of adults in the United States do not use social media?
10. What percentage of Internet users were using social media in 2013?

Think & Share

1. Do you use social media? Why, or why not?
2. What is your main source of information about local and national news?
3. Give examples of people (including yourself) who participate in civic engagement. What do they do? How do they help their communities?
4. Do you think social media is increasing civic engagement or decreasing it? Why do you think so?

Proofreading is an important step in the writing process. After you write and revise a first draft, you need to **proofread** your writing. When you proofread, you read your work two or three times, you look for errors in capitalization, punctuation, spelling, and paragraph formation, and you fix the errors that you find. Some people use a ruler to read one line at a time easily when they proofread. Other people like to read sentence by sentence from the ending to the beginning. This helps to focus on the errors instead of the meaning.

Proofreading Marks

You can use **proofreading marks** to mark the mistakes that you find. This student has written an essay about an important decision in his life. His teacher used proofreading marks to mark errors in spelling, capitalization, punctuation, and paragraph formation. Rewrite the essay and fix the errors.

I remember a tim when I had to make a very important dicision. I was an employee in the bigest do nut shop in our city. I workd the night shift. The night manager was very mean. He always yell at employes and made us to work extra hours. I got lots of advice above this situashun. My friends sayd to do nothing or I might loose my job. My family members sayd I should qwit. I didn't follow their advice. Instead one day I went to the shop during the the day and I talk with the Owner. I explain the problem to her very politely. She sayd, "I'm sorry. let me see what can I do. That night I went to work and the night manager wasnt there! he was fired! I found out that I wasnt the first employe to complane The other night shift employes thankd me. Six months later, I was promoted. Now am I the night manager, and Next year Im going to be the manager during the day shift. Im glad I decide to complain when I did. I think I made the right decizun, and my family and friends think so, too.

Proofreading Marks	
≡	capital letter
/	small letter
⌃	add comma
⊙	add period
⌄	add apostrophe
⌄⌄	add quotation mark
⏋	indent paragraph
¶	new paragraph
◯ or sp.	check spelling
ww	wrong word
⌒	close up space
∾	transpose/ reverse
⌿	delete
⋀	insert

Write a narrative essay.

Write: Did you write in your journal about the topic on page 158? If you didn't, write a narrative essay about a time when you had to make an important decision. If you did, expand your journal entry into a longer narrative essay.

Revise: Reread and rethink your first draft. Make some changes to improve it.

Proofread: Exchange essays with a classmate. Read and proofread each other's work. Use proofreading marks to mark errors. Then meet with the classmate and discuss the errors you have found in each other's writing.

Publish: Rewrite your essay and fix the errors. Then share your essay with the class and with other people who may want to read it. As a class, make a collection of students' essays and publish the collection in print or in an online blog or class web site.

> *Narrative essay*: In a narrative essay, the writer tells a true story about his or her experiences. The writer uses the first person (I) to tell the story. The *voice* in the story is the writer's first-person point of view.

Listening Scripts

Unit 1 – Page 6

Carl is going to have a party at his apartment this Saturday night. This is the list of things that Carl needs to do to get ready for his party. Check the things on the list that Carl has already done.

Carl has already gone to the supermarket. He hasn't cleaned the apartment yet. He also hasn't gotten balloons at the party store. He's bought some new dance music at his favorite CD store. He hasn't hung up the decorations yet. He also hasn't made the food. He has told the neighbors about the party so they won't be surprised when they hear the noise. He'll give the dog a bath a few hours before the party begins.

Unit 2 – Page 19

Listen and choose the best answer based on the conversation you hear.

1. A. By the time we got to the party, everyone had left.
   B. That's too bad.
2. A. I couldn't hear a word he said.
   B. I couldn't either.
3. A. I just interviewed a young man for the bookkeeper's position.
   B. What did you think of him?
   A. Well, he was very shy and quiet, and he was wearing a T-shirt, jeans, and sneakers.
4. A. Could you tell me how I did on the exam?
   B. Not very well, Richard.
5. A. I smell smoke!
   B. Oh, no! The cookies are burning!
6. A. I was so tired last night that I slept twelve hours and was late for work this morning.
   B. Oh. I hope the boss wasn't angry.
   A. No. He wasn't.

Unit 3 – Page 42

Listen and choose the best line to continue the conversation.

1. The packages have been sent.
2. The beds have been made.
3. Our cat was bitten by our dog.
4. My brother was invited to his girlfriend's birthday party.
5. Mrs. Green hired Mr. Fleming as a secretary.
6. Mrs. Davis was hired by Ms. Clark to work in the information technology department.
7. Hello. This is the Worldcom Service Department. Your cell phone has been repaired.
8. Hello. This is Joe's Auto Repair Shop. I'm sorry. We've been very busy. I'm calling to tell you your car is finally being repaired.

Side by Side Gazette – Page 50

Listen to the news reports. Answer true or false.

Good afternoon. This is Gloria Ramos in the WKSB radio newsroom with the latest news update. A bicyclist was knocked down in a hit-and-run accident on Jefferson Street this afternoon. A brown van was seen leaving the scene of the accident. If you have any information, the police department is asking you to call 555-1234. Live in the newsroom, this is Gloria Ramos for WKSB Radio News.

This is Kim Crane reporting live from City Hall. A new mayor has been elected. It was a very close race between Joe Murphy and Julie Miller, but now the results are in, and Julie Miller has been chosen as the new mayor. Julie Miller will be interviewed on this evening's news at six o'clock.

This is Stu Brent reporting live from downtown. I'm at the scene of the big fire at the Main Street Marketplace. Five stores at the Marketplace were destroyed in this fire that broke out early this morning. Luckily, no one was injured. The building is now being examined by the fire department. The fire chief is expected to speak at a news conference later this afternoon. We'll bring that news conference to you live when it happens.

This is Brian Adams with a local sports update. After five years as the city's baseball champions, the Washington High School Eagles were defeated by the Lincoln High School Terriers this afternoon by a score of 4 to 3. The Terriers are the new baseball champions. Tune in at 5 o'clock for the complete story.

This is Wendy Chen reporting live from the Museum of Fine Arts. Last night, the museum was robbed, and several important paintings were stolen. The paintings are considered some of the best works by painters known throughout the world, including Picasso, Rembrandt, and Monet. The robbery was discovered this morning when the museum's director arrived for work. The building is now being checked by the police, and information about the missing paintings is being sent around the nation and around the world. Reporting live from the Museum of Fine Arts, this is Wendy Chen for KPLW Radio News.

Unit 4 – Page 61

Listen and decide where the conversation is taking place.

1. A. Could you please tell me if this book is on sale?
   B. Yes, it is.
2. A. Can you tell me where the bananas are?
   B. Yes. They're in the next aisle.
   A. Thanks very much.

3. A. Do you know how much this shirt costs?
   B. I'm sorry. I don't work here.
4. A. Do you know who composed this symphony?
   B. I think Beethoven did.
5. A. Do you by any chance know whether we'll be arriving soon?
   B. Yes. We'll be arriving in ten minutes.
   A. Thank you.
6. A. Who knows how a heart works?
   B. I do.
   A. Please tell us.
7. A. Do you know how much longer I'll have to stay here?
   B. Just a few more days.
   A. Oh, good.
8. A. Do you have any idea when the bus from Detroit arrives?
   B. I'm not sure. You should ask the man at the ticket counter. He'll know when the bus arrives.

Unit 5 – Page 76

Listen and choose the statement that is true based on what you hear.

1. If it weren't raining today, we'd go to the beach.
2. If we had enough money, we'd buy a new car.
3. I'd be very happy if Mrs. Carter were my English teacher.
4. If the company's profits increase, we'll receive bonuses.
5. If I weren't allergic to trees, I'd go hiking with you this weekend.
6. If I didn't have to work tonight, I'd invite you to go to the movies with me.

Side by Side Gazette – Page 82

Listen to the Tempo Airlines automated telephone system. Match the numbers and the menu instructions.

Thank you for calling Tempo Airlines—the airline that puts passengers first! This call may be monitored to ensure quality assistance. Please listen carefully to the following menu:

If you are calling for information about today's flights, press 1.

If you are calling to make a reservation for a flight in the United States or Canada, press 2.

If you are calling to make a reservation for an international flight, press 3.

If you are calling to make a reservation for a Tempo Airlines Vacation Package, press 4.

If you are calling to enroll in the Tempo Airlines Frequent Flyer Program, which gives you awards for all travel on Tempo Airlines, press 5.

If you want to hear a list of rules for checking in at the airport, press 6.

If you want to speak with a customer service representative, press 7.

To hear this menu again, press 8.

If you are not calling from a touch-tone phone, please stay on the line and a Tempo Airlines representative will be with you shortly. Thank you for choosing Tempo Airlines.

Unit 6 – Page 93

Listen and choose the statement that is true based on what you hear.

1. If I got a dog, I'd probably be evicted from my apartment building.
2. I wish I worked the day shift.
3. If I weren't a teacher, I'd probably be a musician.
4. I wish I didn't have to take biology next semester.
5. If I could type fast, I'd be able to get a better job.
6. If they lived in the city, they'd be able to sell their car.

Unit 7 – Page 105

Listen and choose the statement that is true based on what you hear.

1. A. If I were rich, I'd travel around the world.
   B. Really? That sounds like fun!
2. A. Why didn't you e-mail me?
   B. I would have e-mailed you if I hadn't forgotten your e-mail address.
3. A. How did you enjoy the soccer game?
   B. It was all right, but I wish we could have had better seats.
4. A. Those boys are making a lot of noise in the hallway again.
   B. I know. It's terrible. If they weren't the landlord's children, I'd tell them to be quiet.
5. A. You know, I wish I had taken a computer course when I was in college.
   B. Why do you say that?
   A. If I had, I would have gotten the job I applied for.
6. A. Happy Birthday, Johnny! Now blow out the candles and make a wish.
   B. I wish Grandma and Grandpa were here for my birthday party.

Unit 8 – Page 115

Listen and choose the statement that is true based on what you hear.

1. A. I've been in the office all day. I wasn't aware that it had snowed.
   B. I wasn't either.

2. A. Have you heard the news?
   B. No. What?
   A. Our supervisor is in the hospital.
   B. Oh. I didn't know that. That's too bad.

3. A. Do you know about the special sale?
   B. No, I don't.
   A. You can buy two jackets for the price of one this week.
   B. No kidding! That's great!

4. A. Hello.
   B. Hello, Tim? This is Barbara. I'm afraid I won't be able to have dinner with you on Saturday. I have to work.
   A. Oh. That's too bad.

5. A. Sherman quit his job!
   B. Really? What a surprise!

6. A. We've moved!
   B. Oh. I didn't know that. Where to?
   A. The other side of the town.

Side by Side Gazette – Page 128

Joe Montero is the office manager at his company. Listen to his voice mail messages. Why did each person call?

You have six messages.

Message Number One: "Hello. This is Jim Gavin. I'm one of the new employees on the third floor. I have a question. Why was three hundred and fifty dollars taken out of my paycheck? If you have time today, could you please call me at extension 45? Thanks very much." [*beep*]

Message Number Two: "Hi. This is Denise. I'm sorry, but I won't be able to go to the meeting this afternoon. I just found out about the meeting a half hour ago, and I have to pick up the boss at the airport. Let me know how the meeting goes." [*beep*]

Message Number Three: "Hi, Joe. This is Patty in Accounting. I see that you've just ordered one thousand pens for the office. I'm calling to let you know that we still have enough pens from our last order, so we won't need any more pens for a few more months. I've canceled the order. Okay? Thanks." [*beep*]

Message Number Four: "Hello. This is Jane Adams calling from the president's office. You told me yesterday that the painters would begin painting the president's office today, but they haven't arrived yet. Please let me know when they'll be here. Thank you." [*beep*]

Message Number Five: "Hello. This is George Johnson. I wanted to let you know that I won't be in the office tomorrow morning. I have to go to a doctor's appointment. If you need to talk to me, you can reach me on my cell phone at 881-595-7472. Thanks." [*beep*]

Message Number Six: "Joe? This is Michelle Mills. I really need to talk with you as soon as possible. I've been offered a job at another company, and I don't know what to do. I'd really like to stay here, but they're offering me a job with more responsibilities and a higher salary. Please call me back so we can set up a time to meet. Thanks." [*beep*]

Unit 9 – Page 141

Listen and decide who is speaking.

1. A. I did well on my exam, didn't I?
   B. No, you didn't.
   A. I didn't?! I'm really surprised.

2. A. The mail isn't here yet, is it?
   B. No. Not yet.
   A. That's what I thought.

3. A. You've received our supervisor's memo, haven't you?
   B. Yes, I have.

4. A. You know . . . that suit looks very good on you.
   B. You're right! It DOES look very good on me, doesn't it!
   A. Yes, it does. I wonder if it's on sale.
   B. Let's ask somebody.

5. A. You were driving more than seventy miles per hour, weren't you!
   B. I guess I was. Are you going to give me a ticket?

6. A. I have some good news!
   B. What is it?
   A. You're fine. You can go home tomorrow.
   B. I can?!
   A. Yes, you can.
   B. I'm very glad to hear that.

Listen and choose where the conversation is taking place.

1. **A.** Do you realize what you just did?
   B. No. What did I just do?
   A. You put too much pepper in the soup. Our customers will be sneezing all night!
   B. Oh. I'm sorry. I must have had my mind on something else.

2. **A.** I'm sorry. I must have thought this seat was mine.
   B. That's okay. Don't worry about it. I'm getting off soon anyway.

3. **A.** You know, I really don't feel like shopping today. Could we go someplace else and take a walk?
   B. Sure. That's fine with me.

4. **A.** What are you going to have?
   B. I'm not sure. If I hadn't had the chicken every day last week, I'd have the chicken.

5. **A.** Excuse me. You just put my shirts in your machine.
   B. I did?
   A. Yes, you did.
   B. I'm really sorry. I thought they were mine.

6. **A.** If I had known this was going to be so boring, I wouldn't have bought a ticket.
   B. I agree. I wouldn't have bought one either.

These people are calling the service department of the Supersonic Electronics store. Listen to the service department's automated telephone system. Which person is going to press each number?

Thank you for calling the Supersonic Electronics Service Department. Our menu has changed, so please listen carefully to the following options:

If you are calling about a personal audio device such as a portable CD player, press 1.

If your call is related to a VCR or DVD player, press 2.

If you need assistance with a digital camera or video camcorder, press 3.

If this call is about a cellular phone, press 4.

If you are having a problem with a desktop computer or a notebook computer, press 5.

If you are calling about a telephone answering machine, press 6.

If you would like to speak to a customer service representative, press 7.

If you would like to hear these menu options again, press 8.

To end this call, please hang up.

Thank you for calling the Supersonic Electronics Service Department.

Vocabulary List

Numbers indicate the pages on which the words first appear.

fire (v) 28
fish (v) 131
fit 159
fix 41
flash 30c
fly (v) 2
focus 50
focus on 144c
follow 14c
force 78a
forget 14a
form (v) 46a
found 45
gain 46b
get 1
get accepted 71
get ahead 144c
get along with 73
get back 64c
get depressed 103
get into fights 14a
get involved 14c
get kicked 108a
get laid off 12
get lost 15
get married 13
get out 30c
get paid 73
get ready 6
get scared 28
get searched 99
get stopped 99
get stuck 64a
get stuck in traffic 15
get up 19
get worse 69
give 4
give a bath 6
give back 138
give birth 48
give blood 4
give out 1
give up 144c
go 1
go away 20
go back 64c
go bicycling 82
go bowling 82
go dancing 10
go fishing 4
go home 84
go on a safari 17
go out 7
go swimming 131
go through 30a
go to sleep 13
grab 78a
grow 2
grow up 71
guarantee (v) 64b
hammer (v) 79
hand in 14a
hand over 15

handle (v) 124c
hang 13
hang up 6
happen 11
have 4
have trouble 14b
hear 12
help 14a
hide 35
hijack 46c
hike (v) 22
hire 39
hit (v) 28
hold 30c
hold hands 65
hold together 47
hold up 49
hook up 155
hope (v) 30c
hurt (v) 50
ignore 78c
imagine 50
implant (v) 159
impress 127
improve 64c
include 14c
increase (v) 46a
indicate 108b
inflate 127
influence (v) 49
inform 162b
inhabit 48
inhale 108e
injure 12
insist 64c
inspire 49
install 44
interview (v) 49
introduce 46a
invade 45
invent 33
invest 46a
investigate 64c
invite 36
involve 47
irrigate 47
issue (v) 30c
jam (v) 64a
jog 25
join 14c
judge (v) 46b
keep 14c
keep a record 94c
keep away 108d
keep informed 158a
keep out of reach 108d
keep peace 46b
keep to 94c
keep track of 94c
kid (v) 9
kill 46a
kiss (v) 121
knit 89
knock down 38
know 5

label (v) 144a
land (v) 46a
last (v) 46a
launch 46c
lay off 12
lead 30c
lead to 108b
leak (v) 7
leak out 64a
learn 14c
leave 11
leave behind 144c
leave on 122
let (someone) know 30c
liberate 45
lie (v) 127
lie in bed 77
lift 108a
lift up 82c
lift weights 72
light up 81
like 5
limit (v) 14c
list (v) 108b
listen 14c
live (v) 7
locate 48
lock (v) 122
look 8
look forward to 82
lose 14b
lose my balance 149
love (v) 79
lower (v) 144b
maintain 48
make 6
make a difference 14c
make a wish 70
make friends 144c
make room 94c
make sure 14b
make the bed 35
make use of 50b
manage 90
march (v) 89
marry 52
match (v) 144b
mean (v) 53
measure 78c
meet 6
mention 13
miss (v) 20
misunderstand 149
mix up 128
monitor (v) 82
move 5
move away 111
move out 138
move up 144c
mow 92
mug (v) 28
need 6
need to 14c
negotiate 46a
network (v) 144c

notice (v) 30c
obey 108e
observe 140
obtain 64b
occur 94c
offer 37
open (v) 44
operate 64c
order (v) 30c
oversee 124c
oversleep 15
owe 26
own 5
pace (v) 142
paint (v) 33
park (v) 131
participate 12
pass (v) 158a
pass by 70
pass out 82c
pay (v) 28
pay attention 14c
pay off 81
perform 12
permit (v) 43
persuade 50d
photocopy (v) 124c
pick out 155
pick up 14a
plan (v) 12
plant (v) 13
play (v) 5
play baseball 22
play basketball 108a
play frisbee 137
plug into 82c
point out 28
polish up 125
pour 121
practice (v) 18
prefer 144c
prepare 12
preserve 48
press 78a
pressure (v) 76
prevent 78b
process (v) 128b
produce (v) 46a
program (v) 155
promise (v) 64c
promote 36
proofread 124c
protect 46a
provide 14c
publish 49
pull 47
pull over 30a
punch (v) 159
purchase (v) 78c
push out 78a
put 28
put up 104
quit 67
rain (v) 13
raise (v) 85

reach 62
reach a verdict 158b
react 108d
read 6
realize 18
rebuild 44
receive 42
record (v) 159
recruit 162c
reduce 94c
re-elect 97
refer 158a
refuse (v) 15
register (v) 44
regret (v) 67
rehearse 12
reject 37
relate 162
relax 127
relieve 108d
remember 26
rent (v) 13
reopen 44
repaint 13
repair 40
repeat 78a
replace 42
reply (v) 126
report (v) 30c
represent 50b
require 43
reschedule 127
resolve 64c
respect (v) 158a
rest (v) 122
restore 82c
result (v) 64b
retire 7
return 20
rewind 149
rewrite 41
ride (v) 2
ring (v) 79
risk 108d
rob 37
roll (v) 89
run 4
run away 28
run by 98
run out of 94c
run over 38
run up 28
sail 11
save 47
save money 79
say 14b
say hello 98
scan 159
schedule (v) 124c
scold 101
screen (v) 160
search 99
see 3
seek 124b
select 49

sell 9
send 6
separate (v) 46b
serve 43
set (v) 1
set off 99
set on fire 107
set up 1
settle 45
shake hands 15
share 92
ship (v) 64b
shoot 46d
shop (v) 159
shorten 82d
shout (v) 74
shovel (v) 22
show (v) 14c
shrink 99
shut down 99
sign (v) 57
sign onto 162c
sing 2
sit 60
sit down 121
skate (v) 22
skateboard (v) 130
ski (v) 29
skip 15
smell (v) 64a
smile (v) 23
sneeze 65
snore 7
snow (v) 70
solve 64c
sound 78c
speak 1
speak up 64c
speed (v) 30a
spend 13
spill 47
splash 38
spoil 67
stand 30c
stand out 125
star (v) 135
start 11
stay 6
stay home 17
stay up 67
steal 38
step (v) 149
sting (v) 38
stop (v) 13
store (v) 78b
strengthen 48
study 7
submit 30c
succeed 14c
supervise 124c
supply 108b
support 14c
suppose 84
swallow 108e
sway 50b

sweep 34
swim 1
swing (v) 79
take 8
take a break 3
take a walk 27
take an interest 14c
take care of 26
take control of 94c
take down 13
take in 41
take inventory 1
take lessons 103
take off 11
take orders 8
take out 35
take part 160
take up 47
talk 14a
talk about 14b
taste (v) 137
teach 87
tease 14b
telecommute 161
tell 6
tell time 47
test (v) 78c
thank 40
think 21
throw 80
throw away 80
throw out 108d
tie my shoes 135
tie up 49
tilt 82c
tip over 13
touch 108a
train (v) 12
transfer (v) 49
translate 124c
travel 30b
treat (v) 108d
trim 94c
trust 78c
try 28
tune in 50
tune up 42
turn (v) 47
turn off 150
turn on 47
turn to 30c
type 89
unbutton 82c
understand 26
update 124c
urge 156
use (v) 6
value (v) 14c
vary 126
verify 160
visit 14b
volunteer 14a
vote (v) 52
wait 7
waive 94b

wake up 13
walk (v) 38
walk away 30c
walk into 108a
want 10
warn 122
warrant (v) 64b
watch (v) 71
watch TV 14c
water (v) 47
water-ski 5
wear 4
weigh 62
win 18
wind up 22
wish (v) 90
withdraw 144b
wonder 20
work (v) 7
work out 64c
worry 26
worship 48
wrap 81
write 1
write down 94c
yell 15

Ailments, Symptoms, and Injuries

ailment 108d
allergic reaction 108d
allergy 108d
arthritis 108d
bleeding problem 108d
brain damage 78a
break (v) 22
bump (n) 108a
carsick 65
chicken pox 145
cold (n) 14b
common cold 135
cough (n) 108d
diabetes 108d
diarrhea 108d
disease 99
dizziness 108d
dizzy 108d
drowsiness 108d
drug abuse 108d
fever 108d
flu 12
headache 20
heart attack 22
heart disease 108b
high blood pressure 108d
hurt 22
illness 94c
injury 108e
kidney disease 108d
measles 60
medical condition 159
nervous 108d
overdose (n) 108d

native 43
natural 49
near 64b
neat 108e
necessary 124b
neighboring 46a
nervous 108d
new 3
next 70
nice 68
noisy 92
normal 78b
nosey 93
nutritious 14c
off-site 124c
old 5
only 121
on-site 124c
open 14c
original 44
other 14b
out of order 153
outdoor 13
outgoing 73
outstanding 50
overcooked 129
overdue 94c
overnight 153
overseas 21
own 14c
paid 144b
part-time 83
passive 50
perfect 135
personal 14b
physical 14c
pleasant 141
poisonous 108e
polite 122
political 33
poor 56
popular 70
positive 84
possible 14b
preferred 124b
pregnant 60
prepared 13
previous 18
professional 118
proficient 124c
promising 49
public 43
punctual 129
qualified 128d
quality 82
quick 78a
quiet 14c
rare 99
ready 6
rear 42
reassured 122
recommended 108b
religious 14b

remote 159
required 124b
responsible 46c
retail 128c
rich 70
right 20
routine 30c
rude 28
rusty 13
safe 30c
same 94c
scary 24
Scottish 47
separate 161
serious 108d
several 44
sexual 158c
shaped 50b
short 32
short-term 144b
side-to-side 50b
similar 80
simple 79
single 87
sleepless 108d
small 47
smart 71
social 14c
soft 101
solid 82b
sorry 12
sour 137
spare 92
special 13
specific 14c
step by step 128c
strong 14c
stuck 15
sunny 66
sure 20
swollen 108a
talented 136
tall 56
temporary 124b
terrible 23
thoughtful 141
tiered 94b
toll-free 64b
total 158a
toxic 82b
true 12
trustworthy 126
twin 50b
unable 14c
unaware 115
unbelievable 9
understanding 28
unemployed 46a
unfair 140
unhappy 14b
unlimited 47
unresponsive 82c
unused 144b
unusual 127

upstairs 111
used 70
valid 124b
variable 94c
vegetarian 5
visible 48
visual 48
web-based 124b
wet 105
willing 14c
wonderful 13
wooden 47
world-class 50b
world-famous 50b
worse 69
wrong 23
yearly 73
young 14c

Describing with Adverbs

accidentally 38
accurately 141
actively 50
actually 14a
again 50
almost 38
alone 114
already 6
always 13
annually 50c
appropriately 125
approximately 48
automatically 64c
away 11
away from 78b
back 30c
back and forth 142
badly 50
behind 78a
below 78a
better 16
carefully 16
certainly 18
close 72
closely 124a
comfortably 19
commonly 50
completely 26
confidently 16
conservatively 125
correctly 144a
currently 78c
definitely 18
differently 18
directly 126
downstairs 153
dramatically 159
early 13
economically 46b
enough 16
exactly 103
extremely 13
far 150
fast 16
finally 38

firmly 126
fortunately 14c
frequently 94c
grammatically 82
hard 13
high 48
honestly 14c
however 13
immediately 78c
indoors 13
instantly 159
instead 14c
inward 78a
just 14c
late 6
lately 14b
later 50
legally 158b
legibly 16
lightly 126
likely 125
loud 16
luckily 50
naturally 162c
nearby 150
neatly 125
never 8
officially 44
often 14c
on time 11
only 30c
openly 14c
originally 79
particularly 70
past 148
patiently 60
physically 49
politely 30c
politically 46b
poorly 14c
possibly 55
pretty 28
probably 6
promptly 108e
properly 82b
quickly 13
quite 28
really 14a
recently 4
regularly 108a
safely 30c
separately 144a
shortly 60
simply 56
sincerely 14b
slowly 137
so 24
softly 19
soon 16
specially 162b
still 13
straight 30a
suddenly 46a
through 22

Occupations

Parts of the Body

People

Irregular Verbs

be	was/were	been	leave	left	left
become	became	become	lend	lent	lent
begin	began	begun	let	let	let
bite	bit	bitten	light	lit	lit
blow	blew	blown	lose	lost	lost
break	broke	broken	make	made	made
bring	brought	brought	mean	meant	meant
build	built	built	meet	met	met
buy	bought	bought	put	put	put
catch	caught	caught	quit	quit	quit
choose	chose	chosen	read	read	read
come	came	come	ride	rode	ridden
cost	cost	cost	ring	rang	rung
cut	cut	cut	run	ran	run
do	did	done	say	said	said
draw	drew	drawn	see	saw	seen
drink	drank	drunk	sell	sold	sold
drive	drove	driven	send	sent	sent
eat	ate	eaten	set	set	set
fall	fell	fallen	sew	sewed	sewed/sewn
feed	fed	fed	shake	shook	shaken
feel	felt	felt	shrink	shrank	shrunk
fight	fought	fought	sing	sang	sung
find	found	found	sit	sat	sat
fit	fit	fit	sleep	slept	slept
fly	flew	flown	speak	spoke	spoken
forget	forgot	forgotten	spend	spent	spent
forgive	forgave	forgiven	stand	stood	stood
freeze	froze	frozen	steal	stole	stolen
get	got	gotten	sting	stung	stung
give	gave	given	sweep	swept	swept
go	went	gone	swim	swam	swum
grow	grew	grown	take	took	taken
hang	hung	hung	teach	taught	taught
have	had	had	tell	told	told
hear	heard	heard	think	thought	thought
hide	hid	hidden	throw	threw	thrown
hit	hit	hit	understand	understood	understood
hold	held	held	wake	woke	woken
hurt	hurt	hurt	wear	wore	worn
keep	kept	kept	win	won	won
know	knew	known	wind	wound	wound
lead	led	led	write	wrote	written

Skill Index

BASIC LANGUAGE SKILLS

Language Arts
Embedded questions, 82a
Prepositional phrases, 162a
Punctuation, 50a
Quotation marks, 128a

Listening, 6, 19, 42, 50, 61, 76, 82, 93, 105, 115, 128, 141, 151, 162

Pronunciation, 14, 30, 46, 64, 78, 94, 108, 123, 144, 158

Speaking
(*Throughout*)

Idioms, 49, 81, 127, 161

Reading/Document literacy
Abbreviations:
  Help Wanted ads, 124b
  Weights and measurements, 108b–c
Articles/Academic reading, 14c, 30c, 46a–c, 47, 48, 64c, 79, 80, 94c, 108d, 125, 126, 144c, 158a–b, 159, 160, 184
Bank brochure, 94b
Bus schedule, 30b
Chart, 79
Checklist, 6
Cloze reading, 92, 115
Email, 50, 82, 128, 162
Employee manual, 144b
Fire safety poster, 78b
Food labels, 108b–c
Graphs, 125, 159
Health information, 108b–c
Help Wanted ads, 124b
Historical site information, 44–45
Instruction manual, 78c
Legal services brochure, 158c
Letter, 50, 82, 128, 138–139, 162
List, 6
Medicine labels, 108d
Memo, 140–141
Messages, phone, 114
Notes to school, 14b
Nutrition information, 108b–c
Resume, 124c
Safety poster, 78b, 108e
Schedule, bus, 30b
Schedule, train, 30b
Signs, traffic, 30a
Stories, short structured, 6, 13, 18–19, 21, 28–29, 38, 39, 42, 56, 57, 60, 70–71, 76, 88, 92, 93, 100, 101, 104–105, 114, 115, 119, 122–123, 138–141, 150–151, 156–157
Traffic signs, 30a
Train schedule, 30b
Want ads, 124b
Warnings on medicine labels, 108d
Warranties, 64b

Writing
Cloze writing, 92, 115
Compositions, 19, 45, 105
Directions, 30a
Email, 50, 82, 128, 162
History essay, 45
Instructions, 144a
Journal writing, 13, 30, 46, 64, 77, 94, 108, 123, 144, 158
Letter, business, 128d
Letter, parts of a, 14b
Letter, personal, 139
Lists, 14a, 64a, 78b, 108a, 124b, 158c
Memo, 141
Note to a child's teacher, 14b
Procedures, 144a
Story, 21
Writing process, 50d, 82d, 162d

NUMBERS/NUMERACY/MATH
Address numbers, 124b–c
Dates, 46a–c, 47, 124c
Food labels, numbers in, 108b–c
Money, amounts of, 94a–b, 144b
Percents, 108b–c
Salary, 144b
Statistical information, 79, 125, 159
Telephone numbers, 124b–c, 158c
Time, 30b, 158c
Time zones, 184
Vacation time, workplace, 144b
Warranties, numbers in, 64b
Weights and measures, 108b–c

LEARNING SKILLS
Academic concepts and reading
  topics:
  Body language, 126
  Budget-planning strategies, 94c
  Career advancement, 144c
  Civic rights and responsibilities, 158a–b
  Community outreach program, 30c
  Consumer rights, 64c
  Geography, 48
  Health information, 108d
  History, U.S., 46a–c
  Inventions, 47
  Job interview skills, 125–126
  Music, 79
  Nutrition information, 108b
  Parenting, 14c
  Police, interactions with the, 30c
  School success, promoting children's, 14c
  Statistical information, 79, 125, 159
  Technology in our lives, 159
  Technology innovations, 160
  Time zones, 184
  U.S. history, 46a–c
  Wishes, making, 80
  Wonders of the world, 48
Charts, information, 79, 94b
Diagrams, 78b–c
Graphs, statistical, 125, 159
Map, drawing a, 30a
Map of the United States, 184
Timeline, 46c, 47

LEARNING STRATEGIES
Assessment (Tests and skills checklists), 14d, 30d, 46d, 64d, 78d, 94d, 108f, 124d, 144d, 158d

Community Connections tasks, 30b, 78a, 94a, 108a, 158c

Critical Thinking / Problem-solving, 14a–c, 30c, 64a–c, 108b, 124a, 158b

Culture sharing, 48, 80, 126, 160

Interviews, 9, 49, 81, 127, 161

Picture dictionary vocabulary lessons, 1, 15, 31, 51, 65, 83, 95, 109, 129, 145

Projects, 108a, 158c

Teamwork, 14a, 64a, 78a–b, 94a, 124a–b, 144a

Grammar Index

Topic Index